Successful Ocean Game Fishing

Successful Ocean

WITH SELECTIONS BY NELSON BENEDICT /

CHARLES R. MEYER / HARRY BONNER /

LARRY GREEN / RUSSELL TINSLEY /

FRANK T. MOSS

Game Fishing

VIC McCRISTAL / MILT ROSKO /

NORMAN PHILLIPS / MARK J. SOSIN /

International Marine Publishing Company

CAMDEN, MAINE

TO MY WIFE, MILDRED,

*who knows what it is to stand radio listening watch
through stormy days and dark nights,
this book is affectionately dedicated.*

Contents

Preface

FOLKS WHO NEVER FISH FIND IT DIFFICULT to understand why others spend so much time, money, and effort trying to catch alive what they can easily buy dead in the fish market. At one time sport fishing was called a sport of the idle rich. Now, with more than 30 million anglers participating in the United States on salt water and fresh, this "sport-of-the-rich" idea has been quite thoroughly debunked.

At present it is fashionable among non-fishing sociologists and the new breed of recreation engineers to describe fishing as a throwback to a primordial food gathering instinct that must be humored in a certain class of people, because, in getting their kicks by subduing wild game, they work off potentially destructive social tensions.

Fishermen can tell you why they go fishing—to catch fish. Of course, other factors enter into the fishing that are not always seen at first glance.

Some men go fishing to get away from shrewish wives and contentious offspring.

Some women go fishing because it affords a wonderful way to put down overbearing husbands and draw attention to themselves.

Quite a few people fish because, like Greta Garbo, they want to be alone.

And there are those to whom the catching of the fish is secondary to being a leader of successful fishermen, with the prestige that comes with the leader's prowess in teaching others how to overcome complicated fishing problems.

But beyond these reasons is the basic one that while you are fishing you are divorced from the complications of everyday life, for a few hours the master of your actions and your soul. That nature supplies you with fish that are fun to catch and good to eat, and that your peers applaud when you are successful, add the vital germ of incentive to the fishing.

When folks first realize that they have been bitten by the fishing bug, the catching of the fish is so exciting that larger goals loom only dimly on the horizon. But as familiarity with successful fishing sets in, most anglers become aware that over a period of time they have been unconsciously absorbing lessons of nature, developing a feeling of kinship with the wild creatures of streams, lakes, and the ocean.

This awareness adds depth and scope to the enjoyment of their fishing. Some press on to become tournament anglers, revelling in the competitive application of personal and team fishing skills. Others discover the layman's level of the great field of marine science, assisting programs of scientific investigation by participating in fish-tagging, and by volunteering boats and manpower and serving on the governing boards of institutions of marine learning and research.

The great majority are content quietly to seek greater understanding of fish, fishing equipment, and fishing techniques, not so they may go out and catch every last fish in the water, but to increase their satisfaction by becoming proficient at more challenging ways of fishing.

This volume does not pretend to reveal every answer to all of the problems of fishing. It does try to cover the basic points of offshore and inshore salt water boat fishing, while introducing a number of ideas and bits of insight that seldom are described adequately in print. It aims to encourage fishing under the accepted rules of sportsmanship and conservation of species and habitat.

Since most sport fishermen are philosophers at heart, as well as being practical souls, the book is arranged with informative, how-to chapters blended with stories that convey the mood and feeling of fishing. It's relatively easy to tell where, when, and how to catch fish, but not always as easy to tell why fish do or do not bite, and why certain methods are more productive than others. The book is designed to bridge this information gap.

Special thanks should be expressed to Critchell Rimington, Publisher of *Sportfishing* and *Yachting* magazines, for permission to use articles that were originally published in those periodicals. Thanks are due also to the following writers who have contributed substantial portions of the book: the late J. Nelson Benedict, Harry Bonner, Larry Green, Vic McCristal, Charles R. Meyer, Norman Phillips, Milt Rosko, Mark Sosin, and Russell Tinsley.

The oceans are the last frontier still open to most modern men for individual exploration. Present day boats, motors, and fishing and navigation equipment have put this mysterious, exciting frontier within reach of almost all who have a yen to discover for themselves the true identity of the sea and its denizens.

The purpose of this book is to help make that discovery a little bit more joyous and complete.

Successful Ocean Game Fishing

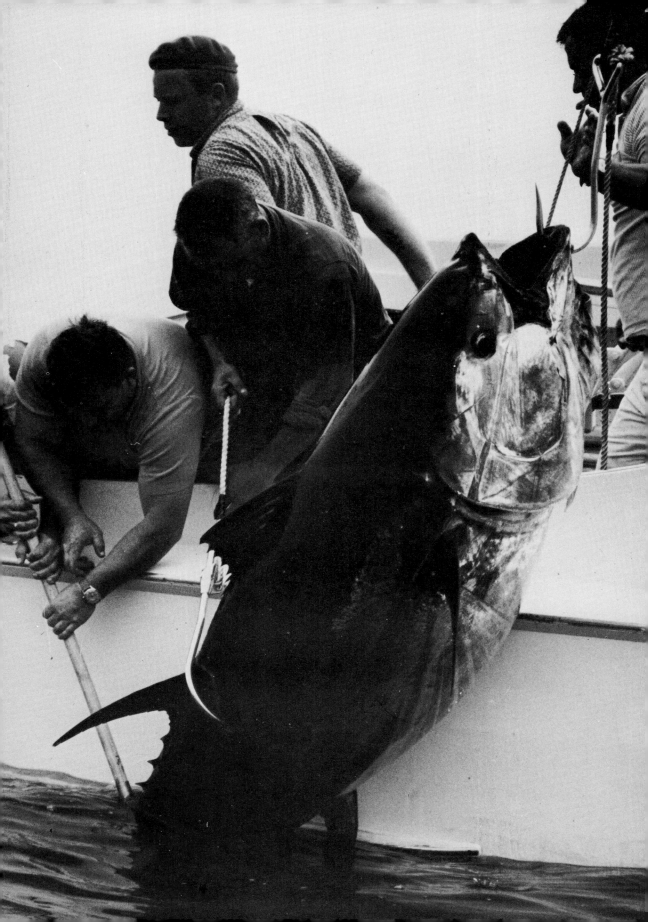

FRANK T. MOSS

1 / Big Bad Bluefins

A FEW YEARS AGO, DURING AN EAST COAST tournament, a weary angler battled a big bluefin tuna for more than ten hours before the crew finally mercifully cut the line to save the fisherman from what looked like an impending heart attack. What made his defeat doubly bitter was the fact that on the same day a bantamweight of an angler named A. M. "Whizz" Whisnant whipped a 542-pounder in the sizzling time of 12 minutes flat.

When extremes of performance like these occur you can't blame folks for asking questions.

Is it true that the supposedly big, bad bluefins are actually pushovers for an athlete with a fast boat and the proper kind of super-tackle? If so, then how do you explain the day-long struggles that have sent strong men to the hospital and others back to golf?

Not often have the true answers been aired in print. Luck plays a big part, but so do the factors of physical condition, personal fishing skill, and a certain special understanding of the basic construction and nature of these remarkable fish. Just as a girl who knows judo can floor a masher twice her size, so can a knowledgable fisherman whip a quarter-ton fish in what appears to be impossibly fast time by using the tuna's power and speed to accomplish its downfall.

Make no mistake, these are the most powerful fish that swim. Few fish carry streamlining to such perfection. The tiny dorsal fins fold down into slots in the back. The curved pectoral fins fold back into shallow depressions in the flanks like the diving planes of a submarine. The outer surface of the eyeballs are flat and flush with the surface of the head. The surprisingly small, trim tail is an oscillating propeller as efficient as any man-made rotating propeller.

The closest thing to a tuna that man has been able to contrive is the naval torpedo. As far as chemistry is concerned, both tuna and torpedo are fuel-burning engines that consume oxygen at a prodigious rate while driving the engine forward at speeds of between 40 and 50 knots. The torpedo carries spare oxygen compressed in a bottle or in the form of hydrogen peroxide, but the tuna has to extract oxygen by passing sea water over its gills.

And herein lies the tuna's great weakness.

From the time a tuna is hatched until the moment it dies it must swim forever forward through the water to maintain the flow of water over its gills. It is not able to "breathe" while motionless in the water in the manner of a goldfish in a bowl. It will suffocate if brought to a prolonged standstill in the water. What this means to the fisherman we will quickly see.

Suppose an enemy were to tie your hands behind your back and tape your nose and mouth tightly shut. Then suppose he were to give you a jolt in the backside with an electric cattle prod. You could probably uncork at least a 50-yard sprint without breathing, running on oxygen "borrowed" from your blood and other tissues. If this evil person kept after you with the prod he would quickly drive you to the point of collapse from lack of oxygen.

At this point, if you were able to get your hands free and rip off the tape, your labored, automatic breathing would eventually restore you to the land of the living. But if the tape were not removed you would surely die. This is the "secret" of how supposedly lucky fishermen manage to kill big bluefin tuna in such shockingly fast time.

The secret is to drive the tuna into making run after screaming run until the hooked fish is on the verge of collapse from lack of oxygen. How do you gag the tuna? He gags himself whenever he puts on a burst of speed. In order to protect his gills and perfect his streamlining he automatically clamps his jaws tightly shut when he shifts into overdrive. Like the gagged sprinter, he burns up body oxygen at a terrific rate with no way of replenishing the supply until he slows down.

In the early days of sport fishing, people believed that only by sheer muscle power could one overcome a big tuna. But in the mid-1920's there emerged a new class of big game fishermen who were sure there had to be a way of taking these powerful fighters on tackle lighter than the enormous 20/0 line winches then popular.

Skippers like Tommy Gifford and Bill Hatch, working with anglers of the caliber of Mike Lerner, Lou Marron, and Papa Hemingway, discovered that big tuna could be caught faster with lighter tackle if the boat were used to chase the fish and if the angler employed tactics to keep the fish running until it reached the point of collapse from anoxia.

This proved to be the most exciting fishing these men had ever known, because it also soon became apparent that the fish were frequently capable of figuring out what the men and the boats were trying to do to them, and certain smart fish tried every trick in the book to avoid crossing the dangerous threshold of oxygen starvation. This rare excitement helps to explain why civilized men and women are willing to undertake the frustrations, uncertainties, and heartbreaks of fishing for the big, bad bluefins.

Present-day tuna fishermen now widely understand the jujitsu tactics that are used to capture giant bluefins in swift time. The easiest way to describe these tactics is to recount the fishing trip on which Whizz Whisnant performed the 12-minute feat mentioned at the start of this chapter. I was Whisnant's skipper that day and had a flying-bridge view of everything that happened.

There were four of us on my twin-screw fishing cruiser, the *Kuno II*, and we were drifting and chumming at Shark Ledge, off Block Island, where a very large body of big tuna was living and feeding. The chum was a thin soup of ground menhaden mixed with seawater. The bait was a live whiting jigged up from the bottom by Joe Pollio, my regular mate. Assisting Joe was Jim Schwarz, a husky young Montauker.

Whisnant was fishing his own personal tuna rig, a 12/0 Fin-Nor reel loaded to the bars with 39-thread linen line. The reel was mounted on a Tycoon fiberglass rod with roller guides. The tip had a rated weight of about 30 ounces. Whizz had placed the rod in one of the fighting chair rod holders and was standing at the boat's side, tending the live bait with the fishing line in his hands like a hand line.

Suddenly he grunted and heaved back strongly on the line with both hands, setting the hook in the mouth of the tuna that had picked up the live bait several fathoms below the surface. Before I could get the motors started he had leaped into the chair, grabbed the rod,

Nova Scotians take their tuna aboard the hard way. A stout rope is passed through the gills and mouth. Several men haul on this while others fasten to the tuna with long-handled gaffs. All hands heave together and the fish comes sliding in with a rush. Tuna as heavy as 800 lbs. are boated this way.

stripped Whisnant's reel clean. But it kept changing course at radical angles and twice I was hard put to keep from running over the line.

All the while Whisnant sat in the chair, alternately reeling in slack line with the speed of a motor winch and laying back on the harness straps to wait out another wild, tearing run. Finally the tuna sounded deep and lay doggo, refusing to run any more.

"Stop the boat!" commanded Whisnant, the line almost straight up and down from the tip of his rod over the stern.

I recognized the problem. The tuna was winded, but not yet at the brink of collapse. Whisnant's task was to goad it into more oxygen-burning runs before the tuna could gather its strength and assume command of the situation.

Shoving the drag lever to the maximum position, Whizz lifted his body from the seat with straightened legs, pitting his full weight and strength against the fish. The taut line hummed and twanged as he plucked at it with his fingers as if it were a harp string. Then he began rocking back and forth against the pull of the rod, sending powerful humming shocks down the line to the fish.

After delivering a half-dozen such shocks, he suddenly sat down in the chair, released the drag to low tension and shouted, "Get away from him—fast!"

I shot the boat ahead. The sudden slackening of line tension after all that humming and banging with the rod evidently made the tuna believe it was now free. It uncorked a final, desperate run.

An angler at Conception Bay, Newfoundland, sweats out the last few moments of a fight with a big bluefin. Straps of the kidney harness carry weight of rod and fish, leaving the fisherman's hands free to manipulate the reel and guide the line evenly onto the reel's spool. Glove protects the left hand.

buckled in the harness straps, and was striking the fish heavily with the rod to goad it into action. Action is what we got.

The fish took off at top speed directly toward several nearby drifting tuna boats. As the engines fired into life I pushed the throttles up into the corner and flung the boat after the fish. She was only a 12 knot cruiser, but she must have looked like a Gold Cup racer coming head on.

The drifting boats quickly opened up a hole to let the fish and us go roaring through.

The next few minutes were a blur of action as the wild fish dashed first one way, then another, trying to get away from the maddening pull of the line and the pursuing boat. If it had had the wit to concentrate all its power and speed in one straight run it surely would have

This time, instead of permitting the tuna to take line under moderate tension, Whisnant pushed the drag down to maximum and the tuna slowly churned toward the surface, drawn upward by the flattening angle of the line caused by the forward motion of the boat. The fish now was too far gone in anoxia to realize what was happening.

It broke water 50 yards astern, the blunt bullet head coming clear of the surface before falling sidewise into a swoon. The fish lay there inert while Whisnant winched it to the boat's side with quick, short pumps of the rod. Jim Schwarz grasped the leader and held the tuna close while Joe Pollio made fast to it with the flying gaff.

As the gaff struck home my right thumb closed on the stem of the stopwatch. When I paused to record the fighting time I found that the sweep hand had stopped just a few seconds short of the 12-minute mark.

Some critics, observing the regularity with which certain anglers dispatch big bluefins in cigaret-smoking time, have accused these fish of being "over-rated" when it comes to measuring true fighting ability. The common mistake is to compare tuna with trout or salmon on a supposedly pound-for-pound basis. No such comparison can be made, and the majority of these critics are persons who have never caught a big tuna and who don't intend to risk a heart attack or what they think is their professional standing by trying.

Bill Carpenter, President of the International Game Fish Association (IGFA), has caught hundreds of these huge, powerful fish, many of them in extremely fast time. He claims the full-grown bluefin is the only fish in any ocean, with the possible exception of the large Pacific black or blue marlin, that fully justifies the use of 130-lb. class tackle.

Many experienced tuna anglers now fish regularly with 80-lb. class tackle, and quite a few are experimenting with 50-lb. equipment. The latter appears to be about the lower limit of tackle that can be used successfully against these very strong fish, because of the terrific tension that must be applied at times to turn or hold the fish.

One drawback to the use of tackle in the 50-lb. class and under for big bluefins is a flaw inherent in IGFA fishing rules. Under IGFA rules, with 80 and 130-lb. class line a double line of 30 feet may be employed with a leader 30 feet long. With line of 50-lb. test and under, double lines of only 15 feet and leaders no longer than 15 feet may be used. In the case of fishing for big bluefins, this rule puts an unintentional extra handicap on the 50-lb. tackle fisherman.

Big bluefins are notorious for being nasty alongside the boat. With 130 or 80-lb. line, it is often possible to get a few turns of the 30-foot double line on the reel, enabling the angler to use double the amount of drag tension that can be used with a single line. With a double line only 15 feet long, it is next to impossible to get some double line on the reel so that this extra drag tension can be applied to hold a bad fish that is ready to be gaffed, but wants to go the other way. It is hoped that a change in IGFA tackle rules may soon correct this unintended tackle rule inequality.

The ultimate challenge is to take one

A. M. "Whizz" Whisnant (left) and the author with the 542-lb. bluefin that Whisnant caught in 12 minutes fishing time off Block Island, R.I. A former member of the United States tuna team that fished the Alton B. Sharp matches at Wedgeport, N.S., Whisnant was one of the early exponents of driving big tuna to the point of oxygen starvation, making very fast captures possible.

Stern door in this modern tuna cruiser makes it possible to slide the fish into the boat's cockpit directly from the water. Door does not weaken boat's transom if properly installed. Some builders now offer stern doors as part of their line of "optional" equipment. For comparison with a typical hoisting arrangement, such as the well-known gin pole, turn back to page 2 for a close-up of a big bluefin being prepared for lifting into the boat with a rope fall.

of these mighty fighters from a boat with no power at all. Many people don't realize that Commander Duncan Hodgson's IGFA former world record bluefin, a 977-pounder caught at St. Ann's Bay, Nova Scotia, in 1950, was hooked and fought from a rowing cutter.

The late Harry Alfandre once fought and lost from a 14-foot rowing sharpie a tuna that competent observers swore would have topped 1,200 lbs. Later, his 15-year-old son Ronnie captured a 600-pounder from the same sharpie in the very professional time of 30 minutes.

Fishing for these monsters requires that the angler be in top physical and emotional shape and have the best in boat, crew, and tackle. More fishermen have suffered strokes and heart attacks while fighting big tuna than while fighting any other species of large game fish.

Proving that small boats are practical for tuna, provided they are properly handled, Dr. Oswald B. Deiter of New Jersey caught this 597-pounder from a 19-foot MFG outboard at Conception Bay, Newfoundland, in 1965 on 130-lb. line.

This high-speed Enterprise fisherman is typical of modern boats built for big game fishing under tournament conditions. Fishing is invariably done at moderate trolling speeds, but the ability of modern boats to hold good cruising speeds in any reasonable sea and weather has extended their ranges.

FRANK T. MOSS

2 / Evolution of the Sport Fishing Boat

THE IDEA OF DESIGNING AND EQUIPPING A boat to meet the special requirements of sport fishing was born in the early 1930's. Before then, a boat for pleasure fishing was any old crock too far gone for cruising or commercial fishing. Charles Frederick Holder wrote in 1905 of fishing off the California coast for marlin and tuna from explosion-prone naphtha launches and one-lung, make-and-break gasoline skiffs. Distillate that leaked into the bilges helped mask the aroma of bait.

Between World Wars I and II, in the early days of the Bamboo Age of sport fishing, anglers and professional fishing guides became dissatisfied with what then passed as fishing boats. Designing a boat from the keel up for fishing was still a radical idea, so existing hulls were rebuilt to reflect their owners' thoughts of what made better fishing boats.

Comfort was secondary. Converted office swivel chairs were installed sans cushions lest anglers fall asleep and miss a strike. Bare feet were an advantage when scrambling up the cabin side to the rudimentary flying bridge. One swordfisherman installed a telephone pole, climbing spikes and all, to serve as a lookout tower. When the phone company took to creosoting its poles to discourage termites, the puzzling loss of straight poles near some fishing ports ceased to be a problem.

As fishing boats go, some of the old conversions were surprisingly effective. My own first command was a converted Bliss torpedo retriever, model of 1918,

that had been revamped as a charter fishing boat not long after the repeal of Prohibition. She did 14 knots with a straight-eight motor out of an old Packard and caught bluefish and tuna like a demon.

New Englanders tended toward converting small commercial fishing hulls. Draggers up to 35 feet and 45 feet were likely material. Maine lobster boat hulls were especially sought for their good looks, seakindliness, and fair turn of speed with moderate power. New Jersey fishermen turned likewise to the home product and developed outstanding conversions of the famous lapstreak Jersey sea skiffs. In fact, some of the earliest boats built expressly for sport fishing were launched in the early and mid-1930's at small New Jersey boat yards.

Chesapeake fishermen favored the motorized deadrise and the distinctive, round stern North Carolina deadrise launch. Floridians utilized every old cruising power boat they could lay hands on, thereby sampling what was good and bad from a score of boat building sources. Fishermen along the Gulf of Mexico motorized local shoal draft crab and shrimp sloops. On the West Coast, particularly in the San Francisco Bay region, Greek and Italian styles of commercial tuna and salmon trolling boats carried over into the burgeoning sport fishing fleet.

Thus, until the early 1930's, sport fishing craft in the United States were a motley group reflecting extremely varied design backgrounds. Then, immediately after the repeal of Prohibition, a new influence began to assert itself in sport fishing boat design.

Among the better things spawned by the Great Drought of Prohibition were the light, fast, highly efficient rum runners that so radically changed the power boat picture during their brief, spectacular career. No boats like them had existed before. *Grey Ghost, Whispering Wind, Running Wild,* their names evoked visions of speed and clandestine adventures. Powered by two, three, or even four thundering Liberty airplane engines, they ran away from anything the outclassed Coast Guard could field to try to catch them.

Repeal beached the fast thunderbirds. Canny charter skippers and offshore game fishermen quickly bought up the long, lean hulls. Out came the bulky, balky, gas-gulping Liberty motors. In went converted Cadillacs, Packards, Buicks, Oldsmobiles, truck motors, tractor diesels, and early prototypes of the V-8 automotive-marine power plants that are so successful today.

The converted rum runners were not fast in terms of their original designed speeds, but they were bigger, lighter, and a lot faster than many of the old commercial hulls that they replaced. Offshore fishermen at last had boats capable of operating 30, 40, and 50 miles at sea in any reasonable weather, and of pounding home at better than a slow crawl when the going got dusty.

After Repeal, boat yards that had been busy building rum runners now had to scramble to keep from going under. Many were just shaking off the financial wreckage of the Great Depression. Those that were able got into the business of building yachts and sport fishing craft, incorporating into the new pleasure craft lessons learned from commercial boats and rum runners.

Now, for the first time, a dedicated sport fisherman could order a boat that

W. E. S. Tuker's famous Copigue *was converted from a working launch, but her humble origin did not keep her from piling up a magnificent record off the Chilean coast, catching swordfish in the days before World War II. Power was a Ford conversion, outrigger was a slender shaft of Calcutta bamboo.*

During the early days of sport fishing, many boats were converted from small contemporary commercial fishing craft. *Gail Ann* follows the lines of a traditional New England dragger. Her long career saw her eventually donated to the University of Rhode Island for use as an auxiliary research vessel.

Bounder, owned by the late restaurateur Jack Reiber, was originally a Chris-Craft double cabin cruiser of pre-World War II vintage. Addition of a small flying bridge atop the deckhouse, and chairs in the cockpit, made a useful if unconventional sport fisherman of her. She is shown trolling at Montauk Point for bluefish, at which she achieved a high degree of success.

was not a marine hybrid, but a vessel specifically designed with a fisherman's requirements in mind. Companies like Matthews, A.C.F., Elco, Baltzer-Jonesport, Chris-Craft, and Consolidated found that there was money in the sport fishing market.

The new sport fishing boats were not complete fishing machines as we know them now. After an owner got delivery of his vessel he usually had to add such refinements as outriggers, fishing chairs, hoisting gear, fish and bait boxes, and rod holders. But the new boats were a big step in the right direction.

They had commodious, self-bailing cockpits, sturdy deckhouses to support flying bridges and topside control equipment, and comfortable living accommodations below. With constant refinement of hull designs, top speeds of up to 20 knots without excessive power became available. Most important, fishermen with experience were comparing notes and a standardized design was now evolving.

Then came World War II and fishing and boating were knocked into a cocked hat. The Second World War had a direct and profound effect on power boat design. The famous PT boats built by Elco and other manufacturers brought the load-carrying, high-speed, full-planing hull to a peak of perfection. Immediately after the end of hostilities thousands of young men were itching to get back on the water with fast capable sport fishing boats of their own.

Just before the advent of World War II, the top boats of the Miami sport fishing fleet looked like this. Most boats had rudimentary flying bridges. Outriggers were universal, but not a single tuna tower was visible. Speeds of 10 to 12 knots were considered to be adequate. The classic sport fisherman style was starting to develop.

Built in 1946 at Wareham, Mass., the author's 32-foot Kuno typified the new trends in sport fishing boat design of the post-war period. Single screw, with a speed of 15 knots, she was an excellent inshore boat, but small for serious offshore big game work. Towers had not yet been invented. Many such boats carried harpooning gear to use on swordfish if baiting should fail.

Built in the mid-1950s by Wheeler of Clason Point, N.Y., Boma was typical of the fast, comfortable fishermen that discriminating owners were starting to ask for. These distinctive boats combined good fishing design with sea ability, speed, and accommodations for owner's party and professional crew. They could operate up to 60 miles offshore and cruise at more than 20 knots.

At first they had to make do with conversions of older yachts and government surplus small craft, but boat builders, once again scrambling for the civilian dollar, soon began turning out sport fishing cruisers that proved to be a new breed. The old, proven configuration of cockpit, flying bridge, outriggers, and fishing chairs was retained, but new materials, hull designs, power plants, and construction methods resulted in boats that sent old timers home shaking their heads in disbelief.

Some of these new boats were fantastically expensive. The Rybovich Boat Yard of West Palm Beach, Florida, for example, limited its production to a handful of exquisitely finished fishing cruisers each year, but what sea-witches these boats were! Cruising speeds of 20 to 30 knots in any fishable weather were commonplace. The new racers could slam off to the edge of the continental shelf while pre-war tubs were wallowing out to the inner edge of the blue water.

At about the same time the Leek brothers of Lower Bank, New Jersey, started mass-producing their famous wooden Pacemaker fishermen, building into their boats features learned from their own extensive sport fishing ventures. A few years later the Leeks acquired the Alglas Company and began building fiberglass fishing models.

The Hatteras Boat Company of High Point, North Carolina, began in 1960 to build fiberglass fishing cruisers. Fiberglass was then a relatively untried boat material. Here again the practical fishing experience of key company personnel resulted in boats that could be delivered to clients designed and completely equipped for all kinds of fishing.

One of the Leeks' strongest rivals in boat sales and tournament competition was the late Willis Slane whose *Hatterascal* fished almost every important tournament from Cape Hatteras to Florida and the Bahamas.

But perhaps the most striking innovation to blossom in the days of the great post-war boating boom was the fast, non-pounding, deep-V hull, designed by C. Raymond Hunt and popularized by Dick Bertram. The Bertram 31-footer was not large as sport fishing cruisers go, but like the ubiquitous Volkswagen, you found Bertrams slamming along in the darnedest places.

The legendary Captain Tommy Gifford fished a Bertram for years at his Montauk and Florida bases. Bertrams participated at every tournament from Maine to Key West. The late Ray Smith ordered a fleet of six 31-footers when he opened his fabulous Club de Pesca at Piñas Bay, Panama.

Bertrams sold well because they were fast, good looking, tough, almost unstoppable in a sea, and caught fish well.

A similar period of evolutionary growth was experienced among the smaller boats that make up the enormous inshore and fresh water sport fishing fleet. Mainly outboard and inboard-outboard powered, they number in the millions. The Commonwealth of Pennsylvania, for example, registered 100,000 power boats in 1970, 60 per cent of which were said to be used primarily for fishing.

Within a few years the new materials of fiberglass and aluminum proved themselves ideal for construction of small, fast, safe, easily operated power fishermen. An early innovation was the amidships control console at which the steering and motor controls were grouped as they are in most larger power fishing craft.

Down in Florida the demand for fast, shoal-draft, commodious open skiffs that could be used either on the bonefish flats or out in sailfish water sparked the development of handsome, powerful outboard fishermen, true fishing machines in sizes ranging from 19 feet to 24 feet. Most of them now feature a raised forward casting platform and cunningly contrived storage spaces for tackle, fish, and bait.

Among sport fishing boats large and small, the factors that have proved most successful have been the layouts, control systems, and modifications to hull form designed by fishermen, for fishermen. Any fast boat can tow a water skier, but a general utility and water skiing boat does not always give the kind of performance and comfort that fishermen now demand.

So many different types of sport fishing boats have developed in recent years, it's no longer possible to say "sport fisherman" without at least eight different types of boats coming to mind. For example, a New Jersey bass angler will automatically think of a husky outboard or inboard-outboard skiff in the 16-foot to 20-foot range. At the same time a southern California offshore man may think in terms of one of the new, monster, 80-foot super-fishermen that are now being built for the long, exciting runs to Baja California and Mexico.

Here is a breakdown of the eight major classes:

1) *Super-cruisers*, 60 feet–80 feet long. Patterned after the long-range, West Coast party boats, these powerful vessels can base 8 to 15 people in comfort for extended voyages of two to four weeks. Full electronic navigating, communicating, and fish-finding equipment. Some carry Whalers and similar small boats for specialized light tackle fishing. Costs range from $200,000 up.

2) *Tournament fishermen*, 35 feet–60 feet long. Full cruising accommodations for four to six. Equipment for all types of competitive fishing. Towers, radar, loran, electronic sounders, medium and short wave radio telephones. Capable of fishing 50 to 70 miles offshore in good weather. Costs vary from $45,000 to $200,000.

The super-fisherman Give Up, *built in 1970 by Huckins, is 80 feet long with a cruising range of 850 miles at the sustained cruising speed of 21 knots. Accommodations are for up to eight in the owner's party and a crew of two or three. Main engines and auxiliary power are diesel, assuring efficiency.*

This Hatteras 45-foot convertible cruiser is both a family cruising boat and a tournament sport fisherman. The hull is of fiberglass, a material that has met with much favor since its introduction in the early 1960s. The tower, welded of stainless steel tubing, carries the radar antenna on a spider.

3) *Vest-pocket offshore fishermen*, 25 feet–35 feet long. They carry most of the equipment of larger boats, in miniature, and relatively comfortable cruising accommodations for four friendly people. Fast and able in surprisingly rough water. Limited by fuel capacity to a maximum of about 40 miles offshore in good weather. A popular, fast-growing class costing from $12,000 to $30,000.

4) *The big amphibians*, 20 feet–25 feet long. Large trailable outboard or inboard-outboard open or semi-open skiffs. Usually with a center control console and semi-raised forward fishing deck. Most are of fiberglass, feature built-in fish and bait tanks, demountable outriggers, simple but effective electronic gear. Costs range from under $3,500 to at least $8,000.

5) *Large trailable skiffs*, 16 feet–20 feet long. Tremendously popular on inland lakes and rivers, and for protected salt water areas. Most can be equipped with portable sounders, RDFs, citizen's band radio units, popular trolling or casting tackle. Costs, including trailers, go from $1,500 to $5,000.

6) *Small trailable skiffs*, 12 feet–16 feet long. The favorites of salt water surf casters for beach launching. Perfect for two-man fishing operations on sheltered water. Outboard powered, costing from $1,000 to $2,000, depending on trailer, special equipment.

7) *Cartop portables*, 8 feet—12 feet long. These small, one-or-two-man boats can be carried atop a Jeep or station wagon where trailers cannot be towed. Small size restricts types of tackle and fishing that can be enjoyed. Costs range from under $300 to about $700.

8) *Inflatables*, 8 feet—14 feet long. Ordinarily, inflatable boats are not thought of as good fishing boats. Oceanographer Jacques Cousteau proved the value of inflatables for fast skin-diver and fishing research work on the *Calypso*. Can be back-packed into areas where only men and horses can travel. Require some special care, but are surprisingly rugged and safe. Under $300 to about $800 in cost.

What is the outlook for the future? More and better boats are looming on the piscatorial horizon. Franco Harrauer's radical Italian plywood and aluminum sport fishing power catamarans are setting new standards of style, speed, stability, and utility.

Fishing from boats is no longer the prerogative of the rich. Now there is a fishing model available for just about any kind of angling that requires a boat. The evolution of sport fishing boats in the last twenty years has had a stimulating effect on the boat building industry as a whole. Fishermen in particular have benefitted from the effort to build higher performance and greater reliability into boats that have a magnificent heritage to begin with.

A modern offshore sport fishing boat is a self-contained fishing machine. It is also a cruiser with many of the comforts of home. Ed Gruber's famous 42-foot Rybovich-built fisherman Nitso *ranges the Atlantic coast from Cape Cod to Florida, is prepared to fish for everything from sails to swordfish.*

3 / Equipping the Offshore Sport Fishing Boat

JUST AS SPORT FISHING BOATS EVOLVED over a number of years from a variety of sources, so did fishing equipment develop from relatively modest beginnings. The flying bridge, for example, was invented by professional skippers who grew tired of the confinement and poor vision afforded by the conventional deckhouse controls of early converted cruising yachts.

Equipping an offshore fisherman for combined light and heavy duty fishing requires considerable planning. Fortunately, most of the experimental work has been done already and if an owner or builder follows existing, successful models the final result is usually quite workable.

The purpose of any equipment is to enhance the success of the activity. In sport fishing, the equipment of an offshore fishing cruiser can be divided into two major classes—operating gear and fishing gear.

Operating gear is that which is vital to fishing, but is not used directly for fishing. Navigating, communicating and boat-handling equipment are examples. Fishing gear is that which is directly concerned with fishing and which finds little use on a non-fishing vessel. Tackle, outriggers, fishing chairs, and the lookout tower are good examples. The following lists enumerate the important items in each category:

Operating Gear

Flying bridge
Cockpit controls
Cockpit lights
Compasses
Cleaning gear
Washdown pump
Sea temperature gauge
Radio telephone
Radio direction finder
Sounding machine
Loran, consolan, etc.
Radar
Intercom

Fishing Gear

Lookout tower
Outriggers
Bait freezer
Gin pole
Gaffs
Rod storage
Fishing belts
Bait board
Live bait tank
Fishing chairs
Fish box or well
Rod holders
Stern door
Tackle chest
"Rocket launcher"
Fishing harness
Knife rack

The flying bridge is the logical control station for most fishing operations. Naturally, it should be equipped with all necessary navigating, communicating, and fish-detecting aids. If the main radio telephone unit is located in the deckhouse, make sure that a band-switching remote control box is installed within easy reach of the bridge operating station. Modern sounders are compact enough for bridge installation. The space inside a bridge console is usually ample for a sounder, radio telephone, RDF, intercom box, and sea temperature gauge.

Some boat designers have made the mistake of locating the flying bridge steering and engine controls so far forward that the operator cannot see what's going on in the cockpit. A full, unobstructed view of at least the after half of the cockpit, including the entire fighting chair, is a must for successful big game fishing.

Not all offshore fishermen have the lower control station located in the cockpit, but a complete control station close to the scene of fishing action is a great help, especially in competitive fishing where every bit of efficiency counts.

Towers and outriggers are specialized equipment that require treatment in considerable detail. They will be dealt with in chapters to follow. Let us consider now the choice and placement of fishing and fighting chairs.

Popular usage defines a fighting chair as that heavy cockpit chair that is mounted well aft on the centerline and which has an adjustable footrest. The fighting chair is used primarily with heavy tackle for big game. A fishing chair, on the other hand, is any light fixed or portable chair, equipped with a rod butt gimbal, that can be used for light and medium game. Fishing chairs do not have footrests.

The purpose of the footrest of the fighting chair is to enable the angler to lift and brace his feet in such a manner as to place the power and thrust of his legs and thighs in direct opposition to the pull of the line and the rod.

With tackle of 50-lb. line class or heavier, it is customary for the angler to wear a fishing harness. This is a vest or wide kidney strap that has adjustable straps that hook into lift rings on the top of the reel frame. The harness transfers the weight and pull of fish and rod to the angler's back, leaving both hands free for handling the reel and line. For tackle of less than 50 lbs., a lighter vest-style of harness is often used in conjunction with a belt equipped with a rod gimbal. Such a combination is good for stand-up competitive light tackle tournament fishing.

The most useful cockpit chair arrangement has a single centerline fighting chair flanked by two lighter fishing chairs. This permits light or heavy fishing without major changes of cockpit hardware.

A fighting chair is subject to tremendous strain, and it must be carefully installed. Heavy hardwood or plywood doubling pieces are needed under the deck plate, and bronze or stainless steel bolts, *never brass,* should be used. The fighting chair deck plate should be located so that when the footrest is fully extended, there is space for a man to move between the extended footrest and the stern or the portable after fish box, if such a unit is used.

Fishing chair seats can be between 16 and 18 inches to the top of the seat cushion from deck level for comfort. The fighting chair is frequently mounted at a much higher level and, because a footrest is provided, there is no reason for the angler to try to keep his feet on deck. In small boats where there is room in the stern for only one chair, the model to be selected is usually a light fighting chair of fiberglass rather than metal, with an easily dismounted footrest.

Fighting chairs are usually equipped

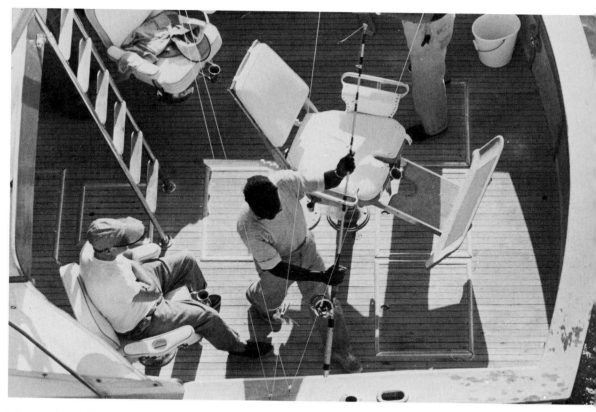

The cockpit above contains a fighting chair and two fishing chairs. This arrangement is ideal for mixed small and big game fishing. Charles Johnson rigged his TX-41 (below) with a single fighting chair for tournament work. Both boats have live bait tanks under convenient cockpit deck flush hatches.

with a rod holder on each arm. Fishing chairs may have a single rod holder or none at all, depending on the owner's preference. The choice of rod holder location for fishing convenience is mainly a matter of providing the best possible combination of rod placements that can be worked out for the kinds of fishing at hand.

If you expect to do considerable trolling for school tuna and similar fish, you will need a rod holder arrangement that will give good spread to the trolling lines and their respective rods. Angle-mounting certain holders helps, especially in smaller boats where at least two rods can be "wung out" from the corners of the stern to act as their own miniature outriggers, providing a non-tangling trolling line spread.

The new, flush-mounting rod holders are very popular. They can be installed at a wide variety of effective angles, and, because there is no exposed tubing or metalwork, there is little chance of an angler hurting himself by bumping into one of these holders in a rough sea.

For general purposes, the following rod holder arrangement works well for both big and small game fishing:
- Fighting chair: one holder on each arm rest.
- Fishing chairs: one holder on the outboard arm rest.
- Across stern: three or four flush-mounted holders.
- Cockpit sides: one outrigger rod holder each side.
- Flying bridge: pair of light holders for bait rods.

A new Florida development is the so-called "rocket launcher" rod holder arrangement. This is primarily a convenient way of mounting three, four, or more holders inside the cockpit for competitive light tackle stand-up fishing, where chairs are not used on sailfish, white marlin, and the like.

The "rocket launcher" is nothing more than a narrow board, either curved or straight, that is mounted flat in a thwartships position on top of a metal tube that fits into what is normally the fighting chair deck plate. The height of the board is about 32 inches above the deck. Several flush-mounted rod holders are arranged along the board in such a manner that their respective rods are held in a fan-shaped arrangement pointing toward the stern. The rods thus held look somewhat like slim missiles poised for launching, hence the descriptive name.

It is frequently necessary to stow a fairly large and bloody catch. The built-in stern fish box, popular a number of years ago, is seldom seen in modern fishing cruisers. A portable, insulated fiberglass deck fish box is more versatile. Drainage is achieved by short pieces of rubber hose thrust out through the stern scuppers or connected to stern drain fittings. Several manufacturers make deck fish and ice boxes in a variety of sizes and styles.

A fiberglass fish box liner makes an excellent under-deck fish well where there is space enough for such an installation. An under-deck fish well should be high enough in the hull to afford positive gravity drainage. Drains and water intakes must have sea cocks for safety. To be effective, any deck or under-deck fish storage container should have at least six cubic feet of capacity.

One advantage of the under-deck well is that it can be used as a live bait tank. Pacific anglers, experts at live bait fishing, usually prefer a deck-mounted live bait tank. Several portable models are now offered in one-scoop, two-scoop, and larger sizes, equipped with their own water circulating pumps, drains, and insulation. The "scoop" is the West Coast standard bulk measure of live bait and is about two-thirds of a bushel.

Equally important to stowing the catch is preservation of bait. Modern fishing

Nothing beats a light, insulated ice chest of the beverage cooler type for keeping the day's supply of trolling outrigger baits in perfect condition. Mullet and mackerel may be packed on shaved ice and kept several days, but squid should be wrapped in plastic to keep it from direct contact with ice.

The portable combination ice and fish box shown below is a manufactured job available in several types of finish. Drains can be led out through boat's scuppers. Foam interlining provides a good degree of insulation. When boat is not actively fishing, box acts as gear locker or can be left ashore.

Fall of this side-mounted gin pole is shackled to a standard sailboat type of boom end fitting at the top of the gin pole. The pole may be made of solid fir, oak, or ash, or it may be hollow-built like a sailboat spar of pine or cedar. Gin poles of aluminum or stainless steel may also be purchased.

Plastic has invaded the trolling lure market, and here are samples of what a modern fisherman may keep in a tackle locker. Pictured are artificial squid, bally-hoo, flying fish, mackerel, and eels. Dolphin has a nylon-covered wire leader. Other leaders are made up from a heavy-gauge nylon monofilament line.

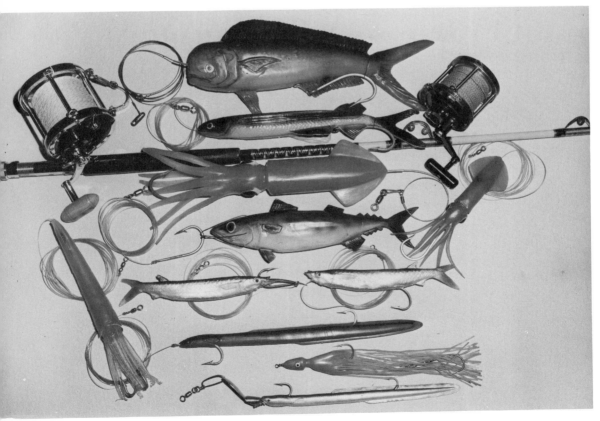

cruisers think nothing of working hundreds of miles from bait sources, now that small, reliable freezer units are so readily available. There is a wide choice of portable, built-in, or single-unit freezers powered either by the boat's 12 volt d.c. system or by 115 volt a.c. supplied by a shore connection in port and an auxiliary generator while underway.

The average boat bait freezer is capable of freezing at least two bushels of bait. The day's working supply, however, is usually kept on ice in a Styrofoam or foam plastic deck cooler. Some builders are now offering as optional equipment a combination freezer and tackle locker unit that can be installed in the cockpit well forward, and which forms a very handy tackle-fixing and bait-rigging station. One handy location for such a unit is beneath the ladder leading to the flying bridge.

The contents of the tackle locker, and miscellaneous cockpit equipment merit special consideration. Here is a list of important items:

Tackle Locker

Parallel jaw pliers
Bait knives
Cutting board
Bait needles
Backbone remover
Leader material
Ferrule cement
Small gas torch
Spare lines
Friction and plastic tape
Fish scaler
Outrigger release clips
Pork rind
Tagging kit
Whetstone
Reel wrenches
Reel spare parts
Reel lubricant
Crimping pliers

Assorted hooks
Assorted connectors
Assorted swivels
Hook disgorger
Assorted sinkers
50-lb. hand scale
Rod winding silk
Silk preserver
Monel wire line

Cockpit Equipment

Assorted hand gaffs
Flying gaff
Billy club
Dip net
Hand buckets
Boathook-line pusher
Jaw hook (for big tuna)
Tail ropes
Fish-lifting straps
Deck mop and scrubber

Getting small fish on board is usually easy if suitable hand gaffs or a dip net are handy, but boating big fish can be a problem. One answer is the stern door, a door cut into the stern that can be swung open at deck level, permitting big fish to be hauled in bodily after being killed. Stern doors are fine when they can be designed into a new hull, but often prove difficult to install in an existing hull.

For lifting big fish nothing beats the old fashioned side-mounted gin pole. The pole should be tall enough to give seven or eight feet of clear space between the cockpit side deck and the lower block of the two-blocked fall. A good choice of material is a clear oak 4 x 4, 12 to 14 feet long, stepped on the cockpit deck and secured to the deckhouse edge or overhang by means of a heavy bronze or stainless steel "U" strap.

The top fitting can be a specially cast bronze item, a suitable masthead or boom-end ring with shackle eyes, or a plain, heavy galvanized eyebolt. A four-part rope fall using half-inch nylon rope and double-sheave blocks will lift 500–600 lbs. without trouble. A six-part fall using the same rope rove through triple-sheave blocks will handle 1,000 lbs. Two or three manufacturers now offer all-metal fish-lifting davits that are very satisfactory when properly installed.

You'll also need light and heavy hand gaffs, a dip net, and a flying gaff if big game is your target. Make the flying gaff safety line from flexible bronze cable at least ⅜ inch in diameter, or from nylon yacht rope at least ⅝ inch in diameter. It may be up to 30 feet long and is shackled into the eye that is welded to the gaff hook shaft.

The final touch in the well-equipped fishing boat's preparation is the manner in which the working tools of the fishing trade are stowed in the cockpit. Gaffs should be handy, but out of the way. Small metal, wooden, or plastic hangers attached to the cockpit sides under the side deck overhang take care of these important units. The bait knives should be stowed in a safety knife caddy close to the normal bait-rigging position. Cleaning mops and scrubbers should be where they can be grabbed when needed, but not be underfoot.

Stowing rigged fishing rods is no problem if rod racks are installed under the deckhouse overhead. Some manufacturers now offer stock fishing models with special rod and reel lockers built into the deckhouse sides. At least one tackle maker can supply overhead rod hangers specifically designed to fit that company's IGFA class tournament tackle.

One item not found on every fishing boat, but which is a real work-saver, is a small electric sea water pump with a cockpit discharge valve and suitable washdown hose. Tuna blood can be sprayed away in seconds while it is still wet. Given a chance to set, it's as tough as varnish to remove.

A smart owner planning to equip a boat for offshore fishing first decides upon his fishing ambitions and needs, then plans an equipment layout that will afford maximum efficiency at minimum expenditure of physical effort. Modern tackle and equipment for fishing is so versatile it's difficult to outfit a sport fishing boat these days that won't do well in a wide variety of fishing situations.

4 / Tackling Billfish

I WAS A GUEST ON A SPORT FISHING BOAT sailing out of an East Coast port and we had been doing well with the school tuna while keeping an eye peeled for a swordfish or whatever billfish game might come our way. Trailing from our outriggers were a rigged eel and a rigged squid, both baits being fished from a matched pair of 9/o rigs loaded with 80-lb. test line, certainly a versatile tackle setup for a situation that might see us baiting anything from a 6o-lb. white marlin to a 6oo-lb. broadbill.

Suddenly, someone spotted the slim scythe blade tail of a white marlin cutting the water. Our professional skipper turned the cruiser and passed the squid before the marlin's nose. The fish sounded, then reappeared tailing downwind. On the next pass the rigged eel was presented. The marlin rushed the eel, but stopped short of actual contact and veered into the boat's wake where it inspected the tuna feathers before swinging away on its solitary course.

By this time we were thoroughly aroused, avid to capture this tantalizing fish. To make a frustrating story easier to tell, we spent the better part of an hour chasing and baiting that haughty little white. We gave it everything in the box, to no avail. Then along came another boat that had been invited by our skipper by radio to have a try at the fish, and we watched an almost unbelievable performance.

The other boat picked up the marlin in its wake on the first pass. It was as if a dinner bell had been rung. The marlin charged a flat line bait, dorsal fin erect and colors blazing. In fifteen minutes it had been teased, hooked, fought, tagged, and released while we sat there like the shocked parents of a wayward child asking each other, "What did we do wrong?"

Our captain had an explanation. "We probably bored the fish to death. When the other boat came along with a different combination of motor and wake noise and a different bait pattern, the marlin was disgusted enough to clobber something new."

It was a shrewd, ego-salving remark. The other skipper, whom we tracked down at a shoreside bar that evening, had a different story. "I was fishing with tournament class 20-lb. tackle and leaders of 50-lb. monofilament, not the medium-heavy swordfish gear that you fellows were using. Besides, I was using ballyhoo for bait, flown up from Florida."

His mate, a ham-handed Floridian with a repuation for being able to charm billfish into committing suicide, observed, "Ballyhoo to a white marlin is like grits to a Cracker. A healthy white just can't pass up a good ballyhoo."

This took place a number of years ago and since then billfish have not changed, but advances in tackle and new attitudes toward lighter tackle for billfish have taken much of the old frustration out of fishing for these wonderful fish. It is true that when we go for the giants of the billfish world we need the most powerful tackle we can get—12/o or larger reels loaded with 130-lb. class line, mounted on rods that could be used in a baseball game. But for white and striped marlin, small blues and blacks, sailfish, most swordfish, and the rare, exciting spear-fishes, we don't need such heavy gear.

The following table gives a rule-of-thumb comparison for judging what is now called very light, light, and standard tackle for billfish of average weight classes.

Fish Weight (pounds)	Tackle Rating	Reel Size	Line Class (pounds)
	Very light	2/0	12
Under 100	Light	3/0	20
	Standard	4/0	30
	Very light	3/0	20
100–250	Light	4/0	30
	Standard	6/0	50
	Very light	4/0	30
250–500	Light	6/0	50
	Standard	9/0	80
	Very light	6/0	50
Over 500	Light	9/0	80
	Standard	12/0	130

Modern tackle is so light in weight you don't tire yourself out fighting the weight and inertia of the equipment. Consequently, you can take quite respectable fish standing up, the truly sporty way to fish. With less line tension, the billfish is more likely to put on a good acrobatic display, a prime reason for hooking it in the first place.

The demand for quality reels to handle line in the various IGFA line class ratings has stimulated manufacturers to turn out models that combine smooth brake action with almost indestructible clutch linings and easily-calibrated drag-adjusting levers. Competition in the industry is bringing prices down to where quality game fishing tackle is within the reach of most anglers.

Until about 1950, the only good bill-fishing line was quality Cuttyhunk linen. This type of very-hard-laid line got its name from the fact that it was first laid up by hand on the island of Cuttyhunk, Massachusetts, where it was used for striped bass fishing at the turn of the century.

Cuttyhunk line was stronger wet than dry, quite uniform in quality and very wear-resistant. It had to be cleaned and dried between usings, however, because it was prone to damage from mildew. No manufacturer now makes Cuttyhunk except on special order. The reason is that two very satisfactory synthetic lines, nylon monofilament and braided Dacron, now dominate the line market.

Monofilament is available in sizes of from a pound or two to over 200-lb. breaking strain. It is rapidly becoming the favorite line of billfishermen in line classes up to 30 lbs. For heavier lines, braided Dacron is favored for tournament and other serious billfishing. Being softer than mono of the same test rating, Dacron is easier to drop-back to a fish without backlashing on the reel.

Some experts use 75 to 100 feet of mono spliced on top of a reel full of Dacron line of the same weight class. The best knot for achieving a connection between the two lines is the Albright Special, utilizing at least 40 turns of Dacron around the loop of mono during the making of the knot. The shot of mono on top of the Dacron is said to reduce line failure from surface abrasion under heavy usage.

The fight is over. The flying gaff is fast to the great marlin and the mate is grasping the fish's bill to bring it closer so that the tail rope may be drawn tight around the joint of its powerful tail. Now the angler can rest while the crew does the hoisting, knowing that at last the victory is his.

Light tackle allows a billfish to leap and greyhound to best advantage. This angler is using 20-lb. tackle standing up to take a Pacific striped marlin.

Mono is used almost exclusively with spinning reels and is popular with level-wind reels in the smaller sizes. There are so many grades made that it is possible to find a type of mono for just about any fishing situation including service in salt water fly casting with the so-called "shooting head" fly line.

The new "progressive taper" fiberglass rods have given billfishermen weapons of unprecedented lightness and power. Nowhere is this more evident than on the California and Baja coasts where marlin fishermen habitually use rods of a degree of tip flexibility that would seem excessive to conservative Eastern anglers. But the engineering of these rods is such that as tension on the line increases, extra power in the rod's midsection is brought into play making it possible to find in one rod the flexibility needed to handle light line and the backbone needed to lift heavy fish.

Modern roller guides have almost eliminated the bugaboo of line wear. Ring guides scuff and abrade mono or Dacron line badly, especially under heavy fishing tension. Rollers require cleaning and lubricating several times a season, but with reasonable care will last for years and will repay in saved line many times their slightly higher cost.

In the old days of linen line, fishing rods were rated in terms of tip weight in ounces. Tip weight was then the only positive measure of relationship between shaft power (as defined by tip weight) and the class of line that the rod could handle best. This was misleading because the weight of rod hardware contributes

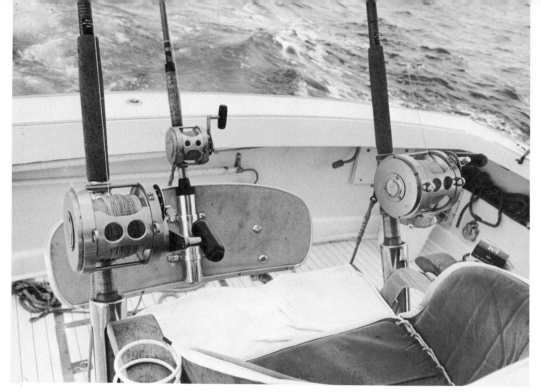

Here's one way of arranging rod holders for instant availability of rods. Holders on chair arms carry matched 50-lb. line class rigs with lines to the outriggers. The holder on the footrest carries a 30-lb. outfit working directly off the stern as a flatline. Gaffs stow under stern covering board.

Crew of the Miss Jeane 7 prepares to release a white marlin caught during a tournament in the Bahamas. Two gin poles provide ample hoisting capacity. Flying bridge seat has box gimbals to permit two anglers to fish light rigs as flatlines from this elevated position, a sporty way to take billfish.

nothing to the power of the shaft.

The smallest linen line ordinarily used was three-thread line, made of 50-leas linen. This tested roughly three pounds per thread, wet, or nine pounds for a three-thread line. All linen lines were classed not by pounds test, but by thread count. Lines of as heavy as 54 and 72 thread were made, testing 162 and 216 lbs. respectively. The standard rod-and-line combinations went about as follows:

Number of Threads	Breaking Strain (pounds)	Rod Tip Weight (ounces)	Equivalent IGFA Class (pounds)
3	9	2–3	12
6	18	4	20
9	27	6	30
15	45	10	50
24	72	16	80
39	112	24–30	130

Since rod materials were not consistent in quality, not all rods of a given weight performed as they should with the lines for which they were supposedly designed. Nowadays, manufacturers have largely abandoned the old tip weight system of rating rods and engineer specific rod models to perform according to dynamic deflection and rate-of-taper standards. The result is a completely integrated tackle outfit of uniformly high performance capability.

Because relatively few anglers can afford a complete personal "wardrobe" of billfish tackle in all of the IGFA line classes, it is important to be able to select equipment that will perform well with the widest logical variety of fish. Following are combinations of tackle that work well for the species and areas mentioned.

White marlin and Atlantic sailfish: Matched tackle in the 12, 20, and 30-lb. classes if one plans tournament fishing. For non-tournament fishing, 30-lb. class tackle is best.

Striped marlin and Pacific sailfish: Matched tackle in the 12, 20, and 30-lb. classes for tournament fishing. Thirty or 50-lb. class tackle for non-competitive fishing, especially if the fish tend to run large.

Atlantic blue marlin, broadbill swordfish: Matched tackle in the 30 and 50-lb. classes for special light tackle competition. Most tournaments recognize 80 or

Dr. Ferdinando Schiavoni, noted Italian sport fisherman, displays a rare short-billed spearfish caught in the Mediterranean. Dr. Schiavoni has been a leader in the development of sport fishing boats and methods in Europe.

The author's former mate, Harry Clemenz eyes a white marlin that he is getting ready to bill off Montauk, N.Y. Tackle here is a split bamboo rod, 15-thread linen line testing 45 lbs., and 12 feet of #9 stainless wire leader.

130-lb. class tackle as scratch equipment for Atlantic blue marlin and swordfish.

Pacific blue and black marlin, Chilean swordfish: These very large, powerful fish are seldom fished for with tackle under the 130-lb. class except by those seeking new records in the lighter class ratings.

There is a growing tendency for billfish anglers to own their own harnesses, thereby assuring a comfortable individual fit. For heavy duty work, nothing beats the "bucket" harness that features a seat built into the kidney belt in such a way that the harness cannot ride up or down the angler's back under heavy strain. It has to be used with a fighting chair to be effective.

Stand-up fishing, on the other hand, calls for a belt socket equipped with a butt gimbal to take the rod butt, plus a light shoulder harness or harness vest. Whether fishing standing up or in a fighting chair, the harness should be adjusted so that the entire weight of the rod and fish may be absorbed by the harness, leaving both hands free.

The rigging of baits and leaders is usually a function of the boat's crew and is discussed in detail later, but few competitive billfishermen travel without a few of their favorite leaders at hand. There is still much difference of opinion about leader material. Some prefer solid stainless steel wire, while others swear by monofilament, braided wire, or combinations of materials for special purposes.

Outriggers, of course, are essential to marlin and sailfishing, but are of lesser importance where swordfish are concerned. The metal lookout tower is now the trademark of the offshore fisherman. A fighting chair is needed with tackle of 50-lb. class or heavier. Most women and many men who are out of condition need a chair with 30-lb. tackle.

As a sport, billfishing has long ago broken away from the aura of exclusiveness. What was once a sport of princes now commands the efforts of many thousands of anglers throughout the world. Few sports can match a light tackle bout with a marlin, sailfish, or swordfish for excitement, suspense, and sense of personal combat. Defeat only goads the loser to greater efforts. Victory brings a sense of achievement afforded by few other endeavors.

5 / All About Outriggers

NOT LONG AGO A LEADING YACHTSMAN, writing in a well-known boating magazine, blew off steam about the "silly outriggers" carried by so many sport fishing craft. He called them status symbols stuck on fishing cruisers to give them a rakish look and to help the crew elevate the laundry on wash day. The gent probably wouldn't like it if someone were to make crude jokes about the "silly spinnaker poles" on his ketch.

The fact is sport fishermen use outriggers to raise, entice, and hook game fish.

The first fishing outrigger was a kite invented by South Sea natives hundreds of years ago to carry a bait far out from the canoe so that timid fish could be lured and caught. When members of the legendary Catalina Tuna Club first started fishing for yellowfin tuna and marlin off the coast of California at the turn of the century, they experimented with kites as a means of imparting lift and separation to trolled baits.

Kites proved cumbersome and difficult to control. It wasn't long before early professionals like the late Bill Hatch were sticking long bamboo poles out from the sides of their boats to achieve the same effect. Early outriggers employed snapjaw clothes pins for line release devices. Modern outriggers are built of fiberglass or metal tubing and have adjustable, spring-loaded release clips, but they work the same way the older 'riggers did.

In operation, the outrigger is lowered to the fishing position on the way to the fishing grounds. The angle of inclination is usually 45 degrees from the vertical, or slightly lower. There is enough after rake to the 'rigger shaft to place its tip at a point opposite or slightly aft of the boat's stern. This prevents the fishing line from fouling on rods and other gear in the boat's cockpit if a knock-down is had on the weather 'rigger on a windy day. It also places the release pins at a point where they are easily observed from the bridge and the cockpit.

The bait—a balao or other small fish—is streamed 60 to 90 feet behind the boat. The bight of the fishing line is then clipped into the release pin of the outrigger. Pin and line are hauled almost to the outrigger's extremity by means of the outrigger halyard, which may be parachute quality nylon cord or heavy gauge monofilament fishing line. The rod is either held in the angler's hands or is placed in a convenient rod holder, ready to be grabbed up when action appears imminent.

The line now extends from the rod tip to the outrigger pin and back to the bait which skips behind the boat, separated from the wake by the reach of the outrigger. Action of the bait is regulated by the length of line originally paid out and also by the speed of the boat, which may be from four to seven or eight knots. Careful skippers mark the correct clip-in point on each outrigger fishing line with a tie-in of light line or a daub of India ink.

When a fish strikes or grabs the bait, the sudden increase of line tension pulls

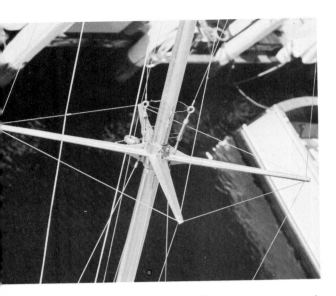

Spreader of this all-metal outrigger is made of cast, corrosion-resistant aluminum. The turnbuckles are wired to keep them from loosening in use.

Hinged upper strut of this outrigger locks when outrigger is lowered into the fishing position, preventing the 'rigger from jumping when boat rolls.

the line clear of the release pin or clip, dropping it to the water. If the fish happens to be hooked, the angler plays it in the normal manner. If not, he must instantly drop-back the bait for a short period of time so the fish can pick it up. If a pick-up is still not achieved, he must then reel in at a moderate rate, hoping to tease the fish into a striking mood while at the same time bringing the bait closer to the boat where it can be watched more easily. The boat keeps moving at trolling speed until the fish is hooked, when the boat is stopped and all other lines and baits are brought in.

Dropping the bait back to the fish with a conventional reel is accomplished by throwing the reel on free spool while very lightly thumbing the spool to prevent a backlash. A blistered thumb is the mark of an overanxious angler who forgets to re-engage the reel clutch or gears before trying to strike the hook into the fish. With a spinning outfit, the drop-back is made by opening the reel's bail. There is no danger of a blacklash here and the reel is re-engaged by giving the reel handle a single quick turn.

All this suggests that effective use of outriggers calls for a well-drilled crew and adequate instruction of guests before going fishing. Outriggers are important when fishing for marlin, sailfish, certain types of tuna, and game sharks like the mako and porbeagle. They are often used for swordfish, although some experts prefer to bait these fish directly from the cockpit.

It is common practice to place rods used with outriggers in rod holders until action develops. When rods are left untended in rod holders, the "click" of each reel must be engaged and the star or lever drag set to a low state of drag tension. This prevents breaking a rod on a heavy, blind strike. It pays to set up a rotating watch system among the anglers so that there will always be one or more alert fishermen ready to take up the outrigger rods when a big fish is raised to the baits.

Sometimes a sailfish or marlin will chase an outrigger bait, but refuse to strike it. When this happens, you may be able to hornswoggle the fish into a striking mood by yanking or "knocking down" the line from the release pin and alternately reeling in and dropping back the bait in a way calculated to frustrate and infuriate the quarry. When the fish comes charging at the bait with mouth open and fire in its eye, drop the bait to it momentarily so the morsel can be grabbed, then strike him quickly when you feel his weight on the line.

Skill with outriggers takes time and teamwork to develop. If a bait starts to spin, it may kink and ruin a valuable line. Hooks pick up grass and weed which

must be cleaned off. The striking drag of reels must constantly be kept at the proper value.

Some fishermen rig two sets of halyards to their outriggers, permitting double the normal number of baits or lures to be streamed at one time. When big school tuna are present, they can often be lured into striking by running heavy Japanese feather lures back to the third or fourth stern wave of the wake, then hauling the lines out on short outrigger halyards so the feathers ride just a yard or so outside the foaming water of the wake.

The second, shorter halyard is often used to troll a hookless teaser. Most deep water anglers agree that teasers definitely do help to raise billfish, although many disagree as to whether teasers cause more tangles than they are worth. It is inter-

Addition of fishing chairs and light outriggers to this handsome Huckins cruiser effectively converts her into a fisherman for small to medium game.

esting to note that a former Cape Hatteras world record 810-lb. blue marlin was caught on a "Knucklehead" lure, one which is essentially a plastic-headed, nylon-skirted teaser with a hook added.

Inevitably, the question of the advantages of trussed outriggers comes up. What do rigidly trussed 'riggers accomplish? For one thing, they accomplish much steadier towing of large baits in rough weather. Outriggers that bend a great deal under bait tension tend to yank the bait bodily out of the water, letting it flop back into the water in an unnatural manner when the 'rigger whips forward. Trussed outriggers are a good deal more expensive than plain bamboo, fiberglass, or metal tube poles. If baits no larger than ordinary mullet, big balao, or medium-sized black eels are to be towed, untrussed outriggers normally work quite well.

Boats as small as outboards and inboard-outboards in the 20-foot class are now being rigged with a new type of outrigger. Here the poles are usually fiberglass units 15 to 20 feet long, the lower ends of which are equipped with special curved butts similar to the curved butts used on some big game rods. The outrigger holder is similar to a flush-mounted rod holder. The lower end of the outrigger curved butt has slots cut into it that engage a cross pin at the bottom of the holder tube. In use, by rotating the outrigger in its holder and engaging the pin slots at various angles, one can wing the outriggers out in the normal manner, swing them back over the stern at a very low angle, or trim them straight up in the air.

Outriggers of this type have proven quite popular on the Great Lakes where planers are used to carry trolling lures down deep and where monumental tangles occur in deep-trolling lines unless adequate separation of the planers is

achieved. (See Chapter 34, "Target—A Record Striper.")

Nova Scotia and Newfoundland tuna fishermen have unique outriggers. The outrigger is not permanently attached to the side of the vessel, but is thrust into a sort of giant rod holder in the corner of the stern. Nova Scotia outriggers are bamboo poles and reach out and aft from the boat's stern like a pair of giant insect antennae in reverse. They are not used in the normal manner.

Instead, a "daisy chain" of herring is rigged to the fishing leader. As many as 12 herring may festoon the leader, but only the aftermost bait contains a hook. Towed from the rearward-tending outriggers, a pair of "daisy chains" creates a splashy, fish-attractive rumpus in the water behind the boat. When tuna rise to, but shy away from, the chain of baits, the boat's mates take the outriggers in hand and, by means of arm motions and body-English, impart extra motion to the "daisy chains."

The system seems to work, for Down Easters have been using it for years.

Several types of line release clips are now available. One resembles a giant clothes pin in shape and grasps the line between spring-loaded jaws in the same manner. Another consists of two plastic rollers that are compressed end-to-end by means of a common, threaded, centerline metal shaft. The line is forced into the slot between the two pieces of plastic, and variable release pressure is obtained by adjusting the compression of wing or ring nuts at either end.

Probably the most popular type of release clip is a small metal-and-plastic cylinder that is tied into the halyard. It has a short, curved, stainless steel line-holding arm, the release tension of which can be adjusted by means of a nut or knurled ring at the end of the cylinder. The release clip is rigged with this arm up in

The fiberglass utility outriggers on this Florida experimental craft swing into fishing position by rotation of the 'rigger shafts in their holders.

the fishing position; a strike drops it.

The beauty of this device is that if the line is placed directly into the arm, the bait can be dropped-back or reeled in without having to pull the line clear of the release clip. On the other hand, if one does not wish the line to render through the clip for some reason, rendering can be prevented by twisting a loop into the fishing line with the fingers. The friction of five or six twists is enough to prevent rendering of the line with even heavy baits.

Outriggers do give a boat a rakish look, and it's true that some hired mates hang wet gloves and freshly laundered skivvies from 'rigger halyards when the owner is ashore. But to an offshore fisherman the outrigger is as much a tool of his trade as a spinnaker pole is to the sailing racer who wants to get the most out of a fair breeze.

Cast bronze outrigger holder of this design is adjustable in vertical and fore-and-aft directions, will take a metal or fiberglass outrigger shaft.

The familiar snap-jaw outrigger clip is a development of the clothes pin clip used by housewives. The tension can be increased with rubber bands.

Wonderful fighters on light tackle, both the Atlantic and Pacific sailfish are regarded as star performers by millions of sport fishermen. Specimen illustrated was caught on spinning tackle from an outboard off Key Largo.

6 / The Sailfish Story

JUST BEFORE THE FLOODGATES OF THE winter tourist season open to spew a tidal wave of sun-seeking humanity upon Florida's southeastern Gold Coast, there occurs a period of relative calm, an interval between mid-December and late January that brings with it what many authorities aver is the finest sailfishing the hemisphere has to offer. This is the great annual meeting between sailfish and anglers that occurs along the edges of the Gulf Stream between Stuart and Boynton Inlet.

Sailfish are found in Florida waters every month of the year. The Atlantic species ranges the Caribbean, appears off Africa's Ivory Coast, pokes into the Gulf of Mexico, summers to some extent off the Carolinas, and otherwise enjoys broad distribution. Yet nowhere else are as many sails available to so many sportsmen as in the area between Stuart and Palm Beach during early winter months.

Contributing largely to the existence of this unprecedented concentration of sailfish is the contour of the coastline. The Gulf Stream edges to within a mile or so of Palm Beach, then starts to bend outward at the reefs off Jupiter before making an even more abrupt turn northward at Stuart. The eddy currents that result entrap great quantities of bait and forage fishes sent seaward from the drainage systems of Lake Worth, the Loxahatchee River, and the confluence of the Indian and St. Lucie Rivers at St. Lucie Inlet.

The catalytic agent that brings about confrontation of sailfish and this great oceanic free lunch counter is the weather. Seasonal "northers," blowing contrary to the current of the Gulf Stream, create heavy ground swells. Sailfish dearly love to ride the crests down-sea.

When a stiff northerly breeze is rattling palm fronds and beaches are bare of bathers, sailfish appear as if by magic, tailing first in platoons, then in companies, and finally in regiments. From obscure staging areas far off Fort Pierce and Cape Kennedy, they react to the lure of turbulent ocean waves to find their way to the lush feeding pastures awaiting them in that elbow created by the Gulf Stream's abrupt northward turn.

If there is such a thing as guaranteed sailfishing, this is it! Tournament fishing, always an excellent criterion of the intrinsic worth of any fishing grounds, has enjoyed a phenomenal record of success off Stuart and Palm Beach. An excellent case in point might be a recent Invitational Masters Angling Tournament sponsored by the Sailfish Club of Florida, located at Palm Beach.

In five days of trolling that January, 46 participants reported 1,138 strikes, fought 439 sailfish, and released 195, all on 12 and 20-lb. test line and barbless hooks.

Anyone can get in on this unique billfishing act, and the more the merrier. The organization ashore and afloat is complete. The local charter boat fleet is unexcelled and fully found, or you can fish from your own boat. Weather permitting, anyone with a fairly decent-sized trailer boat can join the Gulf Stream parade. A surprising number of sails are caught from reef or party boats while live-bait fishing for king mackerel.

Before dwelling upon the mechanics of angling for sails, let's take a brief look at this sterling gamester that has enthralled offshore sportsmen ever since the late, great Captain Bill Hatch first discovered the secret of the "drop-back" in 1916.

Spawning of the Atlantic version of *Istiophorus platypterus* is believed to occur in subtropical waters between May and September. From a lumpy little gargoyle measuring a few millimeters in length at the post-larval stage, the sail attains a length of six feet and a weight of perhaps 20 lbs. in a year's time. Initial spawning takes place in the second year of life, and a mature gravid female may contain several million eggs. Life span seldom exceeds three or four years, a disclosure by biologists that has led to some soul-searching among anglers.

The question raised is why release sails? Ever since the 1930's, anglers have been encouraged to liberate sailfish. Recaptures of tagged fish clearly indicate that sails usually survive release. "Keep them in the Gulf Stream and not on the rack," long has been the slogan of conservation-minded sportsmen.

In recent years, fisheries biologists involved in sailfish investigations have suggested that anglers make very small inroads into total sailfish populations, and that release programs do not contribute materially to the abundance of the species.

Esthetic rather than biological considerations compel anglers to release the majority of sailfish they capture. It may be argued with justification that any fish that fights so spectacularly, and which is so breathtakingly beautiful in form and coloration, richly merits freedom. The sportsman who fishes for sailfish prefers a brief, exciting acquaintanceship, not a permanent conquest.

The allegation that sailfish are inedible is untrue. Smoked sailfish is a great delicacy, and fresh sailfish steaks are held in high regard throughout much of the Caribbean area. The diligence with which Japanese long-line fishermen are pursuing sailfish in all oceans bespeaks a heavy demand for sailfish flesh elsewhere in the world. The long-line fishery is the single gravest threat to sailfish populations, and that of the marlins, everywhere. The rod and reel catch is nothing by comparison.

The compleat sailfish angler can become very basic where tackle is concerned, regardless of whether he is aboard a 40-footer or a seagoing outboard rig. Although sails have been caught on fly rods, ultra-light spinning gear, and bait-casting tackle, the battle is best joined with light trolling equipment balanced to 20-lb. test monofilament or Dacron line.

This calls for a quality rod with a tip weight of three to four ounces, measuring 5 to 5½ feet long. A 2½/0 or 3/0 reel accommodating 300 to 400 yards of line is preferred. Roller guides and tip-top on the rod are good line savers.

The choice of line merits a little careful thought. Dacron has a minimum amount of built-in stretch, unlike monofilament. Crossing of trolling lines or too much tension of the outrigger clip will fray Dacron. Aside from its tendency to stretch, monofilament makes fine sailfishing line, and even this stretch can work to the angler's advantage by acting as a shock absorber on a rough day.

Sailfishing with both lines in recent years, this writer has discovered that he can employ as much as 12 lbs. of striking drag and clamp down to 15 lbs. of fighting drag in the clutches with mono, whereas with Dacron he hesitates to set corresponding drags at more than 8 to 12 lbs.

With tackle of this sort, sailfish should be fought on a toe-to-toe basis, meaning that the angler mounts his rod in a belt gimbal and goes to work standing up. This gives him opportunity to maneuver around the cockpit even on the very roughest days and helps him to counter those ominous lunges into propellers and rudders by sails close aboard.

the "ultimate rig" for sailfish—a 4/0 hook on only three feet of No. 4 wire, a two-fathom shot of 60-lb. test mono with a small, strong snap swivel at the end, blood-knotted to the end of the 12 or 20-lb. test main fishing line.

Choice of bait is traditionally limited to small mullet and balao, commonly called "ballyhoo." Stuart and Palm Beach guides

The miniature tower of this Sea Bird I/O fisherman makes a perfect place from which to run this 20-footer out looking for sailfish in the Gulf Stream.

Terminal tackle has been in a state of re-examination since the advent of the "Venezuelan rig" upon the scene. Venezuelan anglers, among the best light tackle fishermen in the world, recently came up with a marriage of ten feet of 80-lb. test mono and five feet of No. 4 wire to replace the customary fifteen feet of No. 6 or 7 wire commonly used. Also employed were 4/0 hooks, smaller than the 6/0 to 8/0 hooks that were generally considered correct. The result was a quick-fishing rig that got far more strikes from sailfish raised to the baits.

This suggests what might be termed

usually favor the former. De-boning the mullet is no chore (see Chapter 27). Anglers who are their own skippers may purchase mullet already rigged, or can de-bone the bait with a hollow coring tool that can be obtained at any tackle store.

Ironically, sailfish rarely feed upon mullet. Analysis of 240 sailfish stomachs by biologists discovered only a very few mullet, and those specimens were suspected to be baits filched from anglers. Major sailfish foods include squid, octopods, small mackerel-like fishes and, of all things, the paper nautilus. Evident is the fact that sails do much of their feed-

ing well below the surface of the water.

When sailfish are "balling the bait" or charging into dense masses of pilchards, these small fish are excellent bait to have on board. Slow trolling over the outer reefs calls for a live blue runner, while kite fishermen have learned to pin their hopes on live pinfish. The widespread acceptance given to kite fishing in the Keys never has been duplicated at Stuart or Palm Beach, however.

Sailfish are individualists. No two fish seem to react to the bait in the same way. Nor do sailfish always use their rapier bills to stun their prey before turning to eat some. The matter of drop-back, touchstone to all billfishing success, cannot be resolved successfully by merely heeding folklore and counting to ten before attempting to set the hook after the initial strike.

The only proven method of insuring a high ratio of hook-ups for strikes received is to thumb the line lightly with the reel in free spool at the moment of truth when the line falls free from the outrigger, or when a sail belts a flat-line bait. The sail may instantly seize the bait, or it may take its own sweet time—anywhere from ten to thirty seconds. Then it may drop the bait, and the whole procedure must be repeated.

I have watched sailfish toy with baits like kittens playing with catnip mice. Conversely, crash strikes and instant hook-ups are not uncommon and heaven help the angler who has his reel on free spool when this happens. A blistered thumb is guaranteed and a backlash on the spool is a strong probability.

This raises something of a delicate point of order for tyro fishermen aboard charter boats. It is generally agreed that

Freshly hooked sailfish (left) puts daylight under its tail in effort to toss the hook. Boat's mate at right prepares to release the gallant fish.

90 per cent of the fun occurs at the moment of the strike and the subsequent hook-up. An over-eager mate can deny that spine-tingling experience to the angler by grabbing up the rod at the strike, hooking the fish, and then returning the tackle to its rightful possessor. The proper thing to do then is politely to request that whoever hooked the fish must reel it in. This makes the mate look supremely foolish and puts him in his place without precipitating a monumental bicker. The best way to avoid this kind of interference is to inform the crew at the start of the day of your intention to hook your own fish.

The fight itself is a spectacle that everyone enjoys. There is a great showing of silver and royal purple over the white-capped Gulf Stream when the hooked fish takes to the air. Dazzling-fast surface runs are interrupted by greyhounding or corkscrew leaps that may continue right up to the side of the boat. Elapsed fighting time may be anywhere from five minutes to the better part of a half hour with 20-lb. or lighter tackle. When it ends, the angler knows he has been around the track a few times—the Gulf Stream track, that is.

Such is life down Stuart and Palm Beach way when the northers blow across winter's threshold. Early-arriving "snow birds" who huddle around the heaters in their hotel rooms simply don't know what they are missing. It may be nippy on the beach, but those wild, wonderful, spindle-snooted mullet assassins known as sailfish generate enough heat of their own to provide spiritual and physical warmth for any and all acolytes who worship at their shrine.

James H. Kimberley, Palm Beach, Fla., angler, won a light-tackle tourney at Acapulco, Mex., with three sails taken on 12 and 20-lb. class tackle.

FRANK T. MOSS

7 / Navigation for Fishermen

THAT FATHER OF MODERN CELESTIAL navigation, Nathaniel Bowditch, might well turn over in his grave if he could see what science is doing to his beloved art of discovering where in the world one's ship is at. A self-taught mathematical genius, Bowditch in his teens corrected thousands of errors in existing navigation tables, errors that had caused the loss of ships and lives. His simplified system of navigation was published in 1802 under the title of *The New American Practical Navigator*. It is still the basis of celestial navigation today.

A no-nonsense New Englander, Bowditch was a scholar, a master mariner, and yet a man of simple tastes who loved his fishing. On second thought, it's quite possible that if he were alive today he would have nothing but praise for the almost magical electronic aids that sailors and fishermen now use to take the curse out of fog and darkness, and to locate the grounds where fish abound.

The simplest form of fishing navigation is that which uses ranges on shore to pinpoint known fishing spots out on the water. A range, incidentally, is the imaginary line extending through two prominent objects on shore, objects that line up with each other when viewed from the desired location on the water. The further apart the objects, the more accurate the range. Cross two such range lines at the fishing spot and you have a foolproof way of returning to that spot later on, provided visibility remains good. Here is a practical example of how ranges work.

Suppose that you have stumbled onto a rather superior bass rock pile a couple of miles south of a familiar shore and you want to be sure you can come back to this exact spot whenever you want to. If you were to plant a small buoy on the spot this would be a dead giveaway to other fishermen. The only way to establish the spot's position so you can find it again is to obtain at least two ranges on objects ashore, objects easily spotted from the location.

You know that to be fully effective, range lines must lie approximately at right angles to each other. Therefore, while you are still anchored at the new bass spot, you look to the northwest and discover that there's a huge rock on the beach that lies exactly in line with and under the east corner of the new consolidated school on the hill, a mile or so beyond. Here is one excellent range. You don't need the exact compass bearing of this range, but you do need its description, so you write the description into your notebook and even make a drawing to show what the range looks like. Binoculars are a big help here.

Next, looking toward the northeast you discover that the chimney of a house on the beach stands exactly under and in line with a small factory water tower a mile or two beyond. Here is your second range, at right angles to the first. You don't even have to locate the new fishing spot on the chart provided you know the general compass bearing of each range and, in returning to the spot another day, run out on one range until you cross the other.

But what about foggy weather?

In fog and haze, ranges become indistinct or are blotted out completely, and fishermen must use other means to find the good spots. Suppose that one of your ranges is obscured by haze or smoke, but not the other—how would you find your secret bass spot?

One method would be to run offshore directly away from, but in line with, the still-visible range until your running time exactly equals that required to meet the other range at the spot. Then you would drop overboard a small buoy on a light anchor and fish in widening circles from this known spot until you find the good rocks and the bass. Of course, knowing the exact depth of the water at the spot would be a great help, and this informa-

tion should be recorded in your notebook for every such spot that you normally locate by using ranges or a time-and-compass technique.

This is why fishermen keep their electronic sounders going almost constantly while trolling or running between fishing locations. An accurate depth of water is always a wonderful check on any range or line of position. The more you practice coordinating soundings with visual ranges and accurate bearings on known objects, the more accurate your fishing navigation will be.

Without an independent means of electronic navigation like RDF or loran (which we will discuss shortly), foggy weather fishing navigation quickly becomes a guessing game. Fortunately, with an accurate compass, a watch or clock, a chart of the local water, and a

Offshore fishing navigation is a lot more than trusting to luck. Crew of a large Florida party boat uses loran (left) and recording sounder (right) to pinpoint a red snapper bank 40 miles offshore in the Gulf of Mexico.

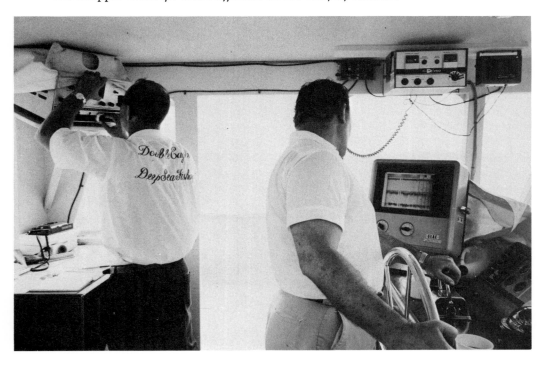

Visual range markers on shore are important to locating some grounds. Here boats off Montauk Point troll the Pollock Rip during an ebb tide. At slack tide they'll continue to fish the spot using shore ranges and sounder.

sounding machine, the coastal fisherman can apply a lot of education to his navigational guesses.

The radio direction finder, or RDF, is a sensitive radio receiver equipped with a special directional antenna that indicates the relative bearing of the shore station, radio beacon, or other vessel to which the unit is tuned. Marine RDF instruments are usually three-band affairs, able to tune in the radio beacon band (long wave), regular broadcast stations, and the 2 to 4 mHz marine radio telephone band. Many sets have a special "sensing" circuit that tells the operator in which of two possible directions the transmitting station lies.

RDF instruments come in a number of sizes and styles. The largest and best are often "automatic" sets that constantly monitor and display the relative bearing of a chosen beacon station without manual adjustment. Manually operated RDF units range from permanent, ship's-power-operated sets costing many hundreds of dollars, down to hand-held, battery-powered units that can be used effectively even from outboard-powered boats.

To be effective, an RDF unit must be accurately mounted with respect to the boat's fore-and-aft centerline. This is because the compass must be read at the instant of taking an RDF bearing so that the compass heading of the signal may be plotted on the chart to establish a line of position. The RDF should be mounted where it is easy to use, but protected from spray and dampness.

If the boat is equipped with a marine band radio telephone and the operator expects to use the RDF to locate other boats, then it is wise to install a heavy knife switch in the radio telephone antenna feedline. Opening this switch when taking a bearing with the RDF on another boat will effectively de-tune the radio telephone antenna system, thereby eliminating the tendency of the RDF to react to your own transmitting antenna, rather than to the signal of the other boat.

There are a number of useful tricks that can be exercised with an RDF unit. Suppose, for instance, that you want to get to a particular navigation buoy that happens to be close to good fishing grounds obscured by fog. The buoy itself has no radio beacon, but there is a radio beacon on the shore not far away. The 2A whistle buoy off the southwestern tip of Block Island, hard on the famous "Hooter Grounds," is an excellent example. Here sport fishing craft find cod, pollock, and snowshoe flounders in the spring.

By consulting a chart of the area (H.O. 1211 will do), you see that a line drawn through the buoy to Southeast Light on nearby Block Island will bear 095 magnetic from the buoy. Boats approaching from the west side of Block Island maneuver so as to get Block Island Southeast Light radio beacon bearing exactly 095 on the RDF and "home" on this heading until they come within sight or sound of the whistle buoy. Of course, wise skippers keep their sounders going to prevent over-running the buoy in very thick fog and getting dangerously close to the shore of the island.

Finding another boat in fog at sea can be tricky if there is much radio traffic on the channel being used. Normally, the boat that is transmitting gives a "long count" of numbers to provide a distinctive signal. The receiving operator rotates the antenna of his RDF so as to receive the "null," or bearing of least signal, of the other boat. At the same time he observes his compass so as to obtain the difference between his ship's course and the relative bearing of the incoming signal, thus obtaining the magnetic bearing of the signal.

The RDF is quite useful when a number of boats are working together offshore in foggy weather, searching for tuna and other pelagic fish. Two or more crossed radio bearings on signals ashore will give a fix from which a course to the home port can be plotted with considerable accuracy. One drawback of the RDF is the fact that it is subject to considerable inaccuracy under some conditions, and errors become larger with increased distance from the transmitting beacon or other radio stations.

Much more accurate is the electronic navigating system known as loran. This is a coined word meaning "long range radio navigation" and refers to a principle of navigation entirely different from either visual observations, radio bearings, or celestial position-finding. Here is a simplified explanation of how loran works.

Imagine two radio transmitters working on exactly the same frequency, one located on Cape Cod and the other at Sandy Hook. One station is the "master" station and the other the "slave" station. At frequent intervals (actually hundreds of times per second) the master station emits a pulse of radio energy that travels through space and is picked up by the slave station. The slave station emits a similar pulse that is triggered by reception of the signal from the master station.

A boat at sea between the two stations, or within their combined field of emission, receives both signals on its special loran receiver. The signals are interpreted by electronic means to provide a readout in numbers that correspond to hyperbolic lines of position printed on a special loran chart of the area. Two such readouts, obtained from two different pairs of loran stations, or, better yet, three, give a fix that is accurate to less than 200 yards under normal conditions.

Using loran, a skipper can proceed directly through fog to a predetermined fishing location, the loran coordinates of which are known. Happening on a good spot, he can take double or triple loran lines of the spot, determining exactly where it is.

Able to obtain only one loran line of position, the skipper can use this in several ways. He can pick up a single loran line that happens to run through a desired fishing spot, then search out the fish along this line by using his sounding machine. He can find his home harbor entrance in thick fog by getting onto and staying on the exact loran line that intercepts the harbor entrance.

By listening to commercial fishermen and offshore loran-equipped sport fishing boats, a smart skipper who does not possess loran can nevertheless pick up valuable information on the radio that may enable him to "home" on the boats in question by heading toward their approximate loran position, if he has a loran chart to interpret it, then using his RDF on their signals.

Modern, digital-readout loran units are no bigger than a small suitcase and cost $1,500 to $2,000. Some operators still use surplus Navy and Air Force loran units. Of these, the APN-9 model has been widely converted to civilian use. These older models are extremely accurate, but require a bit of special training to operate and impose heavy current drains on a boat's electrical system.

From loran, the logical step is to discuss radar. Strictly speaking, radar is not a navigating system at all, but a means of radio detection of objects or land masses

Compass (left), radar scope (center), and flashing sounder (right) occupy the flying bridge control station of this well-equipped offshore cruiser.

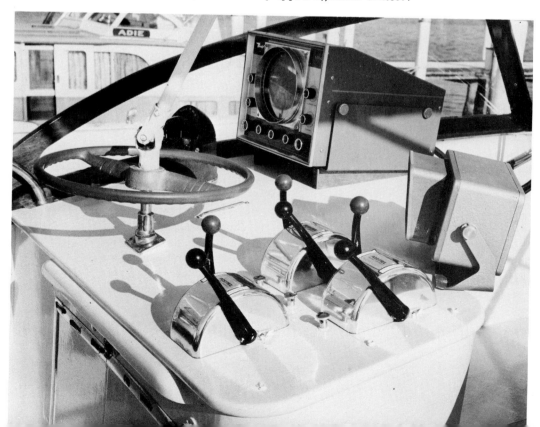

Deckhouse control station of a large Huckins sport fisherman. Loran is the square instrument on counter at right. Underneath is radiotelephone. Radar occupies niche at center with flashing sounder just behind. A VHF unit is mounted overhead. Controls include auto-pilot, sea-temperature gauge.

distant from the vessel. The radar antenna emits a pulsed beam of ultra high frequency radio energy which strikes and echoes back from land, buoys, or other vessels. The instrument detects and displays the returning echo waves, painting a sort of luminous map on an oscilloscope tube. The center of the tube is the boat's location and all bearings are relative to the boat's centerline.

Radar is wonderful for finding your way along foggy coasts, through dangerous intracoastal passages, and through massed fishing fleets. Radar is not cheap. The smallest sets cost upward of $3,000, and most radar installations require an auxiliary power generating source. The sense of security that radar gives, how-

ever, is tremendous. A combination of radar, loran, a good sounding machine, RDF, and radio telephone makes the modern offshore fishing cruiser the electronic equivalent of many destroyer escorts of World War II days.

Fishermen's navigation has come a long way since the time of Nathaniel Bowditch. Anglers now are catching more fish over longer seasons and greater geographical areas than was thought possible just a few years ago. Those who are most successful are the ones who have learned to take the guesswork out of fishing navigation by using modern electronic equipment and plain, old-fashioned common sense. Nathaniel Bowditch would have loved them as brothers.

8 / Big Black Marlin Splash Down Under

FISHING IS A DICEY BUSINESS. THE further you go and the bigger the fish, the chancier it becomes. The only way an angler can reduce those odds is to keep right at it. That was my reason for listening to Captain George Bransford on the dock at Cairns, Queensland, in my homeland of Australia.

"You'd better come out tomorrow," he said. "There's a big high on the map and the weather's going to cut up in a couple of days. And we're hot right now."

I knew very well that the black marlin were out there. Five boats from the Down Under billfish town that day had seen at least twenty huge fish. George had raised eight and had tagged and released two. A couple of his fish had been what he calls "good ones." So, I changed my mind about the pile of mail in my office, especially when I heard that George planned to fish two top American marlin anglers.

Cairns is a long way from anywhere, even in Australia, yet many American anglers fishing it are repeat customers. Bob Walker of Miami and Bill Chapman of New Jersey have fished some of the world's best grounds. This was to be their second look at the newly-discovered marlin ground outside Australia's Great Barrier Reef.

Next morning at seven we climbed down to the cockpit of the 39-foot *Sea Baby II* and changed to boat shoes while the mate, twenty-four-year-old Peter Wright, formerly of Fort Lauderdale, Florida, swabbed out footprints from the non-skid deck. It's a two-and-a-half-hour ride out through Grafton Passage to the edge of the continental shelf. The inshore mountains and islands slowly faded back into the haze.

October is late spring in the South Pacific and the climate is about the same as in Florida, warm and mild. Pete ran out a couple of feather lures on 50-lb. tackle to pick up fresh baits, and settled down to his chore of coring and wiring up a number of mullets. The sea looked good, not smooth, but not rough either.

Bill and Bob climbed up onto the flying bridge to talk with Captain Bransford while the sea slowly changed from inshore green to the deep indigo of marlin water. George Bransford is an old pro at the charter game, and a good one. Of the seven black marlin weighing over 1,000 lbs. taken at Cairns the previous two seasons, five were caught by his anglers. It's not hard to figure why sportsmen come halfway around the world to fish with Bransford.

Twice the feather lures took strikes and were brought in, adding a mackerel and a bonito to the bait box. The baits used on black marlin off Cairns include mullet, bonito, little tuna, narrow-banded mackerel (kingfish), rainbow runners, and even barracuda. The baits normally run under ten pounds, although at times kingfish or small wahoo are used, of necessity at a slower trolling speed.

Fresh baits are easily found on the isolated reefs at the edge of the continental shelf which here slopes down from the 30-fathom line in rough ridges, valleys, and mountain peaks. These slopes are scoured by the East Australian Current, an eddy of the South Equatorial Current. The current washes the shelf outside one of the largest passages through the Great Barrier Reef. The result is one of the thickest patches of big marlin in the world. It's a bad day when you miss seeing at least one or two.

This leads to some odd situations. Mrs. Helen Brown of Nassau, Bahamas, remarked to me one quiet afternoon on the *Marlan*, commanded by young Allan Collis, that she'd only seen "a couple of small fish, about 500 lbs." A day or so later the Aussie record holder Basil Mitchell tagged and released one estimated at 800 lbs., because he wanted to bring in something better.

Anglers have fun talking a new language. Anything under 500 lbs. is "small," around 900 is "fair," over 1,000 is "good," and only the fish that no man can hold are "monsters." What gets you about Cairns is that no one is boasting. You start talking that way for fun, and then come to realize that it's true because that's how big the black marlin are.

Peter finally put the bait rods away and set up the two big rigs as we sped out over the drop-off. Bill Chapman stayed with 130-lb. tackle and Bob Walker chose 80, saying that his slighter frame was not adequate for long-term heavy pressure on the larger outfit. He's a very fit man, but not weighty. Both men settled in beside opulent Fin-Nors, tightly packed with gleaming monofilament line. I climbed up to the flying bridge, out of the way. On fish such as these, the very last thing needed during the first explosive moments in the cockpit is someone snapping a camera.

It was dead quiet. In the distance we could sometimes see one of the other boats. The *Sea Baby* rode easily along the slight ground swell, the sounder clicking away through the background rumble of the two Perkins motors. George watched the water steadily, observing the color changes, drift of currents, and the other intangibles that add up to finding marlin. I focused a short telephoto lens on the baits, a neatly skipping mullet on the 80-lb. rig and a waddling, diving bonito on the 130.

Around 11:30 a marlin struck. Pete and George yelled together as it appeared, spearing down the swell, a brown torpedo that suddenly flashed bright purple and struck the bonito in a spurt of spray. The outrigger clip flipped the line free and Bill struck right on cue. The fish missed and disappeared, possibly stung by the hook. That's fishing, and nobody took it hard.

"Only a little feller—350, 400," Captain Bransford said off-handedly as he switched on the radio to call the other boats.

Snow Goose had seen nothing, *Marlan* had missed a fish and had parted company with a hammerhead shark. Lunch came and went. It was warm out there, and the two anglers sat patiently beside their outfits. I was finding it difficult to stay awake.

At 12:30 we heard that *Marlan* had taken a double strike with fish guessed at 700 and 900 lbs. Both were lost, and we chuckled at the picture of Aussie angler Jack Nixon, an energetic and popular sportsman, with a rod in each hand, wondering which to take.

Pete fussed over his baits, frustrated and impatient. It can seem a long time while the hours slowly tick away. Two-thirty is normal departure time and by 2:15 the ocean was looking horribly empty. Suddenly, I noticed that Brans-

Ed Seay of New Zealand set a 50-lb. tackle class black marlin record at Cairns, Queensland, Australia, with this 1124-lb. monster captured from a sport fishing boat 24 feet long.

CAIRNS GAME FISHING CLUB

ANGLER	E. Seay.
FISH	BLACK MARLIN
WEIGHT	1124lb
TACKLE	50 lb
LAUNCH	"Lucky Strike"
DATE	31-10-69

Is he trying to throw the hook, or is he aiming for the boat? Frightening can be the aspect of a wild marlin that is charging directly toward the boat, body planing over the surface and rapier bill probing for a target.

Whipped but still dangerous, a huge black marlin submits to being held for tail roping. Some anglers consider the black marlin one of three or four species of game fish that fully justify the use of 130-lb. class equipment.

ford seemed intensely preoccupied, eyes busy checking the sounder and the ocean astern.

The fish appeared a moment later.

Sometimes they come slowly with a leisurely inspection of the baits, often so deliberate that they seem clumsy. This one was first a deep, dark shadow in the water far behind the boat, rising after a few minutes of silent following to ride the swell in the center of the wake. Wide and brown with the spire-like tail working easily, it swung across behind the bonito. Bill Chapman poised over his reel, but then the marlin slanted across to the mullet—and took it.

Pete was yelling from the transom as the drop-back line straightened out. Bob Walker was right there striking hard as the *Sea Baby* shot forward. Bransford called for the bonito to be hauled in before the marlin should take that, also. Bill ripped it in as Bob fought his way to the chair, the rod bucking in his hands and line screaming from the reel as the startled fish burst out of the sea.

It already had 200 yards of line and was running and jumping ahead of the boat that was swinging fast to follow the curving line. It burst out again and again a quarter-mile away and it was then, with Bill Chapman fitting the bucket harness onto his partner, that we saw the mullet hanging from the line. Goodby line if one lousy shark, wahoo, or dolphin spotted the mullet. We had to get it first.

By now the marlin's first long rush had ended and we were backing down the line toward the mullet, which slid tantalizingly away as we approached. Pete strained and reached, and finally had it, gingerly reaching first for a knife and then for pliers to cut the wire on the mullet. Nobody said anything as he worked, careful not to touch the line. We all exhaled as one man when he hopped down from the transom, the mullet in his hand.

Captain Bransford was worried by the proximity of *Snow Goose*, which by now had hooked a fish half a mile away. I joked that ours might be the same fish. George smiled.

"Nope. We stand a chance on this feller. That jumping took something out of him and Bob's really fighting. See that 80-lb. outfit? You'll see men with 130-lb. gear not putting that much pressure on a fish."

Soon we were backing again. Bob had lost a lot of line and was worried. George said that it helped to have a fish this size well away from the boat. I knew then that it was truly a "good fish." Bob Walker was working very hard, too hard, I thought, although I said nothing. The harness straps were coming adrift and Pete urged Bob several times to let the boat do more of the work.

His retort was, "If I rest, he rests. I work, he works. I can stand this for two hours. Two hours flat out is better than five at half speed."

He knew what he was doing. Forty minutes had passed. The big ones usually go out for deeper water and this one was holding a steady course, sometimes rising toward the surface, but not jumping. Bob's clothes were sweat-drenched, his face streaming perspiration as he arched slowly back on the rod again and again. The tight nylon whined under the tension. It was George Bransford's turn to worry.

"A good fish can keep this up for hours. Heck, 80-lb. tackle is light stuff on these. A marlin's just as likely to keep swimming all night, then come up in the morning and start feeding on bonito, and hardly bother about the hook."

After an hour the fish suddenly swapped ends, heading toward the coast. We did not know it then, but Bob's hard work had tired the fish thoroughly. Most of the line was back on the reel and he was working harder than ever.

Incredibly, after only an hour and

fifteen minutes the double line appeared. The marlin rose unwillingly as Bob used slow, measured pumps. The boat idled slowly ahead as Pete reached a double-gloved hand for the leader. He won a wrap of the wire, then a second, and the yard-long bill weaved drunkenly.

Pete yelled with pain as the wire crushed through the gloves, but he held on and gained slowly. Beside him, Bill Chapman reached out with the flying gaff. The gap closed slowly as Pete hauled on the wire. Suddenly Bill wrenched back, setting the gaff deep in the marlin's shoulder. The fish lurched away and the rope tightened. Bob Walker stood at the stern, rod clenched in white-knuckled hands, staring at his fish.

"I don't believe it! Golly, what a fish!"

Two small sharks had appeared, bronze whalers following the dying marlin at a cautious distance. Captain Bransford leaped nimbly down to assist with a couple of rope hitches around the great bill, and it was all over. Minutes later we were scooting homeward, slowed a few knots by the great weight trailing astern. Bob Walker reached up to shake hands with George Bransford, beaming his delight. A few minutes later he was lying in one of the cabin bunks, eyes closed, still grinning from ear to ear.

He had reason, as it turned out. On the dock, three hours later, the Cairns club weighmaster, Dick Fitzharding, announced the weight at 1,062 lbs., just two pounds under the existing world record for black marlin on 80-lb. class tackle.

Bob didn't seem to mind the narrow miss at all. He was so lit up with pleasure he almost glowed in the dark as the large crowd of Aussies applauded the catch. Had that bait been a bonito and had it been swallowed—well that's fishing.

Cairns, by the way, is the northernmost city of Queensland, with a population of 25,000. The town is well provided with motel services and has daily prop-jet connections south to Brisbane and Sydney. The black marlin season here extends from September through December, although a few fish seem to be present all year. Bookings for the small charter fleet are pretty solid in season, so quite a few Aussie fishermen are starting to bring their own craft north.

As a black marlin ground, Cairns is at least in the front rank world-wide and probably ahead of the rest. Right now it is the most likely place in the world for an angler to take one of Captain George Bransford's "horrible monsters" and set new tackle class records. There's even a prize of $11,000 offered for the first 2,000-pounder to be brought into Cairns. But it's the fish that are making the big splash Down Under, as you Yanks love to say.

9 / Tuna Towers

I SHALL NOT FORGET THE TIME, YEARS ago, when a sport fishing boat first entered my home port of Montauk wearing a tuna tower. Onlookers stopped in their tracks, transfixed. "What's that—a seagoin' oil drilling rig?" one oldtimer asked.

"Naw, just a mobile osprey's nest," a local wit replied.

The hooting and jeering did not last long, however, once folks became aware of the regularity and precision with which the crew of that boat located and baited underwater swordfish. Nowadays, many owners of deep water sport fishing craft feel positively underprivileged if their vessels do not sport some sort of metallic structure reaching skyward from atop the deckhouse or flying bridge.

The first tuna towers appeared in Florida shortly after World War II. They were designed to combine the height of a mast with the control convenience of a small flying bridge, giving the operator unequalled underwater vision, perspective, and view of the action. Some who saw them then compared them unfavorably with the shapely mast of a Menemsha swordfisherman, but the fishing results the first towers produced soon convinced serious game fishing boat owners that they made up in effectiveness what they lacked in beauty.

Everyone is familiar with the apparent bending of a stick thrust into water at an angle different from the vertical. This optical illusion is due to the refraction of light rays by the water. Where spotting underwater fish is concerned, its effect is to limit the radius of effective underwater observation in direct proportion to the height-of-eye of the observer.

The height-of-eye of a fisherman standing on the flying bridge of a sport fishing cruiser is usually not over 14 feet. The angle of depression from the horizontal that permits sighting of game fish beneath the surface to a depth of about two fathoms is not less than 20 degrees. At an eye-height of 14 feet, this angle permits an effective radius of underwater observation of about 40 feet, giving a circle of effective observation with an area of about 5,000 square feet. Doubling the height-of-eye by placing a tower under the observer and bringing his eye up to 28 feet from the surface increases the radius of effective observation to 80 feet, but quadruples the circular area in which fish can be spotted underwater to about 20,000 square feet.

A further increase of underwater spotting potential results from increased height-of-eye through the resulting reduction of surface interference caused by wind ripples. This factor is hard to evaluate quantitatively, but is an important one. Still another advantage of the tower is the fact that when motor and steering controls are placed atop the tower, the operator's efficiency is greatly increased when seeking out or maneuvering onto game fish.

At this point it might be proper to explain the concentration on *underwater* fish. Everyone is familiar with the classic description of the big game fisherman searching the ocean's surface for the projecting fins of swordfish, tuna, marlin, and the like. In practice, at least half of the successful catches of such species have been made by first spotting fish that were not finning, but swimming several feet under the surface.

The tuna tower does not assist materially in spotting finning fish. A lower height-of-eye puts projecting fins in profile and is better for spotting finning fish, especially at a distance. Therefore smart skippers keep good fin-spotters on the flying bridge level or even in the cockpit, while assigning underwater search to crew members or guests with experience at spotting fish underwater when stationed aloft.

The design and construction of towers involves many important factors. The most obvious is the need to achieve strength and rigidity with light weight and low windage. This requirement has been reached in the best contemporary models through the use of trussed designs in welded aircraft aluminum alloy or stainless steel tubing. The best designs feature double access ladders that form part of the support structure, padded belly rails and sun dodgers for the lookout position, compasses, radio remote controls, intercoms for communicating with the fishermen in the cockpit, a radio antenna mount, a radar antenna mount beneath the lookout deck, and complete motor and steering controls.

Such towers are not cheap, partly because each installation is, in effect, a custom-building job. Prices of up to $10,000 for a fully-equipped tower are not unusual. Some manufacturers of stock fishing boats, however, are now offering standardized towers as optional equipment, a service of considerable value to the prospective fishing cruiser owner. In the early days of tower design, quite a few towers were built of heavy gauge aluminum pipe and cast aluminum awning fittings. Joint rigidity was by means of stainless steel set screws and was not equal to that obtained with welded construction, even though these towers did prove satisfactory in most cases and cost far less than welded construction.

In either welded or non-welded construction, certain precautions should be observed. Only the best materials and workmanship should be used. Each part must be inspected during installation *and during use* for mechanical flaws. Lives may depend on the strength of a weld or the bite of a pair of set screws. The design must be compatible with the size and style of the vessel. Boat designers now prefer to develop tower designs as the general boat design is brought to perfection. Where a tower has to be designed to fit an existing boat, the following planning method can be of considerable assistance.

Obtain a profile photograph of the vessel and have it enlarged to a definite working scale (three-quarters of an inch to the foot is good; each sixteenth of an inch equals one inch full scale). Lay tracing paper over the photo and trace the boat's outline, locating major interior structural members that may be important to the design. Sketch in a tower that is compatible to the boat's structure, complements the boat's appearance, and can be built without expensive alterations to the boat.

The tower should be rigid and capable of retaining its shape without having to depend on parts of the boat's superstructure to perform this function. This may call for imagination in working out stiffening braces to prevent twisting and bending of tower parts in a rough sea. Hardwood doubling pieces should be placed under the side decks or deckhouse top where tower leg members are fastened to the boat.

There are many remote control systems now available. Creating an adequate

View from the tower control station. Clutch and throttle controls are combined
in single levers, one for each engine. Steering is hydraulic. Radio remote control
is in recess to right of steering wheel. This custom built tower is mounted on a
big Huckins sport fisherman. Inner surface of the safety rail is padded for
comfort and safety of the operator when aloft.

control station at the tower deck level should be no problem. The important point is to select controls with a positive neutral *feel* feature so the operator does not have to rely on the sound and vibration of the distant motors to know whether his motor controls are in ahead or astern position, or neutral.

Some installers use a light, vertical section of metal tubing and universal joints to connect the flying bridge and tower steering stations. Others utilize chain-and-cable, hydraulic, push-cable, or electric controls. The plane of the tower wheel should be flat, not vertical. Control cables should be led down from the tower in such a manner that they cannot possibly be used as hand-grabs by inexperienced persons. It is a good idea to cover the ladder rungs or steps with non-skid material.

It is often convenient to mount the radio antenna on the upper portion of the tower. When this is done properly, no ill effects will be noted from a properly tuned transmitter. Antenna stand-offs should be very stout and placed so as to hold the transmitter feed line well away from any vertical metal tower members to reduce stray inductive coupling and loss of transmitter signal power.

Authorities on radio and electrical matters claim that a tower is quite safe in an electrical storm provided it is adequately grounded. In such a case, the tower acts as a gigantic lightning rod, bleeding off surface static charges into the atmosphere and diverting a chance lightning stroke to ground (the ocean) via the grounding system. Naturally, the ground wires connecting the tower to the ship's radio ground plate must be heavy. The through-hull bolt should be brazed, not just soldered, to the exterior ground plate.

Make tower ground leads as short as possible of wire not lighter than #8 where two wires are used, #6 for a single wire. A grounded lightning stroke carries tre-

mendous voltage and amperage and will heat even very heavy wire to the smoking point. Therefore, the ground wires should be led to the ground plate connection through areas easily reached in case of an emergency and well away from fuel tanks, wooden bulkheads, and other potentially combustible members.

In some cases grounding the tower may affect radio transmission adversely. This usually can be cured by placing a heavy knife switch on the tower ground wire line, leaving the switch open except when in an area of electrical storms. A second knife switch cutting the radio antenna into the ground system is often added, and can be used to protect the radio equipment from damage in the event the antenna is struck by lightning.

What effect does a tower have on a boat's speed and stability? Naturally, when you place a weight aloft you raise the boat's center of gravity, altering her stability. Most tuna towers are quite light, however, despite their apparent bulk, and do not materially change a boat's stability except when too many people are allowed aloft in really rough water. The boat may show more tendency to make leeway in a strong wind, but there is little or no "sail effect" because the tower has no aerodynamic shape.

Pitching and rolling in rough seas put the severest strains on a tower. Pounding, especially, puts momentary heavy stresses on a tower structure. An owner with a new tower on his boat is understandably apprehensive the first time he encounters really rough seas, but if his tower is properly designed and made, he will soon discover that it can take as much abuse as the boat. But careful inspection of the tower after a rough passage is still a good idea.

Finding game with a tower requires a new searching technique. The traditional fin-hunter goes slowly, his eyes cocked for the silhouette of a raked, black fin, or the silent, slowly-spreading wake of a fish swimming just under the surface. The tower lookout recognizes these signs and uses them, but he must also train his eyes to react to the vague, purple-blue shape deep underwater that is a cruising swordfish or marlin, or the quick yellowish flash of a tuna's tail finlets.

A very real problem can be that of communicating between the tower and the cockpit. Loud shouting is confusing at best and frequently results in misunderstandings that cost the anglers good fish. The cure is to install an intercom system between tower and cockpit, one in which the loudspeakers are also pickup microphones so no one has to hold a microphone to talk. There are several adequate boat intercom systems available that perform this way.

Tuna towers will never become standard equipment on the great mass of everyday power yachts and casual fishing craft. Yet, with their unique appearance and very real usefulness in certain specialized fishing fields, they have become symbols of the offshore, big game angler.

Radar antenna housing is mounted below upper deck of this welded tower. Ladders are designed to share stress.

On this tower the radar antenna pod is held by metal struts. Sun dodger on top station is recent refinement.

10 / Bait Me a Broadbill

THE FIRST TIME I DELIBERATELY WENT after a broadbill swordfish with rod and reel was back in 1950. I was operating a charter boat out of Montauk, New York, and I was a happy harpooner. With swordfish selling at 50¢ a pound on the dock, a man thought twice before putting a bait to one of those valuable fish. But nagging at the back of my mind was the thought that if certain local fishing characters could take these fish with sporting tackle, so could I. So, when an angler named Murray Rushmore came along voicing a yen to try for a broadbill with hook and line, I swallowed the impulse to tell him he was out of his mind. That decision changed a good part of my life.

As luck had it, we went out and found a big sword that glommed onto Rushmore's squid bait, giving his heavy tuna rod a stiff workout for a couple of hours. With the 350-pounder in the cockpit, I was on top of the world. "Who said swordfish are so tough?" I asked myself.

I could see myself prospering. People would flock to me to learn how to catch the elusive fish. That night I took the harpooning stand off the boat, swearing that from then on I'd bait all the swordfish I met rather than slay them with the harpoon. The decision was fateful, but not in the way I had anticipated. For eight long years I religiously baited every broadbill I found on the ocean—and put not one fish in the boat.

If there was a way to break a line, miss a strike, or otherwise fail to catch swordfish, I found that way. Once, in a black mood, I figured that my obsession was costing me a cool $1,000 a season through lost harpooning opportunities. Finally, to my great relief, an angling friend named Ray Bizzigotti broke the jinx by taking a sword with me on the 4th of July, 1958.

When William Boschen caught the first broadbill ever taken with sporting tackle off Catalina Island back in 1913, he started a chain of events among fishermen that is still being forged in blood, sweat, and tears. Catch statistics support this declaration. Before 1958, the year that saw a phenomenal 120 swords taken by rod and reel at Montauk and Hampton Bays, Long Island, not over 600 of the great fish had fallen to sportsmen using rod and reel. Since then perhaps that many more have been added to the score. This comparatively meager showing is not due to lack of effort. Rather, it is a reflection of the long odds against success with the fish.

Out of fifty fish sighted, you may get the bait in front of twenty, have a positive reaction from ten, hook four, and save one. Thus, an average annual catch of "only" fifty swordfish for all of the major broadbill areas of the country actually represents at least 1,000 baiting attempts and 2,500 fish sighted.

What makes the swordfish so hard to hook and handle? First comes the fish's bill, four feet of boney trouble sticking out in front of its mouth. When a broadbill comes up on a bait and its aim is good, the sword passes *over* the bait so the mouth can pick it up. But if the fish

73

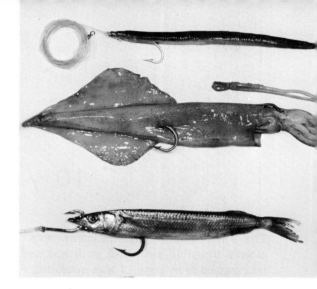

Three prime swordfish baits are (top to bottom); black eel, squid, balao. Eel is rigged with an 8/0 hook plus 15 feet of 100-lb. test mono leader and will attract white marlin as well as swordfish. Balao bait has a doublehook arrangement seldom seen outside swordfish country. The balao is also rigged with 100-lb. mono. Squid has a 12/0 Sea Demon hook on leader made up of 25 feet of 180-lb. test mono line. At far right is a finning swordfish.

is overanxious or not paying strict attention to its aim, the bill can slide *under* the bait and the mouth will snap at nothing but water while the bait slides up the bill to lodge the hook in an eye socket or the root of the dorsal fin, a nightmare situation for both fish and fisherman.

Another factor is the broadbill's penchant for dining down deep on whiting, hake, skates, and other bottom-dwelling goodies, then coming to the surface to burp and bask in the sun. You aren't a swordfisherman until you have spent an hour trying to cram a squid into the mouth of a broadbill too stupid with food to wallop your bait or even get out of the way of the boat.

A third factor is the unpredictable behavior of individual swordfish. Some fish will charge a bait ferociously, all flying spray and slashing sword. Others will turn away from the boat, always presenting the tail to the bait. This is bad because all swordfish have a built-in panic reaction to anything coming up on them from behind. The broadbill's most dangerous natural enemy is the mako shark which aims for the swordfish's tail to immobilize the billfish before it can bring the dangerous sword into play.

To get around these difficulties, experienced anglers have developed a unique baiting system, a technique quite different from that used on marlin. The bait is

seldom trolled, as it is for marlin, but is kept in the cockpit ice chest ready to be streamed as soon as a broadbill has been sighted and the boat brought into a good baiting position. As the boat prepares to cross ahead of the fish, the bait is dropped back 60 to 90 feet behind the boat and held there by the mate who grasps the fishing line.

The mate then hauls down a long loop of fishing line from the rod tip into the water behind the slowly moving boat, using his free hand. As the boat passes the fish, the skipper on the bridge or tower instructs the mate to shorten or lengthen the fishing line, depending on the relative position of the fish, so as to drag the bait 20 to 30 feet in front of the fish.

Just before the fish can grab or strike the bait the mate is told to drop the fishing line into the water. This effectively stops the bait dead in the water, making it easier for the fish to pick it up. The long loop of loose line in the water behind the boat allows the boat to continue moving away without imparting motion to the bait.

As the boat moves away, the mate strips more line from the rod tip into the water behind the boat, watching the loose whorls of line closely for signs that the fish has picked up the bait and is swimming off with it. When this happens, the

74

loose loops and turns of line quickly begin to straighten out.

Waiting out the drop-back, as this maneuver is called, is nerve-wracking. If the fish reappears on the surface, obviously swimming away not hooked, then the boat must be brought around for a fresh baiting try and the line shortened up as quickly as possible. But as long as the fish stays down with the bait there is a good chance that he may pick it up. Many fish have been "blown" by striking prematurely.

When it is obvious that the fish is swimming off with the bait, or when the crew's nerves cannot stand the suspense any longer, the reel's clutch is engaged and the boat is shot forward under power to bring the line tight. The angler strikes hard just once as soon as he feels strain. If he is lucky and has hooked the fish, then he waits out the pounding, jarring rush of the broadbill's first heavy run.

Broadbill, incidentally, are iron-hard around the bill, but have surprisingly soft flesh inside the mouth. Striking drag is usually set by experts at not over 20 lbs. for 130-lb. class tackle, 16 lbs. for 80-lb. class line, and 10 or 12 lbs. for 50-lb. class equipment. The fish make short, heavy runs and do quite a lot of surface charging. About one out of ten will be a jumper. Many roll so much they get the leader and some of the double line

wrapped around the body. Fully half of the swordfish taken by rod and reel come in foul-hooked.

The late Capt. Walter Drobecker, Sr., noted fishing guide, once caught a 400-lb. swordfish entirely single-handed from a Pacemaker fishing cruiser. He was the second man ever to accomplish the feat entirely alone on a boat. He managed the drop-back maneuver by placing the rod in one of the fighting chair rod holders and stripping out the line against a light reel drag and the engaged "click."

Jack Rounick of the Montauk Deep Sea Club back in 1963 became the first angler ever to take three swordfish by rod and reel in one day, strictly under IGFA tackle rules. He fished from his boat *Alligator* under Captain Jack Pierpont.

John Labbat caught a 345-pounder with the writer as skipper on Labbat's very first deep sea fishing trip. *Sic transit Xiphias gladius.*

While many charter boats and some anglers fish for broadbill with 130-lb. tackle, the most experienced swordfish anglers now prefer 80 and even 50-lb. class tackle. The fact that you can't put much line tension to these fish makes it unnecessary to utilize the very large, heavy rigs normally employed on giant tuna and the big marlins. Of course, if you are fishing the West Coast of South America for broadbill in the same league

75

Capt. Jimmy Donovan hauls in leader while Jack Mulqueen prepares to gaff swordfish from Alligator's *cockpit.*

Fish gives them tense moment when it tosses its sword in final attempt to part the leader and win its freedom.

with Lou Marron's 1,182-lb. world record swordfish, you are foolish to fish with anything lighter than 130-lb. tackle.

Reel, rod, and line must be of top quality. Roller guides are now standard on all big game tackle and greatly prolong line life by eliminating the scraping friction formerly encountered with ring guides. A fighting chair with a footrest and a good fishing harness are necessities.

Outriggers are not absolutely essential if the crew is well drilled at baiting the fish from the cockpit. A flying bridge is mandatory for efficient control of the boat, and a tower is a great help for spotting underwater fish. Captain Billy Holzman of Montauk, with more than 40 rod and reel swordfish captures to his credit, admits that more than half of the fish he has hooked were first spotted from the tower, swimming several feet underwater.

The best leader is 25 to 30 feet of 200-lb. test monofilament. Some anglers prefer solid #12 stainless steel wire. Only

a few use cable. The best hooks are Sobey, Martu, and Sea Demon models in sizes 10/0 to 12/0. Squid is excellent bait, as is mullet, mackerel, small bonito, black eel, dolphin, flying fish, and ballyhoo.

Auxiliary equipment includes a heavy flying gaff with 30 feet of nylon rope or bronze cable, a stern door or gin pole for getting the fish aboard, a tail rope for securing the fish after gaffing, and spliced lifting grommets made of yacht rope. The boat should have a radio telephone, depth sounder, and all normal offshore manual and electronic navigating gear.

On the Atantic Coast, swordfish set in off eastern Long Island in mid-June with the peak of the first, heavy run occurring from about June 25 to about July 10. The fish fan rapidly eastward until they fill the great range extending from Block Island to Martha's Vineyard and Nantucket. One seldom has to go more than 20 miles offshore to find them.

Mulqueen swings gaff while Donovan's gloved hands hold the humming leader in this exciting "moment of truth."

Guide Buddy Merritt has come down to the cockpit to help lift the 160-lb. fish into the boat without gin pole.

The best East Coast swordfish ports are Hampton Bays and Montauk on eastern Long Island; Point Judith and Newport, Rhode Island; and Cuttyhunk, Menemsha, Edgartown, Falmouth, and Nantucket in the Cape-and-Islands region. Southern California is witnessing increasing rod and reel swordfish activity with clubs at Balboa, Newport Harbor, and Catalina being the centers of action.

The United States Broadbill Club with headquarters in Costa Mesa, California, has many East and West Coast members. Membership is restricted to those men and women who can prove capture of a swordfish by rod and reel under IGFA tackle rules. The club's purpose is to promote rod and reel fishing for these wonderful fish, discouraging sportsmen from using the harpoon and encouraging them to undertake competitive sport fishing for swordfish.

Heavy commercial long-lining of swordfish in the Atlantic in the early and mid-1960's is thought to have had a detrimental effect on the East Coast stock of mature broadbill. While United States commercial fishermen now find this fishing unprofitable, it is still carried out to a significant degree by Canadians. Mercury has been found in a high proportion of swordfish brought into world fish markets, killing most sales of swordfish in the United States, but foreign markets still utilize these valuable fish.

Let us pray that we have not seen the last of the golden age of the great billfishes such as swordfish. Few thrills in this world can equal what you feel when your line comes tight, the rod leaps and bucks in your hands, and you see that dark, glistening bulk thrusting up out of the sea, slashing right and left with its Excalibur of a sword.

Harpooning is child's play compared to this.

77

The broadbill's bone-hard sword is a deadly weapon. This California sport fishing boat was pierced completely through by the sword of a fish said to weigh around 350 lbs. Oddly enough, little leakage resulted in this case.

Champion fisherman Jack Rounick, left, became the first to take three swordfish in one day under IGFA rules, in July of 1963, fishing with Captain Jack Pierpont off Montauk Point. He is the angler in the photo on page 72.

On the other side of the coin, John Labbat caught this 372-pounder while on his very first offshore trip, fishing with the author out of Montauk.

11 / Using Sounders for Fishing

WHEN THE BRITISH ROMANTIC NOVELIST Rudyard Kipling wanted to portray a sagacious Grand Banks fishing skipper in action, locating fish, in *Captains Courageous*, he described Captain Disko Troop as fingering, sniffing, and even tasting samples of sand and mud brought to the surface by the tallow-filled cup of the sounding lead of the schooner *We're Here*.

Disko Troop existed only in Kipling's fertile imagination, but that canny author was fisherman enough to know the importance of knowing the depth of the water and the character of the bottom, where fish are concerned. The need to know water depth and bottom make-up, in today's competitive fishing, is as great as ever.

Fortunately, modern fishermen don't have to measure depth with slow, often inaccurate lead lines, nor do they have to sniff, feel, and taste bottom samples. Accurate, instantaneous-reading electronic sounding machines have been brought to a high state of perfection in recent years. What's more, the new sounders often do what Disko Troop's lead line could never do—detect free-swimming schools of fish or individual large fish under the boat and report their exact depth with relation to bottom and surface.

Widespread use of electronic sounders developed among commercial fishermen shortly after World War II and spread rapidly to sport fishermen, as smaller, less expensive machines became available. Nowadays, fish-finding with sounders is by no means restricted to ocean fishing alone. Thousands of inland sportsmen on lakes and rivers are having new horizons of fishing knowledge opened to them by the new, portable, battery-powered sounders presently available. We will have a look at practical applications of small modern sounders to small boat fishing after we have explored the way that electronic sounders work and what can be expected of them in the way of fish-finding performance.

The modern electronic sounder (perhaps we should say the modern *sonic* sounder) probes the depths with a beam or broad finger of high-frequency sound. The speed of sound in water is about four and one-half times that of sound in air, or approximately five-sixths of a nautical mile per second.

The sounder works by projecting a pulsed beam of sound directly downward toward the bottom and then picking up and indicating the returning echoes in terms of feet or fathoms of water depth. This readout may be in the form of marks on a paper graph (recording), as flashes of a neon tube behind a transparent, calibrated dial (flashing), as a pointer on a calibrated scale (meter), or as integral numbers on a masked drum (digital readout).

Recorders possess the great advantage of making and preserving a visual record of the depths over which the boat has passed. You don't have to watch a recorder constantly so as to be able to remember what the depth was ten minutes ago. Tapes of often-made passages, such

The numbers on the sounder tape read (top to bottom): 10 06, 20 08, 30 07, 40 09, 50 05, 0 07, 80 03, 90 01, 100 0

Segment from a Raytheon sounder tape gives several examples of bottom and fish as seen by a sounder. The dark, vertical smudge at top right is bait fish close to the surface in a dense school. A large school of large fish on the brow of the drop-off could be pollock, cod, groupers, snappers, or other bottom-dwelling fish. The tiny spike on the small hump close to the left margin could be a single large fish or a shark. The double profile at lower left results when there is a double bounce of echos between the boat's hull and the ocean's bottom.

as entering the home harbor or approaching a favorite fishing spot, can be kept in the log for future reference and comparison.

Flashers, on the other hand, are generally less expensive than recorders, and, while they require constant monitoring to take advantage of their steady stream of information, they are ideal for smaller boats where instant information is more important than a record, and for inshore night fishing. With experience, almost anyone can learn to "read" a flasher so as to obtain a good guess at the character of the bottom and the presence of fish under the boat.

Perhaps the clearest way to describe what a good sounder can do for you is to give a few true illustrations. Charter boat skipper Benjamin Franklin Rathbun of Noank, Connecticut, almost daily runs dangerous Wicopesset Passage at the eastern entrance to Fishers Island Sound. Ben once told me:

"Of all the electronic equipment I have on the *Anna R.*, the machine that's saved my skin most often in thick weather has been my recording sounder."

In the party fishing business, Captain George Glas sails the big, fast, welded-steel catamaran *Hel-Cat* daily from Montauk to Coxe's Ledge, 40 miles from the home breakwater. Fog never stops him. He relies on loran for navigation and radar for safety, but uses an advanced type of sounding machine to locate the schools of cod and pollock that he seeks on that famous deep sea fishing ground.

Famed striped bass expert Coot Hall has for years used flashing and recording sounders while working the treacherous rips and reefs around Cuttyhunk Island, Massachusetts. Expert marlin angler Dudley Roberts Jr. finds a sounder indispensable for following the peaks and ridges of the massive undersea mountain range between Eleuthera Point and Little Cat Island in the eastern Bahamas, along which he raises big wahoo and rampaging blue marlin.

Many owners of sounding machines are prone to speak of their depth sounders as "fish finders." This is stretching a point because in many cases, in order to find or get onto fish, the depth sounder is used to locate the particular rock pile, wreck, hummock, ledge, or reef where fish are known to abound.

The brand-new sounder owner usually starts off by taking more or less random soundings out of curiosity to learn how deep the water may happen to be at any given time or location. But soon he learns to recognize the characteristic profile drawn by his recorder or displayed by his flasher as he approaches a known fishing spot. Once he has learned to recognize profiles of this type he has information of considerable value when it comes to getting onto the good fishing spots during periods of poor visibility when he cannot use ranges on shore for fishing navigation.

Most modern recorders and many flashers have sensitivity enough, within their normal working depths, to pick up and indicate fairly dense schools of small fish or individual large fish swimming clear of the immediate bottom. It takes a bit of experience and skill to tune the sounder to the best "gain" to indicate fish, and to interpret the indications the sounder makes when over fish.

So it is within the bounds of propriety to call depth sounders "fish finders" to the extent that they are used directly or indirectly to locate fish or the grounds on which fish should be found.

As was stated earlier, the sounder indicates the depth by shooting pulsed sound-beams at the bottom, then receiving, amplifying, and displaying the returning echoes. Since the speed of sound in water is a known quantity, it is possible to convert by electronic means the time-lag between outgoing sound pulses and returning echoes, converting the time-lag

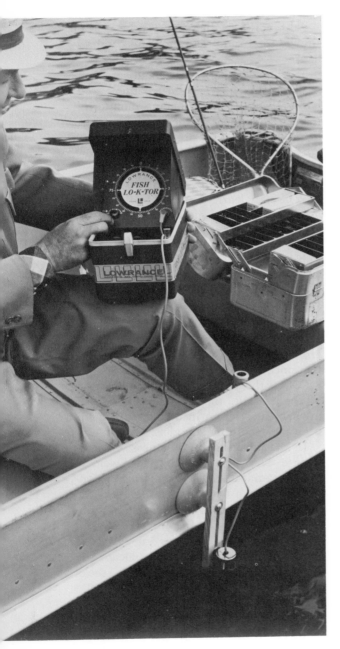

The Lowrance Fish Lo-K-Tor is one of a number of "lunch box" sounders in the low-price range. Powered by its own battery, it gives accurate depth indications to 100 feet, spots fish, and indicates character of the bottom. A transducer holder attaches to hull.

into terms of fathoms or feet of depth.

The actual sound pulse vibrates at the rate of about 50,000 cycles per second (50 kHz). The sound is created in a device called a transducer, usually located in the bottom of the hull external to the boat's skin. The transducer has the property of being able to convert high frequency electromagnetic vibrations into mechanical vibrations that will travel through water, and to receive and reconvert into electromagnetic vibrations the much weaker returning mechanical sound echoes.

This is basically the principle utilized in active sonar to detect submarines and other submerged objects. In fact, certain sophisticated types of fish-finders have movable transducers, or sound heads, that can be aimed horizontally as well as vertically. Commercial fishermen and many large party boats use this equipment, which is a great deal more expensive than the relatively simple sounders on most yachts and sport fishing boats.

Because the transducer measures the depth between its underwater location and the bottom, compensation must be made in the indicator to allow for the depth of the transducer below the water's surface if true water-surface-to-bottom is desired. Otherwise, the transducer gives depth-under-the-keel, which is usually sufficient for most fishing.

What do typical sounders cost? A family sport fishing boat may get by very nicely with one of the new combination flasher-recorders that combine the best features of both instruments. Cost of a good flasher-recorder is about $500. Smaller boats may do well with either permanently installed or portable, battery-powered flashers that can handle water to depths of about 150 feet, and cost from just under $100 to a little over $200.

For deep water work, anything deeper than 240 feet, nothing beats a good recording sounder of the type developed expressly for fish-detection and interpretation of bottom characteristics. These sets are not cheap, costing $750 and up, but their superior performance and versatility makes them well worth the extra money. Meter or digital readout sounders have not achieved wide acceptance among fishermen because of their inability to detect and display fish or tell about the character of the bottom.

The logical location for the sounder is where the boat's operator can observe it easily without having to move from his position of control. This may be within the flying bridge of an offshore cruiser, in or on the center console of a big outboard skiff, or even at the control station atop a boat's tuna tower. The instrument should be protected from rain and flying spray.

Installation should be done by a competent electronic technician, unless you qualify in this department yourself. The battery "hot" line must be properly fused and battery polarity must be strictly observed lest you accidentally come up with a case of reversed polarity and a serious electrolysis condition. Careful attention to installation instructions should prevent any such trouble.

Here are a few tips that will help the relative newcomer to electronic fish finding master his equipment.

Use the machine constantly when you are trolling over good fishing bottom. Use it when approaching any fishing spot that requires anchoring or drifting, and keep the machine going as you fish. Only constant practice will accustom your eyes to the tiny, telltale blips and flashes that indicate the presence of fish or bottom conditions that fish like.

Learn the profiles of approaches to favorite fishing spots, important navigational turning points, and buoys. Learn these profiles from a number of different compass directions. Record them in your log so you won't forget. Fishermen who use flashers constantly soon develop a sort of sixth sense for changes in depth the same way that a good radio operator develops a mental filter for background noise, but responds instantly when his own station is called.

Always check your radio direction finder or loran fixes with a sounding. It's surprising how often a sounding will reveal that you're actually northwest, rather than southeast, of a given radio signal from another boat or a beacon.

Flashers are great for night fishing. Place the instrument where you can observe its winking ruby-red eye comfortably from your bridge or console control station. The ruby flasher light won't affect your night vision and the flasher will keep you on a striper reef or out of treacherously shallow water as no other instrument can.

When trolling deep, use the flasher or recorder to prevent costly hang-ups of tackle on the bottom.

The suggestion is sometimes made that sounders are not "sporting" because they give the fisherman an unnatural eye with which to detect fish, or the habitat where fish should be. Neither the International Game Fish Association nor any other responsible group regulating the rules of competitive fishing has ever condemned electronic sounders as "unsporting."

It is true that sounders have vastly increased the ability of their users to produce good catches under a wide variety of fishing conditions. It is also true that learning to use a sounder to the limit of the machine's ability takes time, patience, and more than a modicum of skill. Experience has shown that the more truly skilled an angler becomes, the less interested he is in trying to catch every last fish in the ocean.

A versatile sounder is this combined recorder-flasher by Apelco. Blips on the tape above bottom are scattered fish. Flasher unit can be operated with recorder shut off, saving paper when a permanent depth record is not required. Price range is about $450.

A simple combination instrument is a depth and temperature gauge made by Vexilar. One side gives temperature at the depth to which the instrument has been dropped. The other side has a liquid-level depth scale. Lowered on a fishing line, it's easy to use.

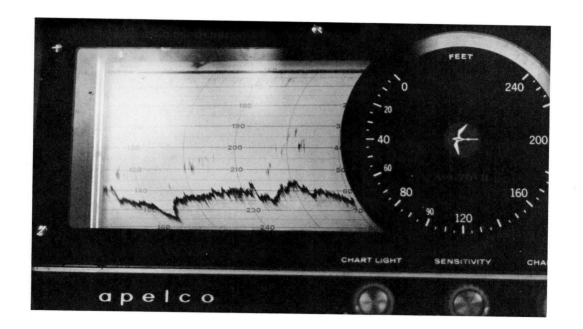

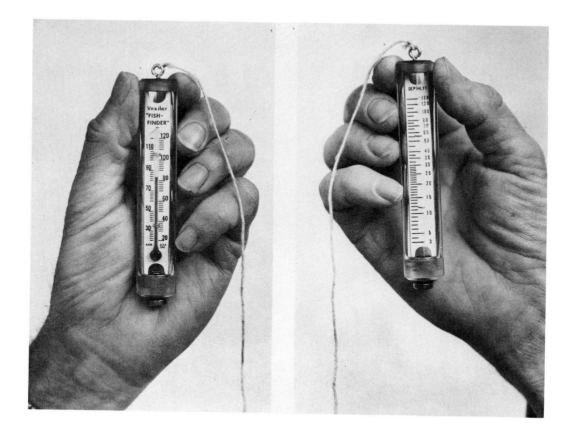

FRANK T. MOSS

12 / Tuna Trolling Tactics

TROLLING FOR SCHOOL TUNA AND BONITO is a very old method of fishing. The ancient Polynesians in their endless voyages across the Pacific evolved effective trolling lures of mother-of-pearl and lines of sennit fiber. In fact, a Tuamotu Pearl, as one class of aboriginal lure is called, is still recognized as one of the very best tuna-catchers ever invented. The Polynesians fished mainly from outrigger canoes and, on long passages, from their big, twin-hulled voyaging canoes.

Modern sport fishermen troll feathered, wooden, plastic, or metal lures from sport fishing cruisers and have discovered that the best results are obtained at a speed consistent with the sailing speed of the ancient canoes—six to nine knots. Modern anglers have developed some surprisingly sophisticated fishing techniques to raise tuna and encourage them to strike the lures, and to locate fish in areas where the schools may be separated by many miles of sea.

From the Atlantic, the Gulf of Mexico, the Mediterranean, the Pacific, and wherever sport fishing for tuna is carried out, a number of relatively simple operating rules have been developed. One of the most important is that every tuna trolling boat has its own best trolling speed.

Unlike some other fish, tuna and related species love the noise and commotion of a power boat's boiling, tumbling wake. Expert tuna skippers carefully experiment with speed and engine revolutions to find the best strike-producing combination for various sea and weather conditions.

It is a curious axiom that old-fashioned single-screw boats with deep, narrow wakes seem to raise and hold school tuna and bonito better than twin screw vessels. I once had a small Cape Cod single-screw cruiser that raised tuna smartly at the relatively fast speed of nine knots. When I switched to a broad-beamed twin-screw fisherman it took me a month to convince myself that the new vessel's best tuna speed was a slower six to seven knots.

One owner of a twin screw cruiser found that his boat catches tuna best when running at seven knots on the starboard engine alone. For some reason that boat catches only half as many tuna when it operates on the port engine alone, or both engines together. There is no standard rule that can be invoked to find out in advance what a boat's best tuna speed and engine combination may be. Experimentation is the only adequate answer, but experimentation can be done with the benefit of a number of helpful guides.

Keeping records of the boat's tuna-catching performance is very helpful. Information that should be recorded includes engine revolutions, boat loading, sea state and relative direction, quantity, quality, and direction of sunlight, and the presence or absence of surface bait fish. Under some conditions you may find that the tuna raise and strike best when the boat is trolling down-wind. Under other circumstances the strikes may come more often when trolling into or away from the sun. A backlog of successful trolling case histories helps greatly in selecting the tactics for any given combination of sea and weather conditions that you may meet.

Tackle for tuna trolling is usually justifiably heavier than that used for live bait fishing for the same fish. There are several reasons for this. First, a boat that is moving forward at eight knots is covering distance at the rate of 800 feet per minute. The forward motion of the boat after a strike is had, but before the vessel can be brought to a stop, tends to strip a considerable amount of line from the reel and to put a heavier-than-normal strain on the rod and line. Loss of line to boat motion from a motionless boat is never a problem.

Another reason is the fact that where one strike is had, more may be expected momentarily. Therefore, the smart skipper does not shut down his motors instantly when a strike is reported, but continues forward, possibly "goosing" the throttles, in the expectation that additional strikes may be obtained from fish that have accompanied the first one into the boat's wake. Naturally, the strain on the tackle can be heavy while the boat is still moving, and the reel must have a lot of reserve line capacity.

A final reason is that under certain conditions it is possible to raise and hold a close-packed school under the boat's stern and literally "bail" tuna into the boat, provided the tackle is equal to the task. More about this later.

Perhaps the most effective general tuna trolling tackle is a 3/0 or 4/0 star or lever drag reel mounted on a fiberglass rod matched to 30 or 50-lb. class line. Roller guides are a must to reduce line friction and prevent excessive line wear. The rod butt should have a slotted fitting at the lower end that will fit standard fishing chair rod gimbals. A 30-lb. test outfit will work well with school tuna and bonito up to 50 lbs. in weight. From 50 to 75 or 80-lb. fish weight, the 50-lb. line class outfit is more appropriate.

For larger school bluefins, ahi (yellow-fins), Pacific and Atlantic big-eye tuna, and very large wahoo in the 80 to over-100-lb. sizes, 50-lb. class tackle is generally considered to be a bit light, unless one happens to be in tournament competition. Eighty pound class tackle is justified on the ground that lighter tackle (except in competitive fishing) takes an unconscionable amount of time to effect a capture of these very powerful fish.

Observers of the offshore scene are usually quick to note that certain boats always seem to strike the first fish and get more strikes over a period of time when fishing is slow. Very often this is because the crews involved employ a lure and line-length pattern that is particularly effective in raising the tuna.

Newcomers to tuna trolling are always surprised at how close to the stern tuna will come to grab a trolled lure. Many fishermen place a row of snap-jaw clothes pins across the boat's stern into which the fishing lines can be clipped. This helps to eliminate jumping of the feathers in a choppy sea and facilitates keeping the lures and lines in a correct trolling pattern. While the boat is actively searching for tuna, but has not yet received strikes, a very effective line-lure pattern is as follows:

Two feather lures will be clipped down to the stern in clothes pin holders, the lines adjusted to place the lures only 15 or 20 feet back from the stern. Two more will be adjusted to ride side by side on the crest of the second stern wave, about a boat's length behind the stern. Two more will be adjusted to troll on the forward slope of the third or fourth stern wave. This varied line length trolling lure pattern is good when fish are scattered or mixed in size and species.

As soon as it has been established that a certain line length produces the majority of strikes, the other lines are adjusted to the same length. This bunching of the lures imparts a sort of school-effect

When this boat slows down on the tuna grounds, her motor and propeller noise and wake should combine to create a sound field the tuna will find attractive.

that very often results in multiple simultaneous strikes and much faster fishing action. The ideal line length usually falls somewhere between the second and fourth stern waves. Outriggers are seldom used with school tuna trolling lures, mainly because nothing is gained by trolling small feather lures in a position widely separated from the fish-attracting wake.

It is absolutely essential that the drag tension of each reel be adjusted to a very low figure. The initial shock of the strike, combined with the motion of the boat, may break a line if the drag tension is set to more than 25 per cent of the line's rated strength. Drags must be readjusted after each fight with a fish before the lures are streamed again.

Experts acknowledge that in many instances more than half of the strikes they get are "blind" from deep-swimming tuna that rise to the wake. When the fish are deep, the trick is to know how to capitalize on blind strikes so as to hook more than one fish at a time. This invariably requires that each rod be handled by an alert angler who has been instructed as to the procedure to be used when the first blind strike is obtained.

At the instant of the first strike the skipper jazzes the throttles a bit, sending gouts of white water into the wake. The angler with the fish on takes up his rod, *but does not increase drag tension* until the boat begins to slow down. Instead, he waits while the other anglers start jigging their rods energetically, causing the lures to dart and leap in the white water of the wake.

Finally, when it is necessary to slow down so the first angler will not run out of line, the skipper does so. Meanwhile he encourages those anglers who have not yet had strikes to continue jigging. In this manner it is frequently possible to fill all of the lines with fish after an initial blind strike has been had.

Once deep-swimming tuna have been located and raised, it is a tremendous advantage if the fish can be held at or near the surface. In the Pacific, where live bait fishing is a widely practiced art, live anchovies are flung overboard to interest and hold the school. Subsequent action is usually obtained by using live baits on heavy spinning or special salt water casting tackle.

Along the mid-Atlantic and northeastern coastal states a different method is employed. The trick is to attract and hold the entire school of tuna or bonito to the stern of the slowly-moving boat by the strategy of keeping at least two hooked fish captive on short lines close under the stern where they act as "leaders" to the massed fish below and behind. This is strenuous, exciting fishing.

When a susceptible school is suspected to be present, the first two or three fish to be hooked are hauled in close to the stern and the other anglers shorten their lines so as to have their lures only a few feet behind the boat's stern. The lures are jigged energetically, especially if the school is seen to rise behind the hooked fish. Very often heavy diamond or butterfish metal jigs, or red cedar jigs, are substituted for the normal feathered trolling lures. These sink quickly to the school of fish and may result in additional strikes.

The throats of fish already in the fish box are cut and sea water is dumped into the box to create a blood slick in the wake. Despite comment to the contrary, tuna will definitely rise to and be attracted by the blood of their own kind under the correct conditions.

Once the school has been worked into a striking frenzy, it is easy to set up a hooking, playing, and gaffing routine that puts a steady stream of fish into the fish box, but keeps live, hooked fish constantly under the stern to act as attractors to the school. Caution must be exercised not to break a line for, if a line is broken, the freed tuna may streak away, drawing the school with it. I have "bailed" as many as 250 school tuna, totaling well over a ton of fish, into a boat in less than an hour using this method.

With respect to lures, few attract tuna better than the tried-and-true Japanese feathered jigs. The most effective colors appear to be: pure white, pure yellow, red-and-white, green-and-yellow, white-and-black, blue, all-black, all-red, in about that order. The experienced tuna man stocks a good variety of colors and sizes. It is common for one color or size to be hot one day, and for a different combina-

tion of tuna lures to be hot the next day.

Leader material may be either stainless steel wire in sizes from #7 to #10, or fairly heavy monofilament. The fishing line usually has a strong snap swivel on its terminal end to facilitate quick lure-changing. Best hooks are the Sobey or O'Shaughnessy models in sizes from 4/0 to 8/0, depending on lure size and the weight of fish expected. Rig tuna lures so they will not spin and ruin the line. Watch for weed or grass on the hooks or feather heads. Dirty lures seldom get strikes.

Among non-feather lures, the time-honored red cedar or white enameled wooden jig is very good. Small plastic artificial squids have proven to be effective when the tuna are actively feeding on squid. Metal spoons are good when slow trolling speeds can be used, but tend to spin and ruin lines at speeds of over four knots.

Finding tuna is easy when the fish are on the surface, actively pursuing live bait fish. It takes a trained eye, however, to locate them when they are swimming and feeding down deep. One sure sign of deep-feeding tuna or bonito is the characteristic oil slick that develops on the surface over a deep-feeding school. This slick often has an odor like fresh-cut melon.

Wheeling and dipping sea birds such as gulls, fulmars, shearwaters, and terns are another sure sign of feeding activity. Sounding machines increasingly are relied on by tuna fishermen to reveal the presence of deep schools. When such schools are located, repeated trolling and turning back and forth over the school often irritates the fish into a rising and striking mood.

Recently, the relationship between water temperature and tuna action has been recognized. Pacific albacore, for example, show strong preference for surface temperatures in the 56 to 61-degree range

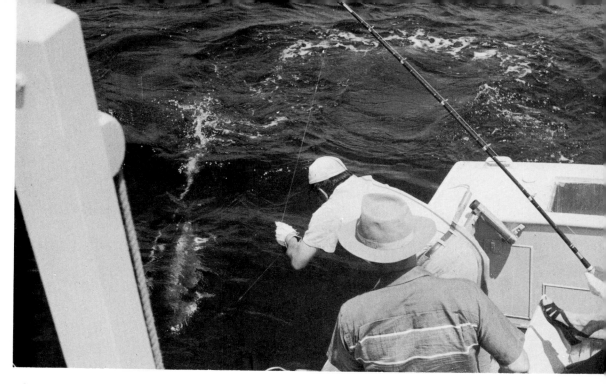

The author's mate, Joe Pollio, gets set to gaff a tough 100-pounder. Tuna of this size class often appear to be particularly difficult to hook with normal trolling techniques, and raise hob with tackle. This fish fell for a small black eel trolled on a long line from an outrigger at nine knots.

Here Joe Pollio shows classic gaffing form. First he hammers the heavy pick gaff into the fish just behind the head, then he hoists fish with a two-handed swing, sliding it head-first into the stern fish box. Tuna here is a 45-pounder that took a yellow feather towed 20 feet back from the stern.

in blue or blue-green water. They almost never are taken in green water or in water under 54 degrees surface temperature. Overflights of the United States National Marine Fisheries Service out of California ports during early and mid-summer are regularly made to find and report areas of favorable albacore water temperatures. Both commercial and sport fishermen take advantage of this information.

A sea temperature gauge mounted on the flying bridge costs less than $50 and provides instant readout of this vital information. Lacking such a gauge, it's relatively simple to dip up water samples in a bucket at frequent intervals and check the temperatures by using an outdoor thermometer. Sea water temperatures are an important part of every offshore fisherman's operating record.

The following table provides some rules-of-thumb for best trolling speeds, line lengths, and working temperatures.

Species	Temperature (Fahrenheit)	Line Length (feet)	Boat Speed (knots)
Bluefin tuna	48–80	15–50	4–7
Yellowfin tuna	60–80	40–60	7–9
Blackfin tuna	60–80	30–50	4–8
Albacore	56–61	30–70	8–10
Bonito (various)	50–80	40–80	6–9

Finding schools of tuna at sea is most often a cooperative venture. This is where the radio telephone and modern electronic navigating devices really pay off. If 20 boats cruise the ocean without communications other than eyesight, the chances are that five will come home loaded, ten will have a fair catch, and five will be skunked. But if they search the ocean by prearranged plan, informing each other of how and where the fish are being taken, all hands stand an excellent chance of bringing home a satisfactory catch.

This suggests that the skipper of a successful tuna trolling boat has to be a great deal more than just a sea-going taxi driver. Many skippers get their greatest satisfaction not from catching the fish, but from solving a particularly complex and puzzling problem that may include reluctant fish, elusive fellow skippers, cryptic radio messages, soup-like visibility, and guests who have to be cajoled into handling the tackle with something approaching a fair degree of effectiveness.

Which leads to a seldom-recognized truth.

Anglers fish to catch fish, but good skippers use anglers as the human tools by means of which fishing reputations are generated. This fishing business does get complicated, doesn't it?

13 / Productive Salt-Water Pan Fishing

BIG GAME FISHING IS EXCITING SPORT, BUT for every big game fisherman there are hundreds of anglers who find their greatest pleasure in angling for the many varieties of salt water pan fish. The smaller species require less elaborate tackle, are usually quite easy to find, and are great for family fun. They are ideal for introducing children to the world of fishing. Not to be forgotten is the fact that the smaller fish are often the best eating.

Almost any good, light rod will do for bottom fishing. Some folks do quite well with light spinning tackle, although my preference is a light fiberglass boat rod and a veteran Penn #155 star drag reel loaded with 20-lb. monofilament or 30-lb. Dacron. This combination will take anything from 1½-lb. porgy to a 20-lb. cod. Modern counterparts of this rig can be bought for not much over $30.

Depending on the season of the year, I stock a supply of hooks, usually of the snelled variety. Some large models I snell myself or rig with light wire leaders. I usually throw the hooks away after a few days' use, finding it better to rerig with fresh hooks rather than suffer along with blunt-pointed, shop-worn hooks that don't work well any more. The following table shows the types and sizes of hook I select for various fish, and the best baits for each.

Fish	Hook Style	Size	Best Bait
Winter Flounder	Chestertown	12	Blood, Sea Worms
Snowshoe Flounder	Chestertown	8–10	Clam, Mussel
Sea Bass	Mustad-Viking	3/0	Clam, Squid
Porgy (Scup)	Sproat	2/0	Clam, Squid
Tautog (Blackfish)	Carlisle	1/0	Green Crab
Fluke	Kirbed Sproat	3/0	Live Killie
Cod	Eagle Claw	6/0	Clam, Squid
Pollock	Eagle Claw	8/0	Squid Strip
Blowfish	Carlisle	1/0	Clam, Worm
Red Snapper	Eagle Claw	8/0	Mullet, Squid
Grouper	Eagle Claw	8/0	Conch, Squid
Rock Cod	Eagle Claw	6/0	Anchovy, Squid
Grunt	Sproat	1/0	Conch, Squid
Mackerel	Treble	10	Metal Jig
Sea Trout (Weakfish)	Mustad-Viking	2/0	Shrimp, Worms
Redfish	Eagle Claw	3/0	Shrimp, Squid
Cobia	Eagle Claw	8/0	Live Pinfish

Fish	Hook Style	Size	Best Bait
Whiting (Eastern)	Mustad-Viking	3/o	Squid
Red Hake (Ling)	Mustad-Viking	3/o	Squid, Clam
Sheepshead	Carlisle	2/o	Crabs, Clam
Croaker	Sproat	2/o	Clam, Squid
Halibut (Pacific)	Kirbed Sproat	6/o	Anchovy, Squid

You'll need a selection of sinkers. Bank sinkers are best for general bottom fishing. They do not catch in rocks as easily as pyramid sinkers. Weights of 2 to 12 ounces will take care of most bottom fishing assignments, although you may need 16 or even 20 ounces for cod, pollock, grouper, or red snapper fishing in very deep water. Fish with the lightest sinker that will hold your rig on the bottom. The "secret" that many successful bottom fishermen practice is to change sinkers as a tide slacks off so they are always on bottom, but not over-weighted.

There are many variations of the typical bottom fishing rig illustrated. This is a single-hook rig that is popular where fish are heavy, and works well on cod, big sea bass, snappers, groupers, and other strictly bottom-feeding species. Off the New England and Long Island shores, cod fishermen often tie a second hook to the line six or more feet up from the bottom. This 8/o Eagle Claw rides on a six-foot leader of 60-lb. test mono that you rig yourself. Baited with a squid head or a strip of squid, it's a killer for pollock.

Many flounder fishermen fish with metal spreaders, but the most successful don't use spreaders at all. Where flounders are big, like the three to six pounders called "snowshoes" that are found off Block Island in May, two big Chestertown hooks bridled together in tandem work well. In this case, the snell of one hook is tied into the snell of the other about six inches up from the second hook. The snell of the second hook is tied into the fishing line about four inches above the sinker. The rig is fished right on the bottom with occasional slow lifts of the rod.

Here's the secret of hooking flounders.

The flounder has a tiny mouth and must suck the bait in before you can hook it. Use *very small baits,* scaled to the size of the fish. When you lift slowly and feel a nibble, resist the urge to strike the hook into the fish. Instead, drop your rod and wait for ten or fifteen seconds. Then lift the second time. If you still feel a nervous nibble, wait again. Strike only when you feel the tug-tug of the fish's weight on the hook. It's as simple as that, and works on other fish, also.

You can attract flounders to the boat by taking an onion sack, weighting it with a brick or two, and filling it part-way with crushed clam and mussel shells. Hang this over the side of the boat and shake it every once in a while to send a cloud of tasty, but not very nourishing shell fragments drifting down-tide. It's another way of chumming.

The same system works well on other species of fish like sea bass, porgies, and weakfish. Crushed green crab shells will bring tautog running. Down Florida way, chumming with small shrimp will bring sea trout and redfish close to the boat, and shrimp chumming in the shallow channels around the bonefish flats on the flood tide will sometimes bring you surprising action with big bonefish coming in from deeper water.

Good baits for salt water pan fishing are easy to gather, or you can purchase what you need at almost any tackle store. Here are some easily gathered natural baits.

Young Scott Green caught his supper, a surf perch and a flounder, using a light, closed-face, spin-cast outfit. Fishing for small inshore species is an ideal way to break children in to the starting phases of sport fishing.

Jigging for pollock and cod is swift sport in cold water sections of the Northeast. This action took place at a college fishing seminar sponsored by Yale University at Wedgeport, N.S. prior to a tuna tourney held there.

Blood worms, skimmer clams, and mussels are the "fat of the land" for most bottom-dwelling fish. One secret of keeping bait fresh is to keep it cold. Pack worms in wet seaweed, store them at 40° to 45°. Freezing kills worms. Clams keep well when salted well and stored in a cool place. Mussels are best stored in a basket of wire mesh that is submerged in clean seawater.

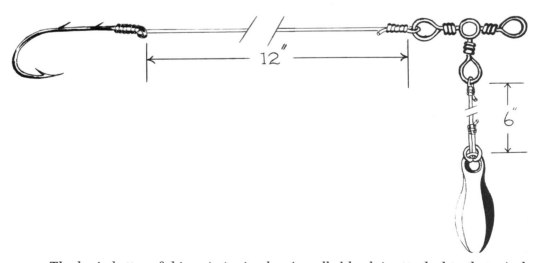

The basic bottom fishing rig is simple. A snelled hook is attached to the swivel. The sinker, heavy enough to hold bottom in the existing current, is also made fast. A second hook can be tied into the line a foot or two above the first. (Incidentally, the artist goofed slightly when he sketched this rig. Were he an experienced fisherman, he would have reversed hook and sinker.)

Mussels. Prime for flounders in the spring. Obtain by raking from rocks or dock pilings at low tide, or along a rocky beach at low tide. Crush small mussels and shells of big ones in an onion sack, as suggested previously. Keep mussels alive by suspending in a wire basket where clean tidal water will flow over them. Treat clams the same way. Clams and mussels will keep several days if bedded in wet sea weed in a cool place.

Clams. Cherrystones and Little Necks are good to eat, and make very acceptable bait if you don't eat them yourself first. Sometimes after a severe storm, you'll find huge surf (skimmer) clams washed up on an ocean beach. Grab them quickly, they're like gold for cod and sea bass. Open them while they are alive and store the whole (or cut into portions) clam meats in gallon pickle jars along with a good ration of Kosher salt. Use at least a pound of salt per gallon. Store in a cool or cold place, but don't freeze. They will last for weeks.

Squid. You can jig your own squid at night in many seaside harbors by going down on the finger piers with a Coleman lamp and waiting for the squid to appear in the water, chasing small bait. Wind solder wire around the shank of treble hooks and make up two-hook or three-hook jigging rigs with a sinker at the bottom to get the hooks down. Snag-hook the squids with the treble hooks, taking care to avoid getting squid ink squirted in your eyes. It won't injure your eyes, but it will make them smart pretty badly. Store the fresh-caught squid on ice wrapped in Saran wrap to keep the squid from direct contact with the ice.

Squid can be deep-frozen and will keep for months. If stored on ice only, it will last up to a week. Iced after thawing, it will last only a couple of days. So cut up and prepare only as much squid as you need for any particular period of fishing.

Killies. These make excellent bait for fluke. You can catch them along the beach of a cove with a small seine, or by chumming the tiny fish into a big lift-net or killie trap. Keep them alive in a well-aerated bait bucket or container. Dead killies are better than none at all for fluke.

Pinfish. These small southern fish (along with small grunts and blue runners) make excellent live bait for larger fish, such as groupers, cobia, red snappers, and amberjack, and can be caught in many southern boat harbors by fishing with small hooks and bits of squid or conch. Keep alive in a bait well or a GI can full of sea water, adding fresh sea water frequently.

Of course, it's often easier to buy your squid, clams, and worms direct from a bait or tackle dealer. Worms should never be frozen; they will keep well at 40 degrees in moist sea weed. Live green crabs keep well in moist weed in a well-ventilated box or crate in a cool place.

A great deal of salt water pan fishing is done by anchoring over a productive piece of bottom. Chapter 7, "Navigation for Fishermen," describes how to record the location of offshore grounds in good weather so you can find them again in haze or fog. For most anchoring, a Danforth or similar anchor of the proper size for your boat is sufficient. For very rocky bottom, select a fairly light stock anchor with thin palms or flukes.

Always make the anchor chain or line fast to the head or crown of the anchor, then lash the line or chain to the anchor's shank ring with some lighter line. This is the so-called "trip-line." If the anchor becomes wedged under a rock, a hard pull will break the trip-line and you can pull the anchor out by its crown, saving a valuable piece of ground tackle.

A method of light pan fishing that has grown in popularity is jigging. Originally, jigging with small metal jigs was confined primarily to mackerel and a few other species. Now we know that we can catch a very wide variety of food and game fish with metal diamond jigs and small trolling jigs. Here's the technique.

Rig a light rod with level-wind or spinning reel filled with 15 or 20-lb. monofilament, or lighter, depending on rod strength. Obtain some diamond jigs with treble hooks. Weights from three to six ounces should cover most jigging situations. Drift the boat with the tide over an area where sea bass and porgies are known to be. Jig a fathom or so above the bottom as you drift, and you'll soon have the porgies and sea bass eating out of your hand.

Drift over blackfish rock areas and catch tautog up to 8 or 10 lbs. on very light tackle this way. Use jigs of six or eight ounces over productive codfish and pollock areas and find out how exciting these "dead" fish can be on light tackle. Here's how to get the best out of your jigging.

Practice the mental "count down" so you can drop your jig to any desired depth without having to go to the bottom first. Jig with quick upward sweeps of the rod at intervals of about every five or six seconds. The fluttering of the jig as it falls in the water attracts the fish. When the jig hits the end of the line, hold the jig stationary for a second or two so a fish can grab it. Then, lift it just a little to test whether you have a fish on before you start the next jigging motion.

Sometimes you can do well by dropping very deep, then reeling in at moderate speed. Touch bottom, then reel in at a speed of about two handle turns per second or one turn for each mental "left, right . . . " of a march step. Count the number of turns you take up to the level at which you start to get strikes. This system is particularly effective on big pollock and cod over deep water wrecks.

Another very effective salt water pan fishing technique employs the use of light spinning tackle and baits such as live shrimp. This is casting work and it takes sea trout (weakfish) and red drum (channel bass) like crazy in southern waters. One real problem is keeping the shrimp alive. There is no magic way to keep shrimp in good condition, but you will lose fewer live shrimp if you change the water often in the shrimp bucket and cull dead shrimp frequently.

In very shallow water wading is often the best way to get close to the fish, but outboard, stern-drive, and small inboard boats work very well in the protected waters where shrimp-casting is popular. A portable shallow water flashing sounder helps tremendously to locate bars, deep holes, rock bottom, and schools of fish or bait.

One of the joys of pan fishing is eating the catch after it has been made. To assure that the fish will be fresh, they should be cleaned as soon as possible after catching. In hot weather, store the fresh-caught fish in an insulated beverage cooler along with a big chunk of ice. Many fishing ports have freezers where a sizable supply of fresh-caught fish can be quick-frozen and packed in dry ice for transportation home.

Important extra equipment for salt water pan fishing includes a bait cutting board, knives, whetstone, dip net, and light hand gaff for big fish. You'll want some extra hooks of the models you're using, mono or light wire for making leaders, parallel jaw pliers, a fish scaler, and a hook disgorger of some kind. All of these supplies can be bought in any tackle store.

Where and when to go fishing? Smart anglers keep an eye on what's doing in the fishing and outdoor columns of local papers. In a new area, it pays to hire a guide for a day or two to learn the local tricks. Supply yourself with adequate charts and from the charts figure out for yourself where the good rips are for trolling or drifting, where to get onto productive sea bass or blackfish rock bottom, and where to find the mud flats that flounders favor.

By all means, keep a record of what you do. Don't trust memory! Obtain a set of Tide and Current Tables for the locality, then compare Table predictions with the states of the tide that you actually observe. Remember, all salt water fish are governed by tidal movements, but fish change habits in different areas, so be prepared for surprises.

Finally, if you're just getting started in fishing, or if you want to get young children started in this great sport, don't sell salt water pan fishing short. The lessons you'll learn and the insight into fish behavior that you'll uncover will stand you in good stead as you progress to more exacting forms of fishing later on.

TROLLING HAS BEEN DESCRIBED AS THE
lazy man's way of fishing. Successful
trollers agree, however, that trolling requires patience, work, tackle skill, and
understanding of the basic strategy of
this kind of mobile fishing. Most fishermen are not afraid to work hard for a
worthwhile fishing reward. A good many
have the patience and tackle sense to
become good trollers. But many don't
know that every move of a trolling boat
must be carefully planned and that constant attention must be paid to observing
and interpreting the signs that signify the
presence and activities of fish.

A boat trolling over fish is in constant
interaction with the fish. Anglers often
do not realize that the fish are keenly
aware of the noise of the boat's propulsion
system and of the pressure waves generated by the hull passing through the
water. This awareness often stimulates
the fish into striking at lures trolled at a
critical distance behind the boat. I saw
this demonstrated dramatically a few
years ago at Montauk, New York, when
a friend arrived with a bass boat equipped
with a small tuna tower and asked me to
guide him and his family for an afternoon
of inshore striped bass trolling.

We took some bass tackle from the
charter boat I was operating and set out.
The weather was beautiful, but too calm

*A fleet of boats can troll over fish without
disturbing them if they keep the noise
field of their boats at a constant low
level. But running wide open over fish
soons puts them down.*

FRANK T. MOSS

14 / The Strategy of Trolling

for good bass fishing. There was no surf to color the water. We could see many big stripers lazing near the bottom. The fish actually opened ranks to let the boat go by, then closed in behind as it passed on. Our long, yellow nylon "Jigit" eels, 120 feet behind the boat, passed right through the fish with nary a strike. I was about to leave to look for more cooperative fish when a look from the tower showed me that the fish were closing in under the wake only 60 feet behind the boat.

Acting on impulse, I called down to the cockpit, asking the anglers to reel in the lines about 60 feet. Hardly had they brought the lures in to this distance when a double strike nearly yanked the rods from the hands of my friend's wife and daughter.

After we had gotten the pair of fish in, we resumed trolling over the fish with the lines carefully adjusted by eye from the tower to put the lures exactly where the stripers moved in from either side to join under the wake. In the next hour, we took eight more good fish while several other boats, attracted by our activity and fishing with identical tackle, but with lines of conventional 100 to 120-foot length, caught nothing.

Unfortunately, there is seldom an easy way to discover in advance how far back from the stern this critical *interaction distance* may be. It has to be arrived at, in most instances, by trial and error.

A similar incident took place at Silver Springs, Florida, when an outboard motor company was taking pictures of some of its models in action. While the mechanics were fussing with a balky motor, the boat operator, who was an inveterate fisherman, decided to do some trolling for bass near a likely-looking weed bed. It didn't take him long to discover that sometimes he got a strike *as he was letting out line*, but not when he trolled the plug at his habitual distance of 80 feet behind the boat. Experimenting, he made passes

with shorter and shorter lines until he discovered that the optimum distance of the plug behind the boat, for those fish, was a scant 16 feet!

What do these examples suggest? They make the general point that when fish won't strike according to a "normal" trolling formula, it pays to experiment. They also make the specific point that anglers very often troll with lines much too long to take advantage of the *interaction effect* of the boat's noise and motion of the fish.

Contrary to the notion implied in the title of Jacques Cousteau's famous book and film, "Silent World," the world of water in which fish live is a relatively noisy one. Visibility is often restricted to a very short distance by suspended plankton, sediment, or other particulate matter. The eyes of most fish are adapted to short range vision. Nature has compensated for this lack of visual range by giving fish extremely sensitive and sophisticated sound-sensing systems. Fish don't have ears. They don't need them. Immersed in an excellent sound-transmitting medium, they are able to "hear" with many parts of their bodies.

The prominent lateral line extending down the flanks of most fish, for example, is a chain of pressure-sensitive pores activating a computer-like network of special nerves. It is a sense organ used by fish to judge the size, speed, range, and identity of objects creating sound or pressure waves beyond the range of underwater vision.

Fish are apparently able to learn to some degree from experience. Anyone who has fished a virgin lake in Canada knows how ferociously the northern pike, lake trout, char, and other species react to their first sight of almost any kind of artificial lure. But a few years later, after the lake has been open to sport fishing on a regular basis, the same fish exhibit more restraint in striking at trolled or cast artificial lures.

Trolling is a matter of putting facts together to achieve the combination that makes fish strike for you when they won't strike for other fishermen.

Many fish show tolerance for man-made aquatic noise and vibration, provided the energy level of the noise does not approach or exceed the discomfort point. Experienced trollers know that a number of boats can troll continuously over schools of stripers, bluefish, tuna, salmon, bass, and other species as long as no boat makes radical changes of speed. But let one maverick boat charge through the area at full speed and the fish usually quit striking and seek a more peaceful area.

On the other hand, fish that have been resting quietly at a favorite "residential" spot may be aroused just enough by the approach of a trolling boat at moderate speed to react favorably toward trolled lures that follow the boat at a critical distance, speed and depth. Trolling may not always be the most enjoyable way to take fish, but there are definite times when it is the only *practical* way to fish. For instance:

● When you have to locate fish that you know are present, but can't spot from the surface.

● When the fish present won't respond to casting or bait fishing methods.

● When your companions are inexperienced at fishing techniques that require a fair amount of personal fishing skill.

● When the presence of many other boats makes trolling the only possible fishing method.

One has but to fish The Race off New London, Connecticut, when the bluefish are in, at Montauk or San Francisco Bay when the stripers are running, or off Miami when the kingfish are abundant to realize that trolling is the last resort of anglers who are forced to compete with vast hordes of boats.

The skill that boat operators exercise when trolling in big groups has a direct bearing on how successful most of the boats will be. Where the boat operators are skillful and obliging, the general catch level is usually higher than where the majority of the operators present are relative newcomers to trolling.

On Lake Michigan, for instance, salmon trolling is a fairly new technique that attracts many boat owners who have little experience at trolling on big water in the company of other boats. On calm days off Manistee, Michigan, huge mobs of small boats congregate where fish are being caught. It's worth your life to hook a salmon. Immediately every boat in sight starts to converge on a common point—your boat. Collisions occur, reverse gears whine, lines tangle, and the shouting is awful. Experienced trollers work under special rules of maneuver when operating in close groups.

● They avoid excessively long lines and try to fish with lines of standard length and lure depth, using uniform speed.

● A boat with fish on is considered to have a prior claim on right-of-way.

● Boats working a small patch of fish form a circle so each will have equal chances at the fish.

● Even if a boat has Pilot Rules right-of-way, it *never* turns in front of another so as to force the other to run over its lines, nor does it turn so short behind the other as to run over his lines.

● Boats approach and leave a trolling area at slow speed to avoid disturbing the fish.

● Anyone who accidentally cuts off another boat's lines immediately stops to apologize and offers to replace the lost items from his own stock.

● Boats running free give trolling boats a wide berth.

● Like good car drivers, good trollers plan their moves in advance and operate their boats in a way that is predictable to other skippers.

The best fishing is almost always away from the mob and the first boat to work over a known productive spot has a tremendous advantage over those that follow. Each group of resident fish usually contain a few individuals that happen to be less lethargic or more susceptible to boat *interaction* than the others. These fish are the ones that strike at the lures as the boat makes the first few passes over the spot.

After a few passes these susceptible fish are caught up, or have been stung into caution by missed strikes, and subsequent passes over the spot fail to produce hits. The smart operator does not waste time raking over the now unproductive spot for hours, but soon moves on to other spots, seeking fresh, responsive fish.

An interesting fact about this sample-and-move-on technique is that back at the spots that have been worked over, fresh fish often become receptive to boat *interaction* and can be caught by revisiting these spots after giving them a suitable rest period. Another interesting fact is that different boats seem to have different effects on the fish. One boat may work a spot to the point of no more strikes and move on, to be replaced by another boat that may immediately pick up fish that failed to interact with the first boat, but were sympatico with the second.

No one can explain why this happens. Fishermen who recognize the situation are content to exploit it when they can.

Smart fishermen also recognize that fish sometimes *signal back to the fisherman* that they are reacting to his trolling, but that something about the lure is not quite right to stimulate them into making more than a tentative swipe at it. Lazy fishermen don't get this message, because they can't be bothered to hold their rods in their hands.

I remember a day when I had a party trolling for bluefish at Cerberus Shoal, out in Block Island Sound. Fish were breaking, but they wouldn't hit anything except small eelskins, and these only sporadically.

Finally, I gave the wheel to one of the men and took a rod from one of the rod holders to have a feel at what was going on. After only a moment I felt a tiny tugging on the line, too slight and tentative to be a true strike. A minute later I felt it again. Reeling in, I found the tail of the eelskin badly frayed by sharp teeth. The other eelskins looked the same way. Obviously, bluefish were nipping the eelskin tails in their classic tail-biting manner, but why weren't we getting them on the hooks?

Experimenting with rod action, I soon found that one short jig of the rod after feeling the slight tugging would immediately result in a heavy strike. Constant jigging got no strikes at all. I had the men hold their rods and make one short jig after feeling the initial faint nip. We caught a swinging load of bluefish before the tide finally gave out.

Modifications of this nip-jig-strike routine have worked for me when trolling eels for stripers, balao or eels for white marlin, feathered jigs with squid strips for pollock, bucktails with mullet strips for barracuda, and with the Burke Tailspin lure for Lake Michigan coho salmon.

There are many natural signs that betray the presence of fish to the observant troller. Gulls and terns dipping into the water, picking up small bait fish, are usually a good sign of large fish beneath the surface bait. This is fine in clear weather, but how do you locate feeding birds in a pea-soup fog? By listening for them, naturally. Gulls make a peculiar keening sound when hovering close over breaking bait fish. Many times I've followed this sound through fog to its source to find bluefish, stripers, pollock, or even tuna feeding under the birds.

Predatory fish often feed so heavily that they create an actual slick of fish oil on the surface. Such an oil slick has a sweet, fruity smell. Follow the odor upwind in fog or at night and you'll soon find the feeding area.

Like every other good trolling place, Montauk Point has definite patterns of tide and sea conditions that make for good or poor trolling. Far from being a method for lazy fishermen, trolling requires constant attention to details, observation of natural events, experimentation with tackle.

On salt water the movements and feeding of game fish are largely governed by the phases of the local tides. Smart anglers plan their trips in advance to take advantage of favorable tide conditions. The Current Tables are of more value than the more widely-known Tide Tables, because the fish are greatly motivated by current flow but little effected by the static height of water level.

Good trollers obtain the best charts they can find of the waters they intend to fish. By using an electronic depth sounder together with the chart, they can locate the productive ledges, reefs, rocky areas, banks, and other bottom features that attract and shelter the fish they are after. Experienced trollers constantly watch the shoreline so as to be able to pick up visual ranges on the spots that consistently produce fish. They note the shape of tide rips over shallow reefs, the profile of such reefs as shown by the sounder, and shore ranges that will pin-point the reef when

the tide is slack, or when there is no surface slop to raise a rip.

Trolling is great fun when the fish are biting easily and any fool can catch a box-full. But the test of the good troller is to produce an adequate catch on the slow days when every fish has to be dredged up from under a rock, as it were, and half the boats come in fishless. Practice the following important trolling rules and you will soon find your catches scoring higher when the fishing is tough.

● When orthodox methods don't produce, *experiment*.

● Learn how to use the *interaction* of boats on fish.

● When fish bite strangely, try to *get the message*.

● Learn to *read the natural signs* that reveal fish.

● Always fish by the rules of *good trolling conduct*.

● Work at trolling, and *trolling will work for you*.

15 / Deep Jigging Gets Them

CAPTAIN LES FLATO WATCHED THE Fathometer graph closely as the *Sea Lion II* lifted her bow into a sea, then slid down into a trough. The recorder indicated 120 feet, then a sharp drop to 140 feet with jagged rocks in between. Suddenly the dark line on the graph plummeted to 180 feet. Here a dark cloud appeared several feet above the bottom and soon a second cloud appeared on the graph at an intermediate level.

Les explained, "Those are groupers, snappers, margate, and gosh knows what else on the bottom. The fish at the 90-foot level are king and cero mackerel and maybe a few blackfin tuna."

I stepped to the boat's cockpit where Mark Sosin, outdoor sportscaster for CBS Radio, and Al Pflueger of taxidermy fame had already sent a pair of bucktail jigs plummeting to the bottom far below. Joining them, I eased a two-and-a-half-ounce Upperman Big Ben bucktail jig into the deep blue water. We were drifting off Walker's Cay, northernmost island of the Bahamas, and we were about to sample a brand new type of fishing—deep jigging along the semi-tropical reefs.

I felt my jig touch bottom and immediately locked the reel in gear, lifted the rod tip smartly, and started reeling the jig back toward the surface Al Pflueger let out a grunt. "Here he is!" His spinning rod arched heavily as a heavy fish engulfed his lure.

"I'm in too!" echoed Mark Sosin excitedly. "Look at this rascal go!"

Line ripped from his level-wind reel as a powerful fish surged downward toward the shelter of caverns in the deep reef. Mark was using 15-lb. test line on a bait casting rig such as you would employ for black bass on an inland lake. Al's spinning outfit was loaded with button thread of only ten pounds test. It was stalemate for a long time before the two anglers started to show signs of progress. Both grinned broadly when we could finally make out the color of big fish far down under the boat.

Finally, Dick Milnarick, the mate, brought Al's fish on board with the gaff. It was a beautifully marked 20-lb. red grouper. Then Mark's fish was thrashing at the surface, a prime 25-lb. Warsaw grouper.

During their ordeal I'd sent my jig twice to the bottom. Al suggested that perhaps I should let the rod tip do more of the jigging work. Al is one of the finest light tackle specialists I've ever fished with. I heeded his advice and began jigging the rod energetically as I reeled in. Whammo! It felt like I'd hooked the Silver Meteor.

From that moment on, everything came up not roses, but groupers, snappers, margate fish, yellowtail, and cero mackerel. It was little short of fantastic, with big fish being fought constantly within sight of the lodge nestled comfortably on the low hilltop on nearby Walker's Cay.

Ralph Mumby, sales manager of a Florida fishing equipment firm, was aboard that day, as was Dan Orr, outdoor scribe for the Scranton, Pennsylvania, "Scrantonian." They'd been resting from the blue water trolling that we'd tried that morning. Soon they, too, were busy with jigging outfits. It was late in the day and we were all getting tired. We were about ready to quit and take our fish back to the island for an evening fish-fry when Mark and I hooked into a pair of real brutes.

We knew they were very big for we could not budge them from the bottom. But we also knew that the fish were not hung up in coral heads because every once in a while we managed to gain a fathom or so of line, only to lose it again. My left wrist was starting to swell and my arms felt as if they were ready to fall out of their shoulder sockets.

It suddenly struck me that this was the very same outfit that I fish with in the spring for flounders, back home in New Jersey. How ridiculous could a fishing situation get!

After a quarter of an hour we figured that we had brought our fish up to about the 100 foot mark, but it was like trying to reel in two very lively GI cans full of concrete. Finally, we were able to spot Mark's fish at a depth of 40 feet or so. Nobody said anything while Mark strained his tackle to the breaking point, the fish slowly giving ground. At last Dick made a stab with the gaff and heaved a 35-lb. black grouper into the cockpit.

My fish came in a few minutes later. Back at the Walker's Cay pier my black grouper tipped the scale to a respectable 44½ lbs.

That night, after we had feasted on six varieties of fresh fish, we fell into a talk-fest about the matter of deep jigging for reef and other bottom-dwelling fish. I wasn't exactly a stranger to the technique, for it is used extensively off northern New Jersey, Long Island, and New England for a variety of species, ranging from mackerel to sea bass, pollock, codfish, porgies, blackfish, and even fluke. But those fish

were small compared to the huge groupers and fast-moving snappers that inhabit the southern reefs. Up north, metal jigs are the most popular jigging lures. Down south, what are normally considered trolling jigs with painted heads and feathered or nylon skirts seem to do the best.

One reason why deep jigging hasn't caught on more rapidly than it has is because the species anglers jig for are more often caught with bait. Furthermore, jigging requires a bit more fishing skill and a lot more muscle than passive bait fishing. But it's terrific sport with light tackle.

Deep jigging isn't really hard to master, and you can do it anywhere you know that a population of bottom-feeding fish exists. You don't need anything more elaborate than regular plug or bait casting tackle. Spinning gear balanced to 15-lb. test line works fine. Rods should be somewhat on the stiff side because you'll be hooking fish a lot heavier than those you usually catch on the same tackle inland. One thing is quite important. The reel must be strong and have a very smooth-working drag. A "grabby" reel may result in a broken line. With spinning reels, most anglers use a manual pickup arm instead of a bail. The roller of a manual pickup arm usually rolls easily, whereas the roller of a bail is often frozen so it can't revolve. This ruins line.

Also important are the knots you use with your line. Southern anglers who jig down deep usually make a long double line so they can put on extra drag pressure when they get the fish up to the surface. The ideal knot for this is the Bimini Twist (see Chapter 25). The double line should be at least eight or ten feet long.

Next, an Albright Special knot is used to attach 12 inches of 30-lb. test stainless steel cable leader material to the end of the double line. The cable is essential in southern waters to prevent cutting the line or leader with sharp teeth or tail

Milt Rosko (left) with the big grouper that he jigged up on bait-casting tackle in the Bahamas. Jigging is effective on many species of game fish.

scutes. The lure is fastened to the end of the wire cable with a crimping sleeve, making a loose loop for the eye of the lure to swing on.

A wide variety of jigs work well. They fall into two groups, the flat or lima-bean-shaped jigs, and the torpedo-shaped or bullet-headed variety. A few are a combination of both shapes. Jig heads are molded of lead and the skirt is usually of bucktail, nylon fibers, or natural died feathers. Sizes range from as small as one-half ounce for shallow water and small fish, to three or four ounces for deep water and large fish. Where small fish are the rule, jigs with hooks of 5/0 or 6/0 size may be used, but I much prefer strong 7/0 or 8/0 in the jigs I use. Most southern fish have mouths large enough for hooks of this size.

Jigs come in a very wide range of colors, and smart fishermen are constantly experimenting with new color combinations. Pearlescent white and medium yellow appear to be the most popular colors among fish as well as with fishermen. You'll find jigs painted with fancy eyes, rings, and scale shadings. These attractions catch more fishermen than fish. There is one important secret that I have discovered, however, that really makes jigs work well.

Jigs having a sparse Mylar dressing in addition to the bucktail, nylon or feathers bring far more strikes than jigs that are not so adorned. Only a few manufacturers use Mylar on their jigs, so very often you have to add your own. I carry one-eighth-inch-wide strips of gold and silver Mylar in my kit and lay five or six strips atop the usual skirt on the jig on either side of the hook and secure them by wrapping them on with two or three turns of white or yellow plastic gift-wrapping tape. This holds the Mylar on tightly and gives a smooth finish.

Mylar's fish-appeal is much greater than plain bucktail and is probably due to its metallic gleam. I've also used strips of Multispectral fish attractor, plastic worms, and even long feathers to give jigs added fish-appeal. It's also true that an energetic jigger hooks more fish than a lazy one. Sometimes fish will respond only to a jig that is reeled upward and jigged at the same time with rod action. At other times steady jigging with the rod at a level where the fish are congregated will do the trick. You have to experiment.

You never know at what level fish may strike. Groupers, snappers, and most reef species will take hold right on the bottom or close to it. King mackerel, jack crevalle, blackfin tuna, and amberjack often strike at intermediate depths. Sometimes you'll get hits as you are about to lift the jig from the water. This means that it pays to work all levels equally hard unless you are concentrating on one level for one type of fish.

What I like most about deep jigging is the variety of fish that it brings. One pleasant afternoon my wife, June, and I fished a couple of miles off the Ocean Reef Club on Key Largo, Florida. Using light jigs in fairly shallow water, and very light tackle, we had jack crevalle, kingfish, amberjack, blue runner, yellowtail, Spanish mackerel, bonito, several species of groupers, snapper, and a barracuda.

Another time we were anchored over a wreck off the Mississippi coast and had red snappers, cobia, blackfin tuna, king mackerel, and one tremendous fish that broke a line. We suspected it was a huge grouper or possibly a jewfish. It probably took a smaller fish on the jig, getting hooked itself.

Florida and the Bahamas are not the only localities where deep jigging works wonders. It's practiced widely on the West Coast for yellowtails, white sea bass, rock cod, and similar species. I've already mentioned the way it's used in the Northeast for cod, pollock, and the like. In The

Race, off New London, Connecticut, it's extensively used with diamond jigs for very big bluefish. It should work equally well wherever there are predatory fish that like small, active food.

Remember one more fact—bring along plenty of jigs! Attrition of jigs, especially over a rough reef, is quite heavy. But you'll have a ball, and deep jigging really gets them, offering a type of action you can't find in any other style of fishing.

Either bait-casting or spinning tackle may be used for deep jigging. Line can vary from 10 to 20-lb. test, provided it matches the rod in use. The lures illustrated are bucktail jigs that work well in southern waters. In northern regions, chrome-plated metal jigs are equally effective on fish.

16 / I'll Take Dolphin

RUSS KINNE AND I WERE FLOATING ON THE clear waters of the Pacific, drifting with the wind and current in a 16-foot fiberglass outboard boat under a rock escarpment along the Panamanian coast. One moment the sea was empty; the next, we gazed down on an incandescent green, gold, and blue-dappled horde of dolphin, the most beautiful fish that King Neptune ever ruled. They were stacked in layers, stratified according to size. Near the surface were 8 to 10-lb. school fish. Beneath them were larger male fish. Lurking deep on the outside edge was the biggest *Coryphaena hippurus* I had ever seen.

He was slab-snouted, long, and very deep in the body. His pectoral fins undulated like the wings of a gull soaring in an updraft. He looked at least five feet long with a weight of 55 or 60 lbs. Abruptly, Russ flipped an oversize Rebel deep-diving plug seaward and a silent underwater eruption ensued.

The monstrous dolphin streaked upward toward the plug with an incredible burst of speed. At the same instant a mob of smaller fish darted forward and one of these slipped in front of the potential record-breaker, grabbed a mouthful of treble hooks, and somersaulted into the air. Russ boated this small dolphin with a grim face, thinking of the tremendous gold-and-azure torpedo that *almost* had

Pectorals spread like the wings of a jet fighter, a small dolphin resists the pull of the leader as mate slips gaff under the beautiful fish's body.

taken his lure. Both of us felt like crying over the probable record that had been lost.

Men have been known to lapse into poetry upon their first exposure to the glamorous dolphin. Lord Byron immortalized the beauty of the dolphin in his "Childe Harold," when he wrote:

> *Dies like a dolphin, whom*
> *each pang imbues*
> *Parting day with a new*
> *color as it gasps away,*
> *The last still loveliest,*
> *'til . . . 'tis gone . . .*

Author Philip Wylie once aptly put it, "I've repeatedly seen anglers lose them because once they sighted these fish their eyes popped, their jaws dropped, and they forgot to go on fishing."

The dolphin is lovelier than any other fish in the sea, yet, pound for pound, this brawling acrobat is stronger than a sailfish with equal if not greater ability as an aerial gymnast. On light tackle it will sizzle off runs with the drag-smoking speed of a bonefish, punctuating this exhibition with jumps that are as spectacular to the onlooker as they are disconcerting and wrist-wrenching to the man behind the rod.

Why don't dolphin receive more publicity within the angling fraternity? Mostly because they are seldom sought as the primary object of an offshore fishing expedition. Deep sea anglers hook many dolphin accidentally while trolling for tuna and billfish. The fight is often conducted from the sit-down comfort of a fighting chair on tackle designed for fish in the over-100-lb. class, rather than on equipment more suited to this ocean-going welterweight. Only recently have anglers with truly light tackle started to realize the great sporting potential of dolphin.

The technical family name of this interesting fish is *Coryphaenidae*, with two specific subdivisions, *C. hippurus Linnaeus* and *C. equisetis Linnaeus*. According to ichthyologist Edward C. Migdalski of Bingham Oceanographic Laboratory at Yale University, *hippurus* has pectoral fins more than half the length of the head. The tongue is narrow, rounded in front, and does not fill the floor of the mouth. There are 55 to 65 dorsal fin rays, 26 to 30 anal fin rays. *Hippurus* is the dolphin most commonly encountered by sportsmen.

In his *Angler's Guide to the Salt Water Game Fishes*, Migdalski explains that *equisetis* has pectorals no more than half the length of the head and a broad tongue, square-cut in front, that fills the floor of the mouth. Fin ray counters will emerge with 51 to 55 rays in the dorsal, 24 to 26 in the anal fin. The smaller *equisetis* grows to a maximum length of about 30 inches and a weight of 5 lbs. Its range is thought to be the same as that of *hippurus*.

The non-scientific offshore angler may find this interesting because heated discussions about the identity of dolphins often take place at such dolphin hot-spots as Diamond Shoals off Cape Hatteras, North Carolina, and the Jack Spot off Ocean City, Maryland, whenever *Coryphaenidae* appear to have missed the annual summer appointment, or to have arrived late in a juvenile rather than an adult stage. Because the migratory routes of these pelagic wanderers are only dimly understood, it may be that there are seasons when only one species or the other

arrives. In other years they may be so mixed together that causal anglers don't take time to differentiate between the two species.

At the present time it's impossible to produce conclusive evidence whether the two species travel together or separately. Until anglers, themselves, learn to tell the difference and report their findings back to interested biologists, the true relationship of these two closely related species will probably remain an ocean mystery.

The mammal (porpoise) and the fish (dolphin) were both called dolphin in ancient heraldry. Here we are talking exclusively about the fish, which is also known as *dorado, dorado de altura, dourade, dorade, coryphene, mahimahi* (Hawaiian), and dolphin-fish.

The all-tackle IGFA world's record, at the time of this writing, was a 76-lb., 12-oz. specimen taken off Bimini in the Bahamas by Charles J. Costello in 1964. This monster was nearly six feet long, with a girth a shade under three feet. A 73-lb., 11-oz. fish from Baja California, Mexico, was caught by Barbara Kibbee Jayne in 1962. Using 12-lb. class tackle, Marguerite H. Barry caught a 55-lb., 2-oz. dolphin at Mazatlan, Mexico, in 1964.

If you search the records for dolphin hot-spots, you'll come up with the Pacific Coast of northern Mexico and Baja California, the Bahamas, southern Florida, and East and West Africa. In the book, *Game Fishes Of The World*, Francesca LaMonte adds Brazil, the Windward and Leeward Islands, the Azores, Canaries, Ecuador, Peru, Chile, the Hawaiian Islands, Fiji, Malaya, the Philippines, Australia, the Indian Ocean, and a couple of other places. In short, dolphin roam the world's tropical and warm-temperate seas.

The fish prefer water at 70 degrees or higher temperature through most of their extensive range. It has been estimated that a full-grown female produces as many as 2,700,000 eggs at one time. The

favorite natural foods are flying fish, mullet, anchovies, sardines, filefishes, trigger fish, jacks, squid, and even occasional pelagic crabs. Deep sea anglers often see dolphin pick up flying fish as these aerialists end a long glide. Imagine the underwater speed of the dolphin to follow and be on the spot to seize the exhausted flying fish!

Watching a school of dolphin attack a trolled bait is spectacular. The next time you're offshore in dolphin territory, put on Polaroid glasses and perch on the flying bridge or the tuna tower, watching the outrigger baits sharply. Dolphin will begin an attack from several hundred feet to one side, streaking in with their stubby dorsal fins knifing the surface. A big fish may take more than one bait, hopelessly snarling the trolling lines.

Because of their proclivity for balao, strip baits, and the like, a large percentage of the dolphin taken in some areas are caught on rigs intended for marlin or sailfish. Unless the dolphin is a very big one, it is usually outclassed by the relatively heavy tackle, and is winched to the boat, rather than being permitted to fight the way it can on lighter tackle. For trolling for dolphin, I favor nothing heavier than 20-lb. class tackle.

While a whole, small mullet or balao is an ideal dolphin outrigger bait, you can make a very acceptable bait from a strip of squid, flying fish belly, bonito belly, or even pork rind, such as the ten-inch "sea strips" sold at many tackle stores. These are available in white, yellow, and blue colors. Yellow is the most productive color for artificial lures. Proponents of yellow argue that dolphin linger around sargassum weed and feed heavily on fish and small shrimp that inhabit patches of

Apparently rising straight out of the water, a large bull dolphin takes to the air after feeling bite of the hook.

this weed and, therefore, have become accustomed to associating yellow with food.

Frankly, I've seen dolphin take tuna feathers, bone jigs, spoons, plugs, and every lure imaginable in a multitude of hues. But sometimes they will be contrary and watch your offerings for minutes without flexing a muscle to strike.

You can expect maximum dolphin action on small whole fish or cut strip baits trolled at five or six knots, 60 to 80 feet behind the outrigger tips. The strike is lightning fast and dolphin usually hook themselves. Immediately thereafter, they take off on an extended run that usually culminates in several high, rapid jumps. Set your reel drag for light tension (unless the fish are quite large). A tension of 5 to 7 lbs, for 20-lb. line is about right. The dolphin's mouth is rather soft and hooks pull out easily.

After the initial, hectic aerial session, a dolphin will often swim with you, periodically turning its broad, flat flank against the pull of the line to test its chances for a fresh break for freedom. When the fish comes in easily, reel as rapidly as possible to maintain a tight line, but be prepared for a sudden, unexpected turn and run. The dolphin will surely make a heavy run as soon as the boat's shadow comes in view.

These are inordinately curious fish. A horde of free-swimming dolphin will follow a hooked member practically to the boat's transom. If you leave one hooked dolphin in the water and cast or troll additional jigs, you can often load every line. Some pros accomplish this by trolling a hand line and keeping a hooked dolphin close behind the slowly-moving boat while passengers cast for its compatriots with light spinning tackle.

Floating weed patches, driftwood, the pilings of offshore oil well rigs, all are special spots for dolphin. Troll your baits close to any floating or drifting objects you find at sea in blue water and you'll stand a good chance of finding dolphin.

Don't spend too much time in any one spot. Dolphin aroused by your baits will probably race in and strike on the first trolling pass. Leader material should be heavy monofilament or light wire because of the dolphin's small, sharp teeth. Sometimes a fish will bite off a lure and immediately turn to grab another with the first still hanging from its mouth.

Schooling dolphin develop a blood lust when large quantities of bait are available during a feeding time. At such times almost anything you throw or troll at them will take fish. Some experienced offshore fishermen, when they find a real school of dolphin, throw chum overboard to hold the fish and tease them into a feeding frenzy.

You'll have no difficulty differentiating between adult male and female fish. The colors of the female are generally less brilliant. The side profile of the female shows a head with an almost circular front profile. The male, by contrast, has a very high, thin "forehead," giving it a squarish forward profile, very high above the jaw line. The height and squareness of the male's forehead becomes more pronounced with age.

Alive, the dolphin is bright bronze-green on the upper surfaces, shading to gold and silver on the belly. There are bright blue phosphorescent spots on each side of the body directly below the dorsal fin, which is purple-blue. As expressed by J. Charles Davis II, in his *California Salt Water Fishing*, "The slowly dying dolphin, with wave after wave of color passing over the body, illustrates the changing condition of the flesh through the changing of certain chemicals in the body as the fish gasps out its life."

Actually, the dramatic color changes the fish can undergo are the result of activity of special pigment cells in the skin. The completely dead fish is a dull,

Dolphin are often considered to be a nuisance because of the way they hit balao and strip baits intended for billfish. Taken on appropriate tackle, they are the equal of any game fish when it comes to aerial gymnastics.

lifeless pewter color. The fading of the color of the skin, of course, has nothing to do with the quality of the flesh on the table, which is very, very good.

Davis suggests that anglers kill their fish and bleed them immediately after capture to enhance the rich, delicate flavor of the flesh. He states that fish allowed to die through natural suffocation are tougher with less delicate flavor than those that have been killed and bled promptly. In any event, the dolphin is a superb food fish that can be broiled, baked, fried, steamed, smoked, and prepared in just about any imaginable way.

For the ultimate in fishing thrills with dolphin, troll for them until a school has been located, then chum the fish to the drifting boat and cast for them with one-hand spinning outfits, 4 to 6-lb. test line, and very small casting jigs. Three or four jumping, cavorting fish on at one time for long periods of time may be the result. Very long runs seldom occur under such

conditions because hooked fish, after they have run off away, invariably circle back to the "protection" of the school.

Average dolphin encountered from charter or private sport fishing boats will go between 4 and 15 lbs. A big male, or "bull," as males are commonly called, may reach 50 to 60 lbs. Almost all dolphin over 40 lbs. are males. The females are usually considerably smaller. Small fish school heavily, but big fish tend to be loners. Explore every weed line and piece of driftwood as a matter of course and eventually you may find a record-smashing old bull waiting in the shadow of the weed or wood, wary of the boat, but covetous of the bait or lure that you will tease him with.

Don't forget a camera and plenty of color film to make a record of the trip. When the folks at home see the slides or movies, they'll be begging to go along with you the next time you go offshore for dolphin.

Dennis Good, of the New Orleans Big Game Fishing Club, caught this marlin 40 miles offshore in the Gulf of Mexico, fishing from a 25-foot Scottie-Craft, back in the summer of 1965. Despite her small size, his boat was equipped for serious offshore work. A fighting chair mounted on the twin-I/O engine box makes possible the use of heavy tackle. Electronics include ADF, VHF, flashing sounder, marine radio. The gin pole is short, but does its work.

FRANK T. MOSS

17 / The Case for the Vest-Pocket Sport Fishing Boat

THE "VEST POCKET" IDEA APPEALS TO people who glory in the myth of the small but invincible warrior, and quite a case can be made for the so-called vest-pocket sport fishing boat. This is a boat smaller than the smallest tournament canyon-runner, very often portable by trailer, but big enough for any inshore fishing and also for offshore work when fish and the weather combine to ring the gong on deep sea action.

Boats of this new, specialized class average 19 feet to 30 feet long and are not noted for fancy accommodations. They are fishing machines in miniature, yet, despite their lack of luxury, they carry all the equipment needed for fishing for anything from stripers, bluefish, and salmon to tuna, marlin, and even swordfish. Outriggers, fighting chairs, hoisting gear, sounders, electronic navigation and communication, even miniature towers—it's all there. And these vest-pocket fishing battlewagons are making news.

Dennis Good brought into the New Orleans Big Game Fishing Club one of the first blue marlin to be caught in the Gulf of Mexico off South Pass, Louisiana, using a 25-foot Scottie-Craft.

Dr. Ferdinando Schiavoni, Italian publisher and captain of his country's international tuna team, pioneered sport fishing for yellowfin tuna in the Mediterranean, first with a big Boston Whaler, later with a 25-foot Pacemaker Wahoo.

Mike Goelet garnered the 1969 Outstanding Achievement Award of the Virgin Islands 4th of July Open Tournament when he caught a 370-lb. blue marlin on 50-lb. class tackle from a 22-foot Aquasport outboard-powered fisherman.

What has made the new vest-pocket fishing boats so popular? First, they are fast and able. In a calm they can eat up the miles at a rate of from 25 to 40 per hour. In rough water at moderate speed, they slide along with no more fuss than boats twice or three times their size. They are hardly vessels in which to push 50 miles offshore in the face of posted small craft warnings, but when handled with reasonable care in reasonable weather, they do a superlative job for those fishermen whose goal doesn't include luxuriating in the comforts sometimes considered necessary for pleasure cruising.

The first secret of successfully rigging and fishing one of these hot little fishermen is to keep the gear light and simple. For example, suppose you have your eye on a sweet little 27-footer that is obviously just the thing for 'long-shore bass casting and light trolling, but you anticipate doing a bit of offshore work, looking for a swordfish or marlin to bait when the weather is good. Should you install a tower or would this be a waste of time?

Sit back and analyze the situation for a moment. Do you really need a tower? Is your offshore fishing experience the kind that has trained your eye to look for underwater fish? If so, then a modest tower in keeping with the size and stability of the boat might be a big help.

On the other hand, if your eye has been

trained to watch for surface-finning fish, a tower on a boat this small may be a waste of material, money, and fishing space. If you feel that you must have a tower anyway, then consider the tower from this point of view: why not construct the tower low enough so it doesn't hurt the boat's stability, and big enough so, in either offshore or inshore fishing, it takes the place of what would be a flying bridge on a larger boat?

This makes sense. All you really need is full headroom under the tower for walking around in the boat. With major steering and throttle controls grouped at the tower console, plus a small sounder, RDF, and radio telephone, your little fisherman will be a versatile boat indeed. Don't forget, however, that unless you also provide operating controls at the stern your vest-pocket fisherman with tower will hardly make a useful boat for single-handed fishing.

Many of the new vest-pocket fisherman designs feature the very popular center-line control console. Some offer single or twin fishing chairs aft of the console. If small game on light tackle is your forte, you'll probably do most of your fishing standing up, so chairs do not assume importance except for comfort on runs between fishing locations. But if medium to big game looks attractive and you plan to fish regularly with tackle of 50-lb. line class or larger, some sort of a fighting chair is almost a necessity.

Dennis Good solved the fighting chair problem in his twin-outdrive Scottie-Craft by installing a very light fighting chair with a removable footrest on a low mount on top of the reinforced engine box. This could hardly be done in an outboard-powered boat, but provided that there is no tower or other structure to interfere with 360-degree fishing from a fighting chair, there is no reason why this unit cannot be mounted ahead of the control console on the raised forward casting deck that many boats of this class carry.

In this case, the heavy duty rod would be fished straight aft over the head of the operator. Once a large fish is hooked, it would be a simple matter to turn the boat so the angler fights the fish over the bow, a tremendous advantage if the water happens to be a bit rough. Outriggers, of course, would be in the way of such a maneuver unless you were able to unship them in a hurry or had just one centerline outrigger that could be swung to either side as necessity might require.

For tackle of 50-lb. class and under, a chair with a footrest is not absolutely required and one or two light chairs aft of the console will equip the boat to handle anything from sailfish and big stripers up to tuna in the 100-lb. class, white or striped marlin, small blue marlin, or even swordfish or any of the medium sized game sharks.

A useful and popular type of vest-pocket fisherman outrigger works this way: The outrigger holders are actually heavy duty flush-mounted rod holders that can be mounted amidships on the boat's side decks. Each outrigger has a curved metal butt section with a slotted rod gimbal fitting at the lower end. The slots in this fitting are made so that the outrigger can be positioned "wung out" in the normal fishing position, swung back low over the stern for passing under bridges, or thrust vertically up in the air over the boat to act as a flag or signal mast. The poles, which may be from 18 to 25 feet long, are of fiberglass or sections of corrosion-proof (usually anodized) aluminum. (See also Chapter 5, "All About Outriggers.")

Clever designers and builders have spent much energy on such items as tackle lockers, bait and fish tanks, fuel and equipment stowage that utilizes every possible inch of space, while retaining a roomy, comfortable, efficient fishing area. Capitalize on this efficiency by placing

The stern of Dudley Roberts' Cuttyhunk bass boat is rigged for easy one-man fishing. Tiller and motor controls are within easy reach of fishing chair.

your working rod holders where they will give spread to your trolling lines and hold your spare rods, all rigged and ready, out of the way of fishing operations.

One angler I know maintains several different tackle boxes, each equipped with all the lures, tools, etc., needed for a particular type of fishing. He is a single-minded person and his multiple tackle box gambit certainly helps to solve the problem of where to stow excess tackle. When he goes out fishing he takes only the box that he needs for the day's work ahead.

The most popular electronic units are small flasher sounders, citizen's band radio units, and portable RDF receivers. Practically all small inboard, outdrive, and outboard power units are now available with alternators, so keeping batteries charged, even at slow trolling speeds, is no longer a problem.

Opportunities for vest-pocket fishing are legion. In Florida, for example, scores of thousands of these small, swift boats fish inshore and Keys waters when it's windy, roam outside for sailfish and the

like when the weather is good. Mid-Atlantic fishermen find these fishing machines ideal for 'longshore trolling and casting for bluefish, stripers, channel bass and the like, and relish them for a quick dash off to the tuna grounds when those gamesters are in.

Gulf anglers use them for everything from sea trout to offshore kingfish and marlin. On the Great Lakes, coho and Chinook salmon anglers are finding the new vest-pocket models small enough for easy trailing, yet husky enough for sometimes tempestuous lake waters. Pacific fishermen use them extensively for salmon, striped marlin, tuna and albacore, white sea bass and yellowtails.

Price ranges are broad, depending on how much boat you want and how much you can afford to put into "optionals." A representative 19-footer with a single 100-hp. outboard, fishing tools, flasher, citizen's band, RDF, and trailer may represent an investment of nearly $5,000. But a 38-foot offshore sport fishing cruiser will cost ten times this figure.

Some big boat fishermen are inclined

to view vest-pocket fishing craft with scorn until they see what these slippery little boats can do. Dr. Oswald B. Deiter, the noted tuna fisherman, for years regularly fished Newfoundland waters from a 19-foot MFG outboard-powered boat that he trailed all the way from his New Jersey home to that distant Canadian isle. Taxidermist Al Pflueger fishes for everything from Florida bonefish to sailfish from an open outboard fishing machine of about the same size.

These boats are tops for light tackle casting where placement of the boat with respect to the fish is important. Witness fly casting for bonefish and permit, plugging for stripers along a rocky shore, or working live bait suspended from a fishing kite for sailfish.

They answer the problem of the man who is itching to get his feet wet in serious game fishing, but can't afford a full-fledged offshore cruiser. Their lack of operating range is often made up for by their ability to be transported to distant fishing grounds by trailer behind the family car or camper unit. If the vest-pocket fisherman looks like your dish, have a good look at the dozens of fine models now being offered by builders. Then select a boat that matches your ambitions and budget.

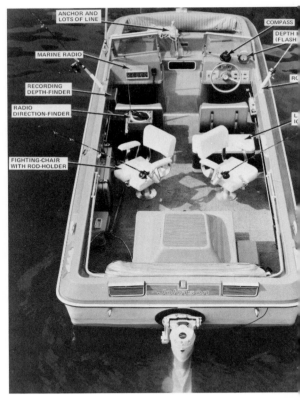

Interesting for its selection and arrangement of equipment is this craft from Johnson Motors. Good example of an equipment layout for inshore work.

This trim craft from the West Coast might almost be called a super vest-pocket fisherman. Motors are placed under flush hatches in cockpit deck.

FRANK T. MOSS

18 / Secrets of Kite Fishing

THE ORIGINAL OUTRIGGER WAS A FISHING kite invented by South Sea islanders hundreds of years ago. Their kites were wonders of primitive simplicity. A thin membrane of fish skin, dried animal bladder, or carefully dried leaf was stretched over a light, flexible reed framework. The kite line and the fishing line were skillfully braided sennit. The purpose of the kite was to carry the bait and fishing line well away from the boat so that wary species of large fish might be enticed and hooked.

The modern fishing kite works exactly the same way. In fact, the reason for the growing attraction of kite fishing among sportsmen is the fact that the fisherman has a special degree of control over the presentation of the bait, and it is exciting as all get-out to watch a sailfish, marlin, tuna, or other active game fish striving to catch the small, agile live bait that dangles in the surface of the water, unable to go deeper because of the suspended fishing line.

Unless you love experimentation for its own sake, you are better off to purchase a kite kit from one of several concerns that manufacture them. The kit usually contains the following items:

● Square kite frame of fiberglass or bamboo tubing
● Special kite cloth covering (light and heavy duty)
● Large wooden kite line reel
● Spool of kite line (usually heavy monofilament)
● One or more fishing line release clips

As with pleasure kites ashore, there is an optimum wind velocity for fishing kites, usually between 10 and 18 m.p.h. Well-engineered fishing kites can be worked in fairly strong winds, but surface roughness decreases the degree of control over the live bait, although a small ripple or gentle swell is desirable. It is possible, however, to reduce, increase, or alter the angle of the apparent wind by moving the boat with, against, or across the existing wind.

I saw this done to perfection a number of years ago when the legendary Captain Tommy Gifford was fishing out of Montauk, New York, one summer. On the tail of a rousing nor'wester Tommy would fish the kite in winds of up to 25 and 30 m.p.h. by using his smallest, heaviest kite and by tacking the boat down-wind so the bait was always broad off one bow or the other. He accomplished a change of tack by bringing the boat completely around up into the wind and then falling off on the other tack. This kept the kite line clear of the boat's tower and outriggers.

When the wind died to almost calm, Tommy supplied wind by running under power at an appropriate speed across or into whatever light breeze there was. This method of fishing was effective against large school tuna, white marlin, mako sharks, and an occasional swordfish.

Essentially the same kite fishing system is used extensively from Miami south into the Florida Keys for sailfish, small marlin, and large non-billfish. It has not caught on in popularity in the sailfish region from

Palm Beach northward to Stuart and Ft. Pierce, probably because other fishing methods have been very productive there.

In action, the kite is flown from the large kite reel which is mounted in the cockpit or on the flying bridge where it will have a maximum free space from side to side across the boat's stern. One or more quick-release clips are attached to the kite line below the kite. Where two or more clips are used, there should be at least 20 feet of separation between them so that suspended baits cannot possibly tangle in the water.

The release clip may be of the spring-loaded outrigger type, through which a fishing line will render freely, or you can use a common snap-jaw clothes pin with a rubber band around the jaws to increase tension. In the latter case a small plastic ring or large stainless steel split ring is slipped into the jaws of the clothes pin. The fishing line is then passed through the ring and the leader and bait attached.

The purpose of a ring or line-rendering release clip is twofold. First, you must have some means of being able to let out line through the release clip as the kite is flown higher and further from the boat. Second, if a shark or other undesirable fish appears on the scene, attracted to the bait, you can often prevent him from taking the bait by momentarily lifting the bait free of the water, winding in some of the fishing line through the ring or release clip.

If a good fish strikes, or if you wish to knock-down the bait to a fish for some reason, the ring pulls free from the clothes pin, or the release pin is yanked open, and the falling slack line gives the fish sufficient tension-free drop-back to grab and swallow the bait.

When two lines are fished from one kite, it is imperative that both anglers hold their rods at all times and keep a sharp eye on their respective baits. The bait should not be supported by the ele-vated fishing line. Almost all of the leader should be held aloft by the kite. With the average height of elevation of the release clip, the bait has quite a large radius of action in which it may swim and dodge in a most enticing way.

A clever angler, by manipulating the amount of line and scope that an active bait has to work with, can tease a reluctant predatory fish into a hunger frenzy. This is done by dropping-back or reeling in fishing line through the kite release clip or clothes pin ring.

Fishermen unfamiliar with the fine points of kite fishing usually don't realize that there are three important ways in which to hook the live bait with the hook. The choice of method will be largely determined by the existing weather condition, whether the kite bait is being drifted or towed, and the type of bait action desired for the fish in question.

Hooked through the back: Here the hook, which may be an Eagle Claw or similar model in size from 4/0 to 7/0, is hooked lightly through the flesh of the back near the forward portion of the dorsal fin. The proper spot is about one third of the distance from snout to tail. This is the natural "pivot point" of the fish's body. Hooked here, the fish has maximum ability to turn right or left, to dive or climb back toward the surface.

This is the ideal hooking position for the bait when there is little or no boat motion, except for wind drift. The hook should be passed through the back meat deep enough to hold well, but not so deeply as to touch the spine.

Hooked near the tail: In this case the hook is passed through the back meat about two-thirds of the way back from snout to tail. This method of hooking is useful where you want the fish to swim fairly deep. It has to be used under conditions of little or no boat movement, otherwise towing the bait through the water will result in an unnatural backward swimming motion not conducive to enticing game fish and bad for the bait because it makes proper breathing difficult.

Hooked through the lips: This method, if done properly, enables the bait to be led through the water in a natural manner since towing tension is applied to the head end. It is especially useful when the boat must move a few miles per hour to maintain apparent wind to raise the kite in calm weather, or when it is necessary to

Capt. Bob Lewis (right) flies one of the fishing kites that he perfected during experiments in Florida. Kites for fishing were invented by natives of the South Pacific centuries ago. Kite today is a long-range outrigger.

Live pinfish (below) is hooked through flesh of back, behind head. Hook is an 8/0 model with mono leader of 60-lb. test. Fishing line is passed through small swivel (below right) held by jaws of clothes pin attached to the kite's tether line. Kite carries bait out, line renders through swivel.

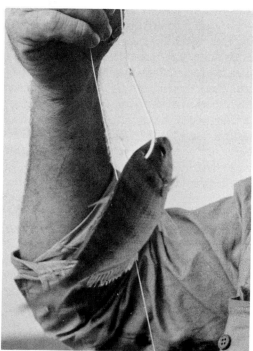

keep the boat moving to cover territory or change fishing location.

The hook should pass through the *lips*, not the fish's jaws. This will enable the fish to breathe in a fairly normal manner. The lips are fragile, however, and care must be taken to prevent jerking the line, otherwise the hook may tear free.

Kite fishing for game fish is wonderful sport when done from relatively small, open boats of the "vest-pocket" type. It can also be done without trouble from larger sport fishing cruisers. In fact, the presence of a tower on a boat is a distinct advantage, because the boat's operator can keep an eye on fish that rise slowly from deep water to a surface bait, thereby advising the anglers of impending action.

Fishing with the kite is also practiced to some degree from land. At Rooikrantz, in South Africa, kites are used to take baits and large spoons out away from the rocks when yellowfin tuna, wahoo, and similar game are working close to shore. An offshore wind is needed, naturally. There are a number of fishing locations where kite fishing might make all the difference between no fish and a real bonanza. Here are some suggestions.

Live bait striper fishing with Boston mackerel, herring, or alewives, on Cape Cod, the Rhode Island shore, Block Island, Long Island, Sandy Hook, or wherever big stripers are known to congregate close to the shore within range of a kite flown from the beach in an offshore wind. The same method can be used to fish in or close to the surf with live bait or surface plugs from a boat further out in deep water, when the wind is blowing onshore.

Live bait fishing for roosterfish along the Baja California coast under the same onshore or offshore wind conditions could be a sleeper.

Fishing for sharks from shore where an offshore wind prevails. One of the real problems of shark fishing from shore is how to get the frequently necessarily large bait out through the surf of breakers. Kite fishing could be the answer, especially where inshore water is shallow and a bait drifted out with balloons might fetch up on and hook the bottom before reaching deep enough water.

Tarpon fishing from shore or boats with baits and light tackle. This has been suggested as one way of solving the bridge-fishing problem in the Florida Keys, especially when it's necessary to fish an up-tide side of the bridge. Wind has to be favorable, naturally, and there must be no high-tension electric power wire in the way of the kite and its lines.

Eel fishing for stripers and big bluefish. Hook the eel in the tail so it will tend to dive deep. Place a split cork on the line far enough up to control the eel's eventual swimming depth. Fifteen feet, for example. When a fish takes the eel, the line falls from the kite release clip, and the split cork is pulled clear of the line by water drag as the fish makes its first run.

Kite fishing is best accomplished with light tackle. Either revolving-spool reels or spinning gear may be employed. The former is easier to use where much manipulation of line length is required. Florida Keys sailfishermen go after sails with kites using tackle in the 12 and 20-lb. classes. Leaders should be as light as possible, as should all portions of tackle that have to be suspended by the kite. Fairly heavy baits can be used provided they are towed out slowly by the kite and no attempt is made to lift them with the kite.

Fishing with a kite requires patience and practice, but gives anglers a potent weapon for catching fish when other methods fail. It is probably for this reason that kites are banned from certain Florida and other fishing tournaments. This doesn't make kite fishermen angry. They know a really good thing when they see it.

F R A N K   T.   M O S S

19 / Understanding Sharks

HUMANS HAVE HELD THE SHARK IN HORRID fascination since the first sailors ventured upon the water in tiny log rafts and skin canoes. Here was a creature large and bold enough to capsize their frail craft and devour the floundering swimmers one by one. It is no wonder that the ancients saw in the shark a sea devil incarnate.

Modern sport fishermen have a different opinion of these swift, powerful predators. In recent years shark fishing with sporting tackle has become popular in many lands. The International Game Fish Association recognizes six species of sharks as game fish. These are:

Mako	(Isurus oxyrinchus)
Porbeagle	(Lamna nasus)
White	(Carcharodon carcharias)
Thresher	(Alopias vulpinus)
Blue	(Prionace glauca)
Tiger	(Galeocerdo cuvieri)

Of these, the mako, porbeagle and thresher are the "most game," because they jump repeatedly when hooked. White, tiger, and blue sharks seldom jump when hooked, but fight a deep, determined battle. Contrary to much opinion, sharks in their natural habitat are not ravening monsters, avid to destroy. They can be excited into a frenzy of feeding and fighting, but as a rule are cautious and not prone to sticking their noses into possible trouble until a situation has been thoroughly investigated.

Sharks are extremely sensitive to sound and vibration in water. Experiments at the University of Miami have proved that sharks are attracted to sources of low frequency sound such as might be made by wounded fish, or by land animals (including men) struggling in the water. Sharks have a highly developed sense of smell which makes chumming a good way to attract them.

Not long ago I spent a day off Montauk with two other well-known shark experts, John Walton and Jack Casey. Casey at the time was shark biologist working from the Narragansett, Rhode Island, Marine Game Fish Research Center, a facility of the Bureau of Sport Fisheries and Wildlife. Walton is a shark angler with several IGFA records to his credit. The object was to chum, tag, and release as many sharks as possible.

During several years of effort, Casey and cooperating sportsmen have tagged and released several thousand sharks in Atlantic waters. The return of tags from sharks recaptured in distant areas is starting to fill out a picture of shark migration, growth, and breeding habits.

On this occasion, Casey and two assistants put several boxes of mixed trash fish and ground menhaden on board Walton's sturdy 45-foot twin diesel fishing cruiser *Chief Joseph Brant III*. The boat is named for one of Walton's illustrious American Indian ancestors. Casey and his assistants planned to fish for and tag the sharks, while John Walton and I chummed and tail-roped the catch.

On the way out Casey prepared dart tags to use on very large sharks and also a new type of plastic fin tag that he was anxious to try. This was an adaptation of the cattle ear tag, used by ranchers to identify beef animals. A quarter-inch hole is punched through the ear of the beef (or the dorsal fin of a shark) and a heavy, plastic stud is pushed through. A second, perforated stud containing an identifying number is locked over the first with a special pair of pliers.

We did not expect to encounter sharks larger than 300 lbs., so we prepared several 6/0 rod and reel outfits loaded with 50 and 80-lb. class Dacron line. Each angler wore a light belt socket. We had left the fishing chairs on the pier so as to have more working room in the boat's cockpit. This meant that the sharks would have to be fought standing up. The hooks were special soft-iron, Japanese long-line models that rust out of a wound in a fish in a short time. Leaders were ten-foot lengths of #10 tinned piano wire.

It was fine weather with only a light surface chop when we arrived at the proper spot, 15 miles south of Montauk Point. With the boat drifting, I started to ladle out a thin soup of ground menhaden mixed with sea water. Casey and his men baited up with whole small butterfish. Two or three stormy petrels, no bigger than sparrows, dipped to the surface, feeding on chum scraps. Suddenly I heard Casey grunt. An unseen fish had picked up his bait. He let it take line, then set the hook. For an instant he was poised there, the stiff rod sharply bent. Then, unexpectedly, a pup of a shark vaulted out of the water nearby, tumbling end over end.

"Mako!" shouted John Walton, his eyes taking in the pointed nose, muscular body, and unmistakable snapping jaws.

A few minutes later, Jack Casey had the angry little shark beside the boat, where Walton slipped a light tail rope over its small body. Nobody ever takes chances with makos. The shark was lifted bodily into the boat, slapped on

deck, and held there by strong gloved hands as measurements were taken and a fin tag applied.

"Forty pounds, male, tag number 105," Casey called out, while I scribbled the information onto a file card.

Then the piano wire leader was cut with pliers and the little mako was dumped overboard, apparently none the worse for wear. The bright orange dorsal fin tag gleamed in the water as the shark slowly swam away. Thus started one of the most hectic, tiring, yet satisfying days of fishing I can remember.

The mako was soon replaced by a school of blue sharks. They rose up from the deep water, attracted by the taste and odor of the menhaden chum. Frequently we had two or three hooked at once and had to spell each other on the rods so aching muscles could rest. Casey and Walton developed a technique of hauling in blue sharks up to 100 lbs. The fish were wrestled into submission on deck, tagged, measured, and flipped free as rapidly as they could be handled. Larger sharks were tail-roped and tied up alongside until quiet. Then fin tags were applied and measurements estimated.

Several fights among free-swimming sharks started over pieces of bait, but came to no real conclusion. The fish seemed to observe a distinct "pecking order" that larger sharks enforced vigorously. At day's end, after dumping overboard the last of the fish bait, a real feeding frenzy began.

Into the dead fish the hungry brutes thrust, snapping and gorging. One large shark, cut off from bait by a smaller one, seized the offender by the back of the neck as a terrier would grab a rat and gave it a good shake. When the big shark let go we could see the bleeding circle of tooth

Awesome is the dental equipment of a mako shark. No scavenger, the mako's diet consists of free-swimming fish.

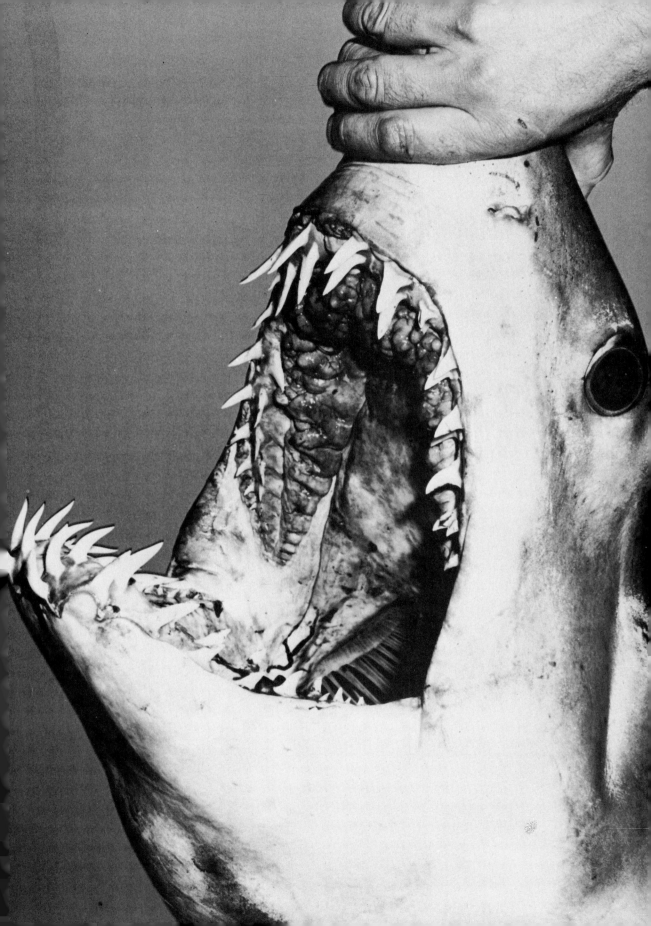

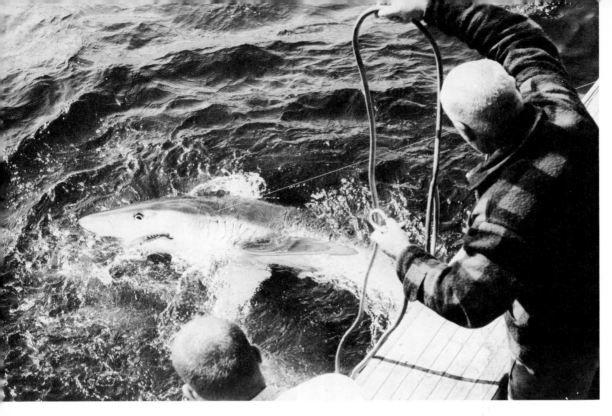

Tail rope in hand, John Walton (right) prepares to lasso a reluctant blue shark hooked during a scientific tagging expedition. Tail rope is bronze wire cable covered with tough rubber. Snap hook at cable end permits noose to be made around fishing leader. The noose is then slipped over head and body of shark and drawn tight around joint of tail. Another shark (below) thrashes alongside. When it is calm a tag will be applied to its dorsal.

marks in the other shark's bright blue skin. The smaller one never stopped feeding.

What are the best ways to fish for sharks with sporting tackle? Chumming with ground fish meal, just described, is good and has the advantage of bringing the sharks close to the boat so the angler may be selective with his bait. IGFA rules permit chumming with whole or ground fish products, but forbid the use of animal or fowl flesh, blood, or other parts.

If you encounter a lone shark while fishing offshore and want to bait it, keep the shark close by and interested by giving it pieces of fish from the fish box or squid from the bait supply until you have a suitable bait ready. Bait a 12/0 or larger hook with a slice of tuna or dolphin belly or with a whole mullet or mackerel, or a garland of several balao. The leader should be 15 feet of heavy wire.

When the bait is ready, put the bait out on the fishing line and troll it *slowly* in front of the shark so the fish can see it flashing in the water and get its scent. When the shark picks up the bait, give it 30 to 50 yards of drop-back on free spool so it may get the bait and the hook well inside. If you strike too soon you may pull the hook clear of the bait and out of the shark's mouth, or the point of the hook may lodge among the shark's teeth, poor holding ground for any hook.

Sometimes a shark will turn away from a trolled bait. When this happens you may be able to arouse its killer instinct by towing a couple of dead tuna or other fish in the wake of the boat after slicing their bellies with a knife to release the blood. Run the boat before the shark so that the shark has to pass through your blood-tasting wake. Be prepared to feed the shark a bait of the same kind of fish as soon as it comes questing down your wake, looking for the source of the blood smell. The boat's speed for baiting sharks should be about four knots.

Sharks do not require elaborate tackle and in some areas are the only really big game available to salt water anglers. The following table illustrates the tackle class and fishing method best suited to various sizes of the six game species of sharks. Non-game species can be taken by the same classes of tackle and fishing methods.

Rods should be of top quality fiberglass,

Species	Weight (pounds)	Line Class (pounds)	Reel	Method
Mako	100– 250	50	6/0	troll, chum
Mako	250– 500	80	9/0	troll, chum
Mako	500–1000	130	12/0	troll, chum
Porbeagle	100– 300	50	6/0	troll, chum
Porbeagle	300– 500	80	9/0	troll, chum
Thresher	100– 250	50	6/0	troll, chum
Thresher	250– 500	80	9/0	troll, chum
Blue	100– 250	30	4/0	chum
Blue	250– 400	50	6/0	chum
Tiger	250– 500	50	6/0	chum
Tiger	500–1000	80	9/0	chum
White	500–1000	80	9/0	chum
White	1000–up	130	12/0	chum

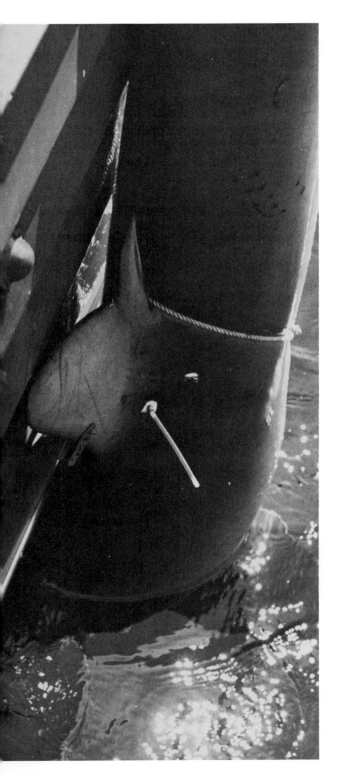

matching the class of line to be used. A rod with stiff action is better suited to sharks than one with soft action. With big sharks it is necessary to use a flying gaff, the cable of which should be ⅜-inch or ½-inch bronze or stainless steel rope. Tail ropes of nylon are also needed. Lacking a proper gaff, you may be able to control a large shark by making a large noose in a long tail rope or dock line and slipping this noose over the shark's head and body, drawing it tight around the joint of the shark's tail. Sharks have great vitality and it is dangerous to take them into the boat before they are thoroughly dead. Big ones may be towed home or lashed to the upright gin pole after being hoisted.

Shark identification can be a problem, especially to those without much experience with the creatures. Following is a brief identification of each of the six IGFA species of game sharks.

Mako: Appears cobalt or purplish-blue on the back, sometimes with a distinct chocolate blue undertone suffused by a sort of lighter blue "bloom" to the skin. Sides shade quickly to white and silver on the belly. Nose is rather sharply pointed. The tail is crescent-shaped and most like that of the swordfish of any shark. There are broad side keels at the tail joint. Special identification point—teeth are long, narrow, very sharp on both edges without saw edges or side cusps at the tooth root. Maximum size, 12 feet long and up to 1,000 lbs. weight.

About to be released, this shark has a cattle ear tag attached to dorsal fin, plus a spaghetti-type dart tag thrust into body at base of dorsal. Recovery of tagged sharks and other fish provides scientists with vital information about migratory routes, growth rates, reproductive success, and other factors. Sportsmen's tagging programs have been very helpful.

Porbeagle: A cold water shark similar to the mako, but thicker in the body. Special identification point—tail joint has two distinct keels on each side whereas mako has one. Teeth are pointed and clean-edged like the mako, but there is a small, distinct side cusp on each side of the tooth root. Maximum size, eight to ten feet long, about 700 lbs.

White shark: Largest of the game sharks, reaches length of between 30 and 36 feet and weight of several tons. Grey to dirty black above, shading to white below. Single side keel on each side of tail joint. Special identification points— large size and aggressive manner, head is very massive and wide when viewed from above, the teeth are symmetrical and triangular in shape with saw edges, small cusps at tooth root.

Thresher: The upper lobe of this unique shark's tail is extremely long, very often as long as the body. It can inflict damaging blows. Black or very dark brown on top, shading to white on sides and belly. Cannot be mistaken for any other shark because of the distinctive tail. Maximum size 20 feet, up to 1,000 lbs.

Blue shark: Bright blue on back, shading to pure white on sides and belly. Long, pendulant pectoral fins may be whitish at the tips in older specimens.

Nose is rounded, may also show some white. Special identification points—the bright blue color and fact that the tail joint has no side keel. Teeth are triangular, small, slightly serrated on the edges. Maximum size 12½ feet, 400–500 lbs.

Tiger shark: Back is brownish or greyish-yellow with distinct "tiger" mottlings of darker color extending down the sides to the yellowish belly. Upper lobe of tail is quite long and horizontally extended with a lateral ridge alongside the tail joint. Special identification points—the distinctive color, shape of tail, and fact that the teeth are saw-edged, and crumpled strongly to one side or the other, depending on which side of the mouth they are located. Maximum size 30 feet long and up to two tons in weight.

Shark fishing can be a great adventure, especially when purpose is given to the fishing by participation in a scientific program such as tagging.

Sharks have a definite place in marine ecology, otherwise nature would not have permitted them to survive for millions of years. Understanding them removes fear and hatred of these remarkable fish, creatures that even now are said to be endangered by man's relentless commercial pursuit of the living resources of the oceans.

Elwood K. Harry, tournament champion and IGFA vice president, illustrates the balancing act that any big game angler may be called on to do if his fish decides to put forth the power at its command. Here a Bahamian tuna is sounding into deep water, testing the 130-lb. class line to its limit, pulling Harry up from the chair seat.

F R A N K   T.   M O S S

20 / Is It the Man or the Tackle?

THE SHEER POWER OF SOME FISH IS amazing. Swordfish harpooners frequently tell of seeing ten-gallon wooden kegs towed completely under by harpooned fish. We can estimate within very close tolerances that it takes at least 85 lbs. of direct downward drag to pull a ten-gallon keg under.

Let's look at this fish-power business a little more deeply. Very little research is available, but a few examples give us some facts to work with. A number of years ago, the radio fishing commentator and writer, Bob Edge, working with Captain Earl Thompson of Liverpool, Nova Scotia, experimented on recording the speed of hooked tuna. He used a rod equipped with a motocycle speedometer to measure the line speed when tuna were hooked with little or no drag tension.

One tuna, which later was weighed in at 59½ lbs., managed to attain a clocked speed of 44 m.p.h. after it had taken out approximately 200 yards of 36-thread linen line. Harlan Major, in his authoritative book, *Salt Water Fishing Tackle,* states that according to experiments he once conducted on the towing strain of bare linen line at various speeds, the 200 yards of 36-thread linen must have exerted a pull of at least 78 lbs. on the fish at 44 m.p.h.

The question comes to mind, "How much real horsepower is expended by a fish exerting a 78-lb. pull on a line at 44 m.p.h.?"

The answer is not hard to discover if we first put down the common formula for horsepower and two necessary definitions:

$$1 \text{ h.p.} = \frac{33,000 \text{ ft. lb.}}{1 \text{ min.}}$$

$$1 \text{ m.p.h.} = \frac{88 \text{ ft.}}{1 \text{ min.}} \quad 44 \text{ m.p.h.} = \frac{3,872 \text{ ft.}}{1 \text{ min.}}$$

The formula for determining power is:

$$P = \frac{D \times W}{T} \div 1 \text{ h.p.}$$

In which:

P = power in h.p.

D = distance (3,872 ft.)

W = line pull (78 lb.)

T = time (1 min.)

The formula can now be expressed as:

$$P = \frac{3,872 \text{ ft.} \times 78 \text{ lbs.}}{1 \text{ min.}} \div \frac{33,000 \text{ ft. lb.}}{1 \text{ min.}}$$

$$P = \frac{302,016 \text{ ft. lb.}}{1 \text{ min.}} \times \frac{1 \text{ min.}}{33,000 \text{ ft. lb.}}$$

$$P = 9.15 \text{ h.p.}$$

So here we have a tuna weighing less than 60 lbs. that expends 9.15 h.p. to haul 200 yards of 36-thread line through the water at 44 m.p.h. This is power expended beyond that needed to overcome the friction of the tuna's body passing through the water. We have no means for measuring how much power the act of swimming takes.

Multiply the fish's weight by ten, obtaining a weight of 600 lbs., about average for giant bluefin tuna, and we see that here is a fish probably capable of pouring out more than 90 h.p. in excess of its own water drag when it has to. No wonder we need piscatorial jiujitsu to catch fish as strong as these!

Thirty-six-thread linen line is rated at 108 lbs. breaking strain. If you were to hook the 600-lb. tuna to some solid object with a length of this line, the fish could most probably break the line in a dead pull from a standing start. Very few men can withstand for any length of time a line pull of 100 lbs. on a fishing rod. Consider the way this pull is multiplied when applied to the man's body.

The rod would be about 88 inches in length, with a distance of perhaps 22 inches from butt gimbal to the lift rings of the big game reel. Thus, while wearing a harness clipped to the reel, the man is working on the short end of a lever that has a length four times the length applied to his body. Therefore, there would be 400 lbs. of tension on the man via the harness straps.

Even with a good harness few men can endure this much pressure for long. The wonderful thing about modern fishing tackle is that it interposes two different types of flexibility between the fisherman and the fish. The first is the spring-like flexibility of the rod itself. The second is the adjustable reel drag that is pre-set to slip at any desired line tension. Together they make the man the equal of the powerful fish.

In discussing the true role of tackle, it is important to understand how line breaks. For instance, we could break a 108-lb. test line with a 10-lb. weight. All we have to do is cut a piece of the line about 12 feet long and make one end fast to a solid object high enough to allow a free fall of 12 feet. Then we tie the other end of the line to the 10-lb. weight, hoist the weight to a point equal to the spot where the first end of the line is tied, and let the weight fall.

In dropping 12 feet, the 10-lb. weight gains 120 foot-pounds of kinetic energy, enough to break the 108-lb. test linen line, which has very little stretch. But try this same experiment with a more stretchy line such as monofilament of the same breaking test, and the line may not break. The extra stretch may be enough to slow the weight down over a slightly longer period of time, reducing the "G" forces to a point less than the breaking strain of the line.

The combination of spring action of the rod, plus the pre-set slip action of the reel drag, plus the elasticity of the line, works to prevent breaking the line despite the great power potential of the fish. To be truthful, the fisherman cannot overcome the fish bare-handed. He has to have the tackle to help him absorb the shocks and hard runs. But it is up to him to operate the tackle with some degree of intelligence.

What does this "degree of intelligence" entail? For one thing it requires proper setting and operation of the reel drag. Harlan Major, in experimenting with linen lines, created a set of curves that shows at what speeds various lengths of line could be expected to break from the friction of being dragged through the water.

The curves are rough and we have no reliable conversion factor to compensate for the lesser water friction of modern synthetic lines, but by interpolating Major's curves and by allowing synthetic braided lines a drag factor of two-thirds that of equivalent linen lines, the following table of velocity versus breaking length was established for each of the IGFA line classes.

Please note that the lengths of line required to break at the speeds given are approximations.

Speed (knots)	IGFA-12 (yards)	IGFA-20 (yards)	IGFA-30 (yards)	IGFA-50 (yards)	IGFA-80 (yards)	IGFA-130 (yards)
10	260	280	315	375	450	560
20	165	190	215	260	300	375
30	130	140	155	200	230	280

What do these figures tell us? Consider this: if you were on a stationary boat, fishing with IGFA-12 line, and had a sailfish on that had taken out a great deal of line, the sailfish could break the line at about the 260-yard mark back from the hook merely by swimming back toward the boat at a leisurely ten knot speed, putting no additional tension on the tackle.

Deduced rule No. 1: *Fight your fish close when using light tackle.*

The first shock of a sudden strike at fast trolling speed is absorbed by the bending of the rod. Line does not start to slip from the reel until rod-bending tension is equal to or slightly more than the initial drag setting.

Deduced rule No. 2: *Keep your rod tip up for maximum spring action at the strike.*

Now we come to the business of reel drag setting. Earlier it was indicated that the striking drag for most species of game fish falls between 20 and 35 per cent of the breaking strain of the line. Let's have an analytical look at what this drag setting talk is all about.

Let's assume we have a big game rig loaded with IGFA 130-lb. line to a full spool diameter of exactly six inches. We are going for big tuna, so we've decided to set striking drag at the 30-lb. mark. This is done with a spring balance in the usual manner. Then we hook a fish. Assuming that the drag adjustment is not changed, what will be the amount of line tension required to pull line from the reel when the spool diameter has fallen to five inches, giving an effective working radius of two and one-half inches?

The formula to use is:

$$X = \frac{A}{B} \times W$$

In which:

$X =$ the new line tension
$A =$ original spool radius
$B =$ new spool radius
$W =$ original drag tension

Therefore:

$$X = \frac{3}{2\frac{1}{2}} \times 30 = 36 \text{ lb.}$$

Carrying this further, we can construct a simple table giving new drag slip ratings for diminishing working radii of the reel spool.

Radius (inches)	Tension (pounds)
3.0	30
2.5	36
2.0	45
1.5	60
1.0	90
0.5	180

Immediately we see that the amount of line tension required to slip the drag builds up very rapidly as the reel spool radius (and diameter) gets down to small dimensions. In fact, we see that at a one-half inch radius the amount of line tension needed to slip the drag becomes 50 lbs. greater than the breaking strain of the line. What useful rule can we rescue out of this situation?

Deduced rule No. 3: *As spool diameter becomes smaller, slack off the drag adjustment to reduce chances of breaking the line.*

By extending this table to the full range of IGFA line classes, and by substituting percentages of full spool radius for spool radius in inches, we get a new table that

Radius	IGFA-130 (pounds)	IGFA-80 (pounds)	IGFA-50 (pounds)	IGFA-30 (pounds)	IGFA-20 (pounds)	IGFA-12 (pounds)
100%	30	20	12½	7½	5	3
83%	36	24	15	9	6	3½
67%	45	30	18¾	11¼	7¼	4½
50%	60	40	25	15	10	6
33%	90	60	37½	22½	15	9
25%	120	80	50	30	20	12

gives the exact drag tension required to slip a reel drag at the designated percentage of full spool, assuming an original drag setting of about 25 per cent of line breaking strain. The 100 per cent radius is the original drag setting for each class of line.

The bottom line of this table gives us a very important clue. Remember that with the exception of the 130-lb. line, we had set original striking drag at exactly 25 per cent of the breaking strain of the line. The bottom line of the table confirms that if the striking drag is set at 25 per cent of the breaking strain of the line, line tension equal to the breaking strain will be reached when spool diameter (or radius) falls below 25 per cent of the original diameter or radius. Equally important is the fact that this applies to other percentages as well. Here are three examples:

a) An 80-lb. test line with drag set to slip at 16 lbs., 20 per cent of breaking strain, will break if the reel spool diameter is reduced to 20 per cent of original diameter.

b) A 30-lb. test line with drag set to slip at 9 lbs., 30 per cent of breaking strain, will break if the reel spool diameter is reduced to 30 per cent of original diameter.

c) A 12-lb. test line with drag set to slip at 6 lbs., 50 per cent of breaking strain, will break if the reel spool diameter is reduced to 50 per cent of original diameter.

What about our question of whether it's the man or the tackle that lands the fish? Some observers think it fashionable to say that it's the tackle, not the man. But we who fish know better. In honestly fought battles between man and fish, with tackle appropriate to the situation, it's the man *plus* the tackle that does the job. The smart angler uses his drag the way a sports car driver uses his gear box.

Deduced rule No. 4: *Plan ahead; fish hard; but take time to think.*

The tail of a tuna or billfish is a highly efficient oscillating propeller.

21 / Yellowtail Fever

A FAINT STREAK OF GRAY MARKED THE overcast eastern sky as the anchor chain of our 65-foot sport fisherman *Betty Lou* rattled into the water at the northern tip of Mexico's North Coronado Island. The locality had been rich with yellowtails during recent days. The calm water, rippled by a light morning breeze from the northwest, promised ideal fishing.

Mexico's Los Coronados Islands are situated just below the United States border some 15 miles from San Diego, California. The area offers fabulous yellowtail fishing when north-bound schools stop over while on their migration in the spring. Catches of 50 to 100 yellowtails by a single boat are not uncommon. After the big migration has pushed through, lesser numbers are taken from fish that remain behind all summer. Autumn sees a big south-bound migration that duplicates the action of the hot spring fishing.

While private sport fishing boats increasingly are fishing the Los Coronados Islands for yellowtails, the bulk of the fishing in recent years has been done by the large and growing fleet of San Diego party and charter boats. The fishing techniques they have developed have had a profound effect on game fishing up and down the coast.

Sea gulls were keening overhead as the deck hand atop the bait tank near the stern threw lively anchovy bait overboard at intervals to attract the hard-fighting yellowtails. The Pacific yellowtail is a cousin of the amberjack and one of the most actively sought species fished for by West Coast sport fishermen. The majority of the 22 fishermen on our boat were busy rigging their tackle or finishing breakfast when the action started. Suddenly a shout of "Hook-up!" came from an angler at the stern.

"Fish boils off the stern!" shouted the deck hand as he flung a ladle of live bait into the water. The water was suddenly full of fast fish streaking after the frightened bait, their sides flashing with golden hues in the growing daylight. Mixed with the yellowtails were a few bonito. It looked as if it would be a real test of light tackle.

Everyone with a live bait in the water was quickly hooked to a fish. Rods arched and anglers shouted. "Hot rail!" yelled a young fellow, making the recognized call for right-of-way among other anglers at the boat's rail. Under and over weaved the fishermen, passing rods and ducking under each other's arms in the mutual effort to prevent a monumental tangle.

I had been one of the first to cast a live anchovy into the melee of feeding fish and had a powerful strike as soon as the bait struck the water. I allowed the fish to take 30 feet of line before I set the hook. My reel had been set for a moderate drag. The reel screamed as my fish peeled off at least 100 yards of line. I followed it toward the bow where several other anglers were fighting fish. My fish was bulldogging on the surface and I decided to let it stay out there for awhile until the mess closer to the boat was cleaned up.

Fishermen bellowed for the gaff as yellowtails were slowly pumped to the surface. In the clear, blue water beneath us the silvery sides, dark blue backs and large, forked, yellow tails reflected daylight brilliantly. Shouts filled the air as thrashing yellowtails were gaffed in over the rail by the dexterous crewmen. Several looked as if they would top the 24-lb. mark. Mixed with the yellowtails were bonitos weighing 8 to 10 lbs. Their small, neat tails beat a rapid tattoo on the deck.

My own fish had tired during the first gaffing spree and its bulldogging waned as I worked it toward the boat. I pumped carefully, aware that at any moment the fish might decide to dash under the boat in an attempt to cut the line on the keel. Luck was with me, however, and soon the mate lifted a sleek 22-pounder over the rail.

"Sack Number Three," I told him as he cut loose the hook that was firmly imbedded in the fish's jawbone.

I immediately set about tying on a fresh hook, choosing a #1 size gold-plated tuna-style hook. This I tied directly to the 20-lb. test monofilament line, using the Improved Clinch Knot. We don't use ordinary leaders on yellowtails, although a few anglers tie in a five-or-six-foot section of 40-lb. test mono between hook and fishing line to act as a sort of shock leader. This is accomplished with the old, reliable Blood Knot.

As soon as I was ready, I went back to my spot at the stern and selected a green-backed live anchovy from one of the wells of the live bait tank. "Greenback" anchovies are usually more active than "blackbacks," and active live bait is what draws and catches the larger fish.

I hooked the bait on by passing the point of my hook under and up through the collarbone area that lies on the right side of the anchovy's head, adjacent to the right gill plate. An anchovy hooked this way lasts longer and stays livelier than one that is hooked cross-wise through the white spot on the bait's nose, another favorite way of hooking this kind of live bait.

At times yellowtails display all the disdain of trout, swimming majestically around the boat, refusing every bait put overboard. At other times they will take only sardines, live squid, mackerel, metal lures, or some other sort of unpredictable forage. All you can do is to experiment and feed them what they prefer at any given time. We were lucky today because anchovies are the most readily available live bait, and the 'tails were grabbing them like hotcakes.

A short cast placed my anchovy close to a pod of feeding yellowtails and bonito. A bonito took my offering and headed for the China Sea. Its runs were fast, but erratic. Streaking in one direction, it would suddenly reverse course and zig-zag back toward the boat. I was hard put to keep a tight line. Pound-for-pound, few fish can outfight a bonito.

Ten minutes later the deckhand gaffed my bonito, a fat 12-pounder that kept on beating its tail even after it had been placed in my big fish bag. It would have been a wonderful fish to take on salt water fly tackle, but a fly rod is no tool for this stand-up party boat fishing.

West Coast anglers have developed a fairly specialized type of tackle for their very sporty live bait fishing. My rod was typical of those in use, an eight-foot model rigged for use with a spinning reel and featuring a fast-taper tip. This combination provides good casting action, yet had solid backbone from the center of the shaft down to the butt for working big fish.

Monofilament lines average 20 to 30-lb. test. Reels must have a working capacity of at least 250 yards. We generally cast out the live baits without weight, although a few anglers use a one-quarter ounce Rubbercor sinker to gain distance. Heavier sinkers are used if the fish refuse to

A Pacific game species, the yellowtail is highly popular among anglers from southern California. San Diego party boats fish close to shore off islands of the California and Mexican coasts. The famous San Diego Yellowtail Derby runs all summer and attracts thousands of anglers competing for big prizes.

come near the surface as they often do.

Having taken two fish with live bait, I decided to give jigging a whirl. Putting away the live bait outfit, I broke out my jigging rod, a ten-footer equipped with a metal spooled conventional reel loaded with 40-lb. test mono. The reel features a very fast 4-to-1 retrieve ratio. The three-ounce blue-and-white metal casting lure had a 4/0 double-strong treble hook in the tail. I fastened this directly to the end of the monofilament line.

With live bait fishing, the bait does the work, but with jigging, you have to keep the lure in constant action. I made a 40-yard cast from the boat and started the retrieve, level-lining the mono carefully onto the reel spool with my thumb. Two bonito rolled and flashed at the lure when a big yellowtail started following it as it flashed through the water. Suddenly, the yellowtail forged ahead, grabbed the metal jig, and dove for the bottom. The rod was almost torn from my grasp.

Down, down went the fish, testing the heavy mono line to the uttermost. It was one of the heaviest yellowtails I could remember having hooked. Down deep, it circled strongly while banging against the line with the characteristic bulldogging yellowtail maneuver. Fifteen minutes passed before I had the fighter up to the surface. Gaffed and deposited on deck, it turned out to be a prime 28-pounder, one of the biggest on the boat that day.

San Diego offers a complete array of party and charter boats from 45 feet to 85 feet in length. Boat accommodations include bunks, galley service, rest rooms, and accurate electronic navigation. Some of the larger boats make limited-passenger fishing trips down to fabulous Baja California. There are very complete facilities in the port at many yacht clubs and fishing docks for berthing and serving private craft. Rental boats are available. The majority of the party boats that fish yellowtails leave between 1:00 and 3:00 a.m.

to allow time for taking on fresh live bait and to travel to the islands for a daybreak arrival.

The yellowtail season extends from mid-March through October. The annual San Diego Yellowtail Derby has become one of the great sport fishing competitive events of the Pacific Coast, and one of the biggest in the world. Anglers vie for weekly, monthly, and "fish-off" prizes worth tens of thousands of dollars.

A California fishing license is not needed to fish in Mexican waters. The necessary Mexican permit is provided by the party or charter boat and the cost is included in the fare. Private fishing boats must register with the Mexican authorities prior to crossing the border, and each individual on board must have a Mexican fishing permit. This can be taken care of in San Diego through the local Mexican official representatives.

Here is a complete run-down of a typical West Coast live bait yellowtail fishing outfit.

Rod: Eight-foot, fast-taper tip for live bait fishing, ten-foot, fast-taper tip for jigging. Jigging rod is matched to 40-lb. line, live bait rod is matched to 20-lb. line.

Line: Quality 20-lb. monofilament line for live bait, 40-lb. mono for jigging and very deep fishing. No leaders are used.

Hooks: #4, #2, and #1 tuna-style single hooks in gold finish for live bait; bronze or nickel finish acceptable. Size 4/0 double-strong treble hooks in nickel finish for jig fishing.

Reel: For live bait fishing, either a heavy duty salt water spinning model, capable of loading at least 250 yards of 20-lb. test mono, or a metal spool star drag "conventional" reel with the same line capacity. For jig fishing, salt water star drag model with line capacity of at least 200 yards of 40-lb. test mono. Metal spool preferred. Some anglers prefer to use 40-lb. test Dacron line instead of mono in line this heavy. A gear ratio of

4-to-1 is preferable in order to achieve a fast retrieve.

Lures: Metal, five inches to seven inches long, purchase locally to get the models that are taking the fish. Weight runs one and one-half to three ounces. Treble hook attached by strong split ring. Colors should be white, chrome, blue-and-white, black, purple-and-white, dark pink, gold.

Yellowtail fishing is not confined to party and charter boat fishing alone. Increasing numbers of private sport fishing boats are discovering the wonderful sport that this swift, hard-fighting fish affords. "Yellowtail fever" is very much a southern California phenomenon these days, a fever for which the cure is simple—go fishing!

Live bait is big business at Western fishing ports. Here a big party boat loads live anchovies before dawn in preparation for a quick dash to the Coronado Islands for yellowtails and other Pacific food and game species.

FRANK T. MOSS

2 2 / Choosing and Using Salt-Water Tackle

IF THERE IS ANY SECRET TO CHOOSING AND using salt water tackle, it lies in knowing how tackle is classified and how to select equipment that will give maximum utility and satisfaction for the money invested.

In talking about salt water tackle for boats we must consider the three major types of tackle employed. "Conventional" tackle is usually considered to be that which employs a revolving-spool reel mounted atop the rod shaft. This is by far the largest tackle class. The next is salt water spinning tackle which differs from fresh water spinning tackle mainly in size and ability to handle heavier fish. The last is the relatively new class of salt water fly rod tackle.

Anglers have discovered that in conventional tackle, especially, there is a direct relationship between the rated breaking strain of the line and the combination of flexibility and backbone of the rod. The latter quality was usually expressed in terms of rod tip-weight in ounces, in the days when rods were built of bamboo. Nowadays, modern fiberglass rod-building techniques have rendered the old tip-weight criterion obsolete, but it is still used in some cases to show variations in strength between different models of a particular line of rods.

Revolving-spool salt water reels are now being manufactured and designated according to the well-known, but frequently misunderstood "o" system of size rating. This system affords a fairly accurate estimate of the line capacity of a given reel. Lines for salt water use are now manufactured mainly to conform to the six International Game Fish Association line classes of 12, 20, 30, 50, 80, and 130 lb. maximum breaking test.

The following table combines the various IGFA line classes with the reel "o" size most commonly used, the approximate reel capacity of modern synthetic line, and the nominal tip weight sometimes recommended for the rod best suited to each class of line. Also indicated are the six unofficial names descriptive of the various line classes.

Fiberglass is now the universally accepted rod-building material. Most quality salt water rods are hollow-built and there is an astonishing variety of combinations of flexibility, backbone, pitch of

Type	Line (pounds)	Reel	Capacity (yards)	Tip Weight (ounces)
Ultra light	12	2/0	475	2–3
Very light	20	3/0	500	4
Light	30	4/0	500	6
Medium	50	6/0	575	10
Heavy	80	9/0	600	16
Very heavy	130	12/0	750	24–30

The salt water fly rod, used here by tarpon expert Stu Apte, is becoming increasingly popular among fishermen who value the quality of the fishing over trying to catch every last fish in the sea.

tip taper, and other important qualities. Fiberglass is impervious to water, cannot rot, and does not take a "set" with heavy use. Fly casting models are so sensitive that the weight of a bee will deflect the shaft. On the other hand, the powerful shafts used for catching very large game fish could be used for crowbars.

Ring guides are a necessity on spinning and fly casting rods, and on revolving-spool surf or bait casting rods, but the availability of inexpensive, good quality roller guides now makes it possible to build what was once considered "tournament quality" into fishing rods priced for the general public. Roller guides perform the important function of reducing line friction to a minimum, thereby prolonging line life and reducing the loss of good fish to chafed, worn lines. When selecting rods for your personal use, look for these marks of quality workmanship:

Roller guides and tip-top of trolling rods matched to the diameter and weight of the rod shaft.

Corrosion-proof stainless steel or Carboloy ring guides where these are necessary.

Guide and decorative windings adequately protected by applications of varnish or flexible lacquer.

Wooden butt section of straight-grained hardwood with appropriate lower end ferrule to fit gimbal of fishing chair, rod holder, or light belt socket.

Corrosion-proof reelseat of chrome plated brass or stainless steel, provided with positive lock ring so rod tip can be locked into position when inserted into reelseat. Lock ring to prevent loosening of reel in reelseat.

Tip dimensions and type of tip action best for the kind of fishing involved.

The latter quality is very important, but is also subject to considerable variation. West Coast live bait fishermen, for example, prefer fairly long, slim tips with considerable flexibility for casting light baits, yet with good backbone in the lower tip section for fighting heavy fish. Modern "progressive taper" or "parabolic action" rods achieve this combination of qualities to a satisfactory degree.

The bait-trolling billfisherman, on the other hand, usually wants a shorter, stiffer rod tip, one that combines flexibility with powerful lever-action to raise fish that are sounded deep, and to apply maximum line tension when this is required. Rods for specialized deep trolling with wire line will be discussed later.

Two basic types of revolving-spool reels are used by salt water sport fishermen. They are really quite similar, their basic difference being the fact that the older,

Good tackle for bonito and related tuna species in the 10 to 50-lb. class is 30-lb. test line with a 4/0 reel and a light trolling rod that matches the line. Roller guides reduce line wear.

Ed Gruber of Montauk's Deep Sea Club caught this 339-lb. swordfish on 80-lb. test line and tournament quality tackle. Tackle of this caliber takes most of the big fish available today, meeting most anglers' big game needs.

long-popular star drag reel achieves drag tension adjustment by means of a "star wheel" attached directly to the reel handle drive shaft, whereas the newer lever action drag reel achieves drag tension adjustment by means of a quadrant lever that is separate from and does not rotate with the drive shaft.

The great advantage of the lever action drag is that the drag can be pre-set to a desired striking drag, which is usually somewhat less than half of maximum drag, and can be returned instantly to this pre-set drag tension without further calibration of the reel. This is a great advantage when fighting a large, active fish, or when it is necessary to re-set the drag to the desired striking drag tension immediately after bringing in or losing a fish.

Striking drag varies with the line class of tackle and species of fish, but is pre-set in this manner: The rod is set up in a rod holder, the line is rove through the guides, the line is hauled from the rod tip using a light spring balance to establish the slip-point in pounds of tension for various adjustments of the drag. The following table gives typical striking drags for a number of species of fish and the types of tackle used to catch them.

Species	Line Class (pounds)	Striking Drag (pounds)
White marlin	30	8
Sailfish	20	5
Blue marlin	130	20–24
Swordfish	80	14–18
Mako shark	50	15
Giant tuna	130	30–40
Tarpon	20	7
Bonefish	12	2–4

These striking drag values are averages. Some anglers use striking drags of greater or lesser figures quite successfully, but the majority of experienced anglers set their drags for these and equivalent species at close to the values given here. An exact ratio between line test and striking drag is not a reliable gauge. The striking drag for blue marlin, for example, is often set as low as 20 lbs., even with line of 130-lb. class, but that for big bluefin tuna may be screwed as tight as 40 lbs. for the same class of line.

Speaking generally, striking drag seldom is set less than 20 per cent or more than 35 per cent of a line's rated maximum breaking strain. Striking drag, incidentally, is equally important with spinning or fly casting tackle. Hand-setting is seldom accurate and may vary as much as plus-or-minus 50 per cent of the desired value, so smart fishermen *always* use a spring balance. The popular "De-Liar" handles weights up to 28 lbs. maximum and is no larger than a package of king-size cigarettes.

Spinning tackle has become vastly popular, especially where casting is employed as a fishing technique. Rods for spinning usually have longer, more flexible tips than those used with conventional reels for trolling or still fishing. This is because the primary purpose of the rod is to cast out a lure that has appreciable weight. Spinning rods in line classes as heavy as 20 lb. and even 30 lb. test are used by some anglers for tournament fishing, but their rather extreme flexibility presents problems when it comes to raising deep-diving, heavy fish.

The same situation is even more true of salt water fly rod tackle. The rather extreme flexibility of the fly rod is a mathematical function of the rod's ability to cast the specific weight of fly line for which it is engineered. The great difference between the fly rod and all other casting rods is that while other rods are built to cast the weighted lure (the line going along for the ride, so to speak), the fly rod is designed to cast the line itself,

the nearly weightless fly going along for the ride.

This engineering incompatibility makes the fly rod a very poor trolling or bait-fishing rod. The rod-handling technique is very different from that of other tackle, although it is by no means difficult for the average angler to master, given competent instruction. The rapidly growing popularity of salt water fly fishing has stimulated a number of manufacturers to develop tackle designed expressly for open water and large fish.

A typical salt water fly rod combination consists of a hollow, two-piece fiberglass rod 9 to 9½ feet long, engineered to work properly with a weight-forward floating or sinking line of #9, #10, or #11 line weight rating. Tapered leaders of from 6 to 9 feet in length are used, and the tackle, for purposes of competitive fishing and record keeping, is rated by the breaking test of the narrowest, or "tippet," section of the leader.

Both conventional and spinning tackle can be badly mismatched as to line class and rod type, and still work fairly well. Fly casting tackle, on the other hand, must be carefully balanced as to line-rod relationship to work properly. To be effective, a salt water fly reel must have a storage capacity of at least 250 yards of 20-lb. test backing line under the casting line, and a drag that can withstand considerable heavy use. A number of excellent reel models are now available.

Like all precision equipment, good fishing tackle needs constant care. Wash your rods and reels in fresh water after use and chamois them dry before putting them away. Linen lines suffer from mildew if not washed and dried periodically. Dacron and nylon lines are more impervious to salt, but never store a salt-impregnated line on a metal reel spool for any length of time. The salt will damage even the best of stainless steel or anodized aluminum spools.

Lubricate your reels according to the manufacturer's instructions, and from time to time put a single drop of light oil on each bearing of the roller guides of your rods. Disassemble the reel from the reelseat before storing tackle for any length of time. Clean the reelseat and give it a light rubbing with Vaseline. Store rods in a cool, dry place, hanging the tips in a vertical position.

Work your tackle hard, but treat it with care and respect, and you will derive great satisfaction from its use on hard-fighting game fish.

THE FACT THAT THE IGFA DOES NOT recognize catches made with wire fishing line does not prevent a great many anglers from utilizing this material for deep trolling and for certain types of very deep bait fishing. In fact, if you were to poll a representative group of East Coast striped bass experts (and some West Coasters, too), asking them what single item of tackle has done most for their specialty, the majority would probably name wire line.

To anglers with only a casual acquaintance with wire line, the stuff does not appear to offer great inducements. "Why not just use trolling sinkers to get the lines down?" is the question frequently asked.

The answer is that trolling sinkers just don't catch many types of fish the way wire line catches them. There is something about the way a trolling sinker sits like a lump on the end of a line that interferes with proper lure action. Furthermore, to achieve the same depth with trolling sinkers that you can achieve with wire alone, you have to put so much lead on the line that holding the rod becomes a tiring chore.

But the most important point to remember about wire line is that it is actually part of a fishing system that is quite different from other methods of deep trolling. Understand the system and you will have wire line in proper focus.

A lead trolling sinker achieves depth by weight. So does wire line. But opposed to the weight of the sinker is water friction

23 / How to Rig and Use Wire Line

and the angle of attack of the line. Wire line does not concentrate the weight all at one spot, but distributes it evenly along the entire length of the line. The water friction of wire is so low as to be almost nonexistent. Every inch of wire contributes to depth. There is hardly any drag at all on the rod from water friction on the line and the considerable drag of a sinker is absent.

Using 50-lb. test monofilament line at the standard speed of three knots, a six-ounce trolling sinker is needed to take a one-ounce lure down 12 feet with 100 feet of mono out. This amounts to a length-depth ration of about 8-to-1. At the same trolling speed 100 feet of .024-inch solid Monel wire, testing about 47 lbs. breaking strain, will take a one-ounce lure down 12 feet, achieving the same 8-to-1 ratio.

One hundred feet of .024-inch solid Monel wire weighs three ounces, so for the same length of fishing line and boat speed the wire line required to take a one-ounce lure down 12 feet weighs half as much as a trolling sinker big enough to take 100 feet of mono and the same lure to the same depth. The parasitic water drag of the wire line is less than one-quarter that of the mono rig with a trolling sinker.

Knowing that under average conditions wire line achieves an 8-to-1 length-depth ratio, it is easy to determine how much wire should be put on a reel for any given depth of water and fishing situation. The following table gives several commonly met examples.

Water Depth (feet)	Best Lure Depth (feet)	Wire Length (feet)
10	8	64
20	17	136
30	26	208
40	35	280
50	44	352

Some anglers fill the entire reel spool with wire. This is wasteful of wire and leads to other complications as will soon be pointed out. My preference in wire line tackle is for a relatively wide-spooled reel with star drag in the 3/0 size. The Penn Senator 3/0 is perfect. The Penn Long Beach #67 is a good substitute. I fill the reel spool about two-thirds full of quality Dacron 50-lb. class line for backing and splice a carefully measured shot of wire, usually 300 feet, on top of the backing.

The reasons for using soft line backing under the wire are these: 1) wire line becomes fatigued and brittle after considerable use and must be replaced. With backing line under the wire, only the actual working part of the wire has to be cut away and discarded; 2) with only as much wire on the reel as is actually needed, salt water corrosion of unused wire is eliminated. Dacron or mono backing lasts indefinitely when treated with normal care.

My tackle locker contains three identical wire line trolling outfits. The rods are fiberglass, with soft action matched to 50-lb. class line. Many anglers prefer roller guides, although I find Carboloy ring guides and a good roller tip-top to be adequate. When I rig wire on these outfits I am very careful to spool exactly the same length of backing on each reel, for a rather special reason. From time to time one breaks a wire while fishing and it is a great advantage to be able to splice on an accurately measured replacement shot of wire without having to go through the line-measuring procedure that is observed on shore.

From experience, I know that with exactly the same amount of backing line on each reel, it takes about 75 turns of the reel handle to spool on the first 100 feet of wire, 72 turns for the second 100 feet, and 68 turns for the final 100 feet. Thus, if a wire is broken, it's simple to trim the line back to the nearest 100 foot mark and add exactly enough to make the line the equal in length of the others.

In rigging wire ashore, here is the procedure to follow.

Select an open area with little pedestrian traffic and measure off a distance equal to the length of wire that you wish to add to the backing, for example, 300 feet. Drive a stout stake into the ground at the 300 foot mark and place a stone or other simple marker at the 200 and 100 foot marks.

Now attach a stainless steel snap swivel to the end of the wire on the storage spool and hook this over a nail head on the wooden stake. Unspool the proper length of wire by walking away from the stake, the storage spool revolving on a pencil or screwdriver shaft so the wire will lay out flat with no tendency to roll or kink. When the proper length has been laid out on the ground, cut it at the 300 foot mark (or whatever other distance has been selected) and splice the wire end to the backing line on your reel.

The splice is easy. Tie a short loop in the end of the backing line. Then, using about a six-inch tag end of the wire, tie the wire to the loop using a becket bend. Draw the becket bend smooth and tight with parallel-jaw pliers. Marry the tag end to the standing part of wire by twisting both parts together equally ("haywire" twist) for about ten half-twists. Finish by taking four or five close finishing turns of the tag end around the standing part. Clip the tag end as close to the main wire as possible and bend the clipped end down flush to eliminate a thumb-slicing burr. This splice will hold at least 90 per cent of the wire's rated breaking strain.

Next, mark your wires at the 100 and 200 foot spots or at other convenient locations if you are putting on less than 300 feet of wire. You can do this by cutting very thin strips of waterproof masking tape and spiral-wrapping the strips around the wire line at the proper spot. Another way to mark the wire is to cut a foot-long piece of wire line and marry it to the main wire at the proper spot in the manner of making a twisted-pair splice, but without cutting the main wire.

Distance marks on the wire are important for determining how much wire you have out at any given time. With two or three such identical wire line trolling outfits, you are now ready to fish the system mentioned earlier. The system is spoiled if you try to combine non-wire trolling gear with your wire lines. The lines won't lie parallel in the water when the boat turns. Tangles and bottom hang-ups will give you lots of trouble. When you fish wire, fish only wire.

Many anglers have trouble putting out wire line. Success comes with practice and it helps to know the correct procedure. First, remember never to put the reel on free spool without engaging the reel's "click" and placing a thumb on the spool so it can't backride when the drag is disengaged and cause loose loops to pile up under the reel bars.

Get the lure overboard, make sure the "click" is engaged, then back off the star drag to a low degree of line tension. *Don't put the reel on free spool.* Instead, thumb the spool lightly and with your free hand strip out wire line from the spool against light thumb and drag tension. When you have 100 feet of wire out the water drag of the lure and the wire should be enough to haul the rest of the wire out without hand stripping.

After enough wire has been paid out for the depth of water, readjust the drag to a moderate value and leave the "click" engaged. You can place the rod in a rod holder, but it is better to keep it in hand, especially if you are using a lure that requires jigging action to work properly.

When fishing two or more wires, make sure that each line is out to exactly the same length. This accomplishes two things. It enables the lines to remain parallel when the boat turns, preventing tangles. It also takes advantage of the "school effect" of two or more lures going through the water in relatively close proximity. This is how you get simultaneous multiple hook-ups.

Variable depth control is quite important and there are a number of ways in which this can be obtained. Length of wire line is one. Raising or lowering trolling speed is another. Raising the speed from three to four or five knots will raise the lures by about one-quarter or one-third, respectively, of the depth held at three knots.

Thus, if you are trolling in 20 feet of water with 135 feet of wire out at three knots, holding a lure level of about 17 feet, and suddenly spot a 15-foot bar or shelf taking shape under the boat (using your depth sounder), you can raise the lures to a safe 12-foot level by boosting the speed up to five knots.

Changing to heavier lures will increase the trolling depth by a factor of about 10 feet per ounce of lure head weight, provided boat speed and line length remain

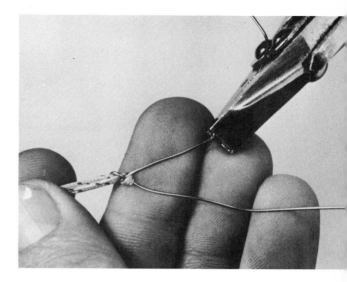

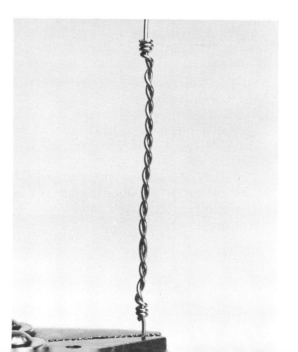

153

the same. Slowing the boat to two knots or less will materially increase lure depth. You must remember that every type of lure has a most-effective trolling speed. Some get hits best at very low speeds. Others work best at speeds as high as five or six knots. The speed requirements of the lures you are using will often determine how much line you must put out to achieve depth.

This leads to another important consideration. *Don't mix lures that work best at widely different speeds.* Troll a selection of lures that works best at the same speed. This will give you a truer indication of the lure preference of the fish. Remember that it's your job to please the fish and not their duty to please you.

One bugaboo of fishing with wire line is how to deal with the kinks that inevitably will be formed in the wire from careless handling. The best method, of course, is to prevent kinks from forming by always maintaining at least a light strain on the wire, and by level-winding the wire evenly onto the spool when it is brought in.

If a kink starts to form, but is still open and not drawn up tight, you can usually unbend the kink by working at it against the way it was made. But if the kink has been drawn tight and the wire distorted, the only recourse is to cut the kink out and splice the wire at that spot—or rerig the wire. Splicing is done this way:

1) Overlap the cut ends of wire by about ten inches and grasp the middle of the overlap firmly with the pliers.

2) Marry one tag end and the main part of the wire for at least twenty half-turns. making the twists smooth and equal.

3) Shift the pliers to the married section and marry the other tag end and its standing part for the same number of half-turns.

4) Finish the splice by taking a few close finishing turns with each tag end,

clipping off the excess and rolling the clipped end down flat with the pliers to prevent forming a burr.

The resultant splice is flexible, will render through rod guides, takes up little space on the reel, and will withstand at least 80 per cent of the line's rated breaking strain.

Another trouble peculiar to wire line is metal fatigue. Soft drawn solid Monel is much more resistant to fatigue than solid copper wire, but even so will turn hard and brittle after prolonged use, especially if constant line jigging is employed as part of the fishing technique. You can tell when Monel or copper wire is getting dangerously brittle by the relative stiffness the fatigued wire has in comparison with fresh, unused wire.

When wire line becomes brittle this way, the best course of action is to remove the wire and replace it with fresh before it starts to break unexpectedly in use. Fatigued wire seldom breaks under heavy stress, although *kinked* wire is seldom more than 60 per cent as strong as fresh wire. Fatigued wire most often breaks under little or no actual strain, whereas kinked wire breaks under heavy strain.

Wire line is used effectively on stripers, bluefish, mackerel, pollock, salmon, kingfish, wahoo, groupers, and in fact just about all species of small to medium game fish that can be taken by sub-surface trolling. Some fishermen use it with heavy sinkers and electric reels for catching red snappers and groupers in waters 600 feet deep.

Braided wire is used to some extent, as is nylon-covered lead-core wire. The latter is widely used in the Great Lakes and some inland waters for salmon and lake trout. On salt water, soft-drawn solid Monel in test ratings of from about 20 lbs. to as much as 80 lbs. is the most popular wire. For most salt water work on small to medium sized fish, wire diameters of .018 inch to .027 inch (approxi-

Ted Sigler, mate of the Montauk charter boat Margaret IV, *demonstrates the pro's way of putting out a wire. Reel's click is engaged, drag is set at low tension. Line is hauled down hand-over-hand at constant velocity.*

mately 26 to 55-lb. test) are the most commonly used.

Using wire imposes certain disciplines upon fishermen. Speeds must be held to exact values for the wire to work. Turns must be made evenly and with wide radius, lest the lures foul the bottom. Depth sounders must be used constantly. Trolling runs over productive areas must be planned in advance, especially when there are other boats about, also trolling deep with wire.

But wire line deep trolling has opened many new areas to productive fishing and has vastly increased the ability of anglers to produce consistent catches under less than ideal conditions. Despite its "illegitimate" status with the IGFA, wire continues to be used because it catches fish, which is what really counts with a great many fishermen.

FISHING LEADERS, OR TRACES AS THE British call them, have a long and honorable history. Izaak Walton advised, "Let your rod be light and very gentle . . . the line, for three or four links toward the hook, should not exceed three or four haires; but if you can Angle with one haire, you will have more rises and catch more fish."

For trout fishing in the very old days, the horse hair leader was the thing. Individual hairs were knotted together to form longer strands. Two strands were twisted, three or four were braided to make leaders that were both durable and cheap. The supply of raw material was inexhaustable.

It did not take fishermen long to discover the superiority of "catgut." This material did not always come from cats. Sheep, lamb, or calf gut worked just as well. The stuff was as intractible as rawhide when dry, but when wet it became wonderfully soft and pliable, permitting a fair degree of control over the cumbersome artificial flies that fishermen were then learning to use. Gut leaders of heavy caliber also became quite popular for salt water fishing. Their durability and resistance to sharp teeth was second only to wire.

The invention of stringed musical instruments like the piano and harpsichord created a demand for quality steel wire. Until fairly recently, tinned carbon steel piano wire was the strongest, most durable material available for leaders for the heaviest types of big game fishing. Its

great fault was the way it rusted, especially in salt water.

Two new materials came to the fore to overcome this defect, stainless steel wire and nylon monofilament. Let us look first at the comparable specifications of piano wire versus stainless steel. The following table gives the diameter and breaking strain for piano wire and stainless steel in the sizes most commonly used for fishing.

Wire Size	Diameter (inches)	Piano Wire (pounds)	Stainless Steel (pounds)
#2	.011	28	27
#3	.012	34	32
#4	.013	39	37
#5	.014	46	44
#6	.016	60	56
#7	.018	76	69
#8	.020	93	86
#9	.022	114	104
#10	.024	136	128
#11	.026	156	148
#12	.028	184	176
#13	.030	212	202
#14	.032	240	232
#15	.034	282	272

A quick glance at the top and bottom lines of the table will show a 1–10 ratio of strength between #2 wire and #15, the lightest and heaviest ordinarily used for fishing leaders. A great deal of fishing can be encompassed between these extremes. For the sake of easy comparison, the 14 sizes of wire mentioned can be divided into five major categories, ranging

24 / Taking the Mystery Out of Leaders

from ultra-light to heavy in use class.

Ultra-light. Wire sizes #2 to #4. These are used primarily to make short, durable end-sections to protect very light fly casting and similar leaders from being cut by sharp teeth or fish scales. One example is the four to six-inch section of #2 or #3 wire made fast to the hook of a streamer fly for use with salt water fly casting tackle.

Another use is the two-foot wire section of #4 wire attached to the hook of a balao or similar bait for 12 or 20-lb. tackle class when tournament fishing for sailfish. Here, the rest of the leader is 40 to 60-lb. test monofilament for a total leader length of 12 to 15 feet.

Light. Wire sizes #5 to #7. Used either full length or in combination with monofilament leaders, usually employed with 30-lb. class tackle. Popular applications are for sailfish, white marlin, big bluefish and striped bass, small tuna, bonito and albacore, Pacific yellowtails, salmon, muskies, northern pike, lake trout, tropical snappers, groupers, and other game fish of this general weight class.

Medium. Wire sizes #8 to #10. Usually used full length for large white and small blue marlin, striped and black marlin to about the 300-lb. limit, small swordfish,

The leader is the vital link connecting the bait or lure and the fishing line. Best salt water materials are nylon monofilament or stainless wire such as has been used to rig mullet for sailfish, marlin, or large tuna.

small to medium game sharks, alligator gars, or any fish that normally call for 50-lb. class tackle.

Light-heavy. Wire sizes #11 to #13. Normally used full length (up to 30 feet) for fish worthy of 80-lb. class tackle such as swordfish, most marlin, large sharks, and tuna to 500 lbs.

Heavy. Wire sizes #14 and #15. Heavier than these, solid wire leaders become so stiff as to defeat their own purpose. These powerful wires are used to make leaders up to 30 feet long for use with 130-lb. class tackle for all record billfish and giant bluefin tuna.

Until quite recently, where flexibility in a very heavy leader was required, stranded or cable-laid wire was preferred. Seven-strand wire has six wires twisted around a seventh that acts as the core. A 6 x 19 cable has six strands of 19 wires each, the strands being twisted around a soft fiber core. A 6 x 37 cable has six strands, each containing 37 wires, laid up the same way. The more wires in a cable of the same diameter, the more flexible the cable is.

Cable leaders can be made up by the rather difficult method of forming the eyes with a Liverpool or gun-factory cable splice. It is a lot easier to make up the eyes with modern crimping sleeves and a crimping tool. The resultant eyes test at least 85 per cent of the strength of the original wire.

Solid wire leaders are seldom made up with crimping sleeves, although heavy-caliber monofilament leaders are frequently made up with sleeves. The common haywire twist is used to make eyes or loops of any desired length in solid wire. Here is a point-by-point description of how the haywire twist is made.

1) You'll need parallel jaw pliers, leader wire, and the snap swivel, hook, split ring, or lure to which the wire is to be made fast.

2) Pass the end of the wire through the eye of the object (or bend it back on itself for about six inches if you are making an open eye). Make sure the working end is at least six inches long.

3) Bend the wire back on itself through the eye of the hook, swivel, or other object. Take hold of the bend with the tips of the jaws of your pliers. Don't try to hold both the wire and the hook eye at the same time. Let the hook eye or ring lie very close to the pliers jaws.

4) "Marry" the wire by twisting *both parts* evenly around each other, not the working end around the main part. Make at least ten or twelve half-twists, laying the turns tightly and evenly together. The resultant "married" part should be at least an inch long.

5) Shift the grip of the pliers to the married part and make four or five close finishing turns of the working end around the main part of the wire.

6) The working end should be at right angles to the main part of the wire. Bend a right angle into the working end, making the bend about one-half inch from the main part with the tip of the bent end now pointing toward the eye end of the main wire and lying parallel with it.

7) Using this angle as a handle or lever, *twist* the working end with a rotating motion of the wrist. It should break off cleanly at the last finishing turn of the eye.

A kink in a wire leader will weaken the leader seriously, and leaders showing evidence of having been kinked or drawn over a hard edge, such as the keel of a boat, should be discarded. International Game Fish Association tackle rules permit leaders up to 30 feet long for lines of 80 and 130-lb. test, and leaders up to 15 feet long for lines of 50-lb. test and under. These rules apply to wire and monofilament leaders, or leaders made up of combinations of materials.

Nylon monofilament is made in so many grades and sizes that trying to give

In attaching wire leaders to spoons, hooks, and swivels, first marry the wire before making the finish turns. Heavy monofilament (below) is often fastened to hook with crimp sleeves.

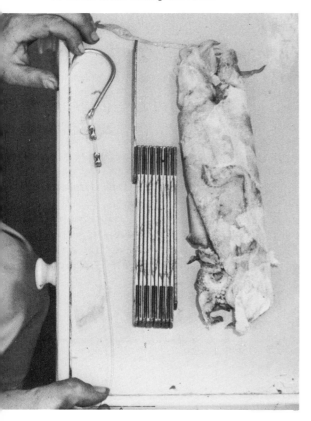

a comparative table of sizes, diameters, and breaking strains would be meaningless. But manufacturers label monofilament quite accurately with the breaking strain of their products. As a rule of thumb it is good to remember that effective leaders average about two and one-half times the breaking strain of the lines with which they are used. The following table gives comparative figures for IGFA line classes and the mono or stainless leaders commonly used with them.

IGFA Line Class (pounds)	Mono Test (pounds)	Stainless Wire
12	30	#3
20	50	#6
30	80	#8
50	120	#10
80	200	#12
130	300	#15

Remember that these are *average* suggestions. Many fishermen prefer to work with leaders quite a bit lighter than the figures given here. Others dispense with leaders entirely for special types of fishing, making the hook fast directly to the line. This works best with monofilament line. But for general fishing the values given in this table will prove adequate if the leaders are made up properly. Following are brief descriptions of several easily made monofilament knots.

Surgeon's Knot. This knot is very simple and results in a loop of any desired size that will test at least 80 per cent of the original strength of the line. Everyone knows how to tie a simple overhand loop in the end of a line. In making the Surgeon's Knot, make *two* twists of the loop around the main part of the line instead of one. Pull the ends together evenly.

Improved End Loop. Stronger but bulkier than the Surgeon's Knot. Make a loop of the proper length, then put your forefinger into the loop at the point where you want the knot to form. Wind the two

The Improved Clinch Knot is used with mono on hooks.

parts of the loop end back around *both parts* of the rest of the line (main part and working end) for five full turns. Pass loop end back through the small loop of two parts held open by your forefinger, pull tight evenly.

Clinch Knot. This is the knot commonly used to make mono fast to any metal hook eye, ring, or connector. Pass several inches of the mono through the eye or ring, then twist the working end around the main part of the line for five or six turns. Pass the tip of the working end of the mono through the open space between the hook eye or ring and the start of the first turn. Pull tight. Clip off the working end to a final length of about one-eighth inch, then singe this short end with a match flame.

Albright Special. This is a special knot used to tie a mono leader directly to a braided Dacron or similar line, thereby eliminating the usual snap swivel or connector. It's a bit tricky, so practice with waste material before you start work on good line and leaders.

1) Double the end of the mono leader back on itself for about ten inches and hold the doubled part in your left hand, the doubled end pointing toward your right hand, thumb and forefinger grasping the doubled mono about mid-point of its length. Lay the Dacron line parallel to the doubled part of mono, going from right to left. Grasp the two parts of mono and the single part of Dacron at the spot indicated with a working end of about ten inches of Dacron extending beyond the grasping point to the left.

2) Continuing to hold the three parts at the point indicated, take the working end of Dacron in your right hand and start winding it around the three parts in the manner of making a whipping, working from left to right back over the two parts of mono and the single part of Dacron. Lay the turns on as smoothly, tightly, and evenly as possible.

3) Take at least 40 and preferably 50 such turns, working toward the loop end of the mono. When the required number of turns has been completed, carefully slide all the turns down the loop toward the right until only the tip of the bend of the mono loop is visible. Pass the end of the Dacron line through this loop to

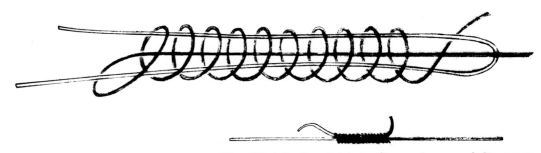

The Albright Special joins lines of unequal diameter.

lock it in place. Locked, it won't slip.

4) Pull the knot as tight as possible, holding *both parts* of the mono with the left hand and pulling on the *main part* of the Dacron with the right. The knot will render down to a very tight, close-fitting whipping of Dacron around the loop end of mono leader.

5) Clip off the tag ends of mono and Dacron, then give the knot one final strong pull on the remaining main parts to make sure the knot will hold and to bury the tag ends.

The Albright Special as described here closely resembles the Bimini Twist, a knot used to make the double line in the end of a fishing line where this line cannot be spliced. The Bimini Twist is described elsewhere in Chapter 25. The Albright Special will hold 100 per cent of the strength of the weaker of the two pieces of material, provided the proper number of wrapping turns have been taken.

Which material, wire or mono, makes the better leader? This question generates argument wherever fishermen get together. As a rule, mono leaders are preferred for their flexibility and apparent lack of visibility in water. Wire is used where there is danger from sharp teeth, fins, or scales.

Where baits have to be changed frequently, as in sailfishing, it pays to make up a number of baits on short wire leaders of the proper wire size, making a small open eye in the upper end of each such bait leader. The main part of the leader is a section of mono of appropriate strength rating. The lower end of the mono has a snap swivel to clip into the wire bait leader and the upper end has a small open loop into which the snap swivel on the end of the fishing line is clipped. This permits quick bait changing without having to fool around with long coiled leaders.

In some instances it is advantageous to connect the line directly to the mono leader, eliminating the line-leader clip. In this case the Albright Special, just described, is the knot to use, if the line is Dacron. If the fishing line is also mono, the proper knot is the old, reliable Blood Knot, described in the accompanying photo.

There's really little mystery to selecting and making up the right leader for any specific fishing situation, once you know the basic facts of leader theory and construction. In all cases let good judgement be your guide, and don't overlook the advice of local experts.

The Blood Knot joins mono lines that have the same or different diameters and is used to make up tapered leaders used with fly casting equipment.

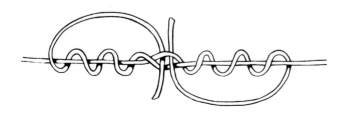

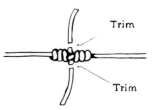

THE BIMINI TWIST IS NOT A WILD
Bahamian dance, although those who try
to do this twist sometimes look as if they
were doing a slow-motion Limbo. It is a
knot developed to make a non-slip, non-
cutting, flexible union of the double line
that terminates most fishing lines. It is
especially useful for making double lines
in Dacron and monofilament that cannot
be spliced.

1) With someone to help you, carefully
measure the double line to be made, allowing up to 30 feet of double line for lines
of 80 and 130-lb. test, or 15 feet of double
line for lines of 50-lb. test and under.
Plan to make the double line a few inches
shorter than the legal maximum.

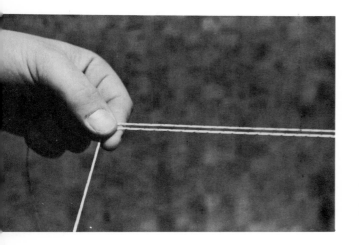

2) Having selected the spot where the
double line knot is to go, have your assis-
tant grasp both parts of the double line
at this spot with the thumb and forefinger
of his right hand, the loop of the line
facing away from him. There should be
at least 16 inches of tag end of line projecting from between his fingers, pointed
to his left where he can grasp it with his
left hand.

3) Now straighten out the loop of
double line and slip the end of the loop
up over your wrist. Maintaining light
tension against your helper's grasp, throw
at least 40 twists into the loop by rotating
your wrist.

25 / Making the Bimini Twist

4) Take the end of the loop and hook it over some solid object such as the top of a handy dock spile. Let your helper maintain his pull against this object while you take a pencil or some other smooth object and place it between the two parts of the twisted loop where the parts come open at the far end of the loop.

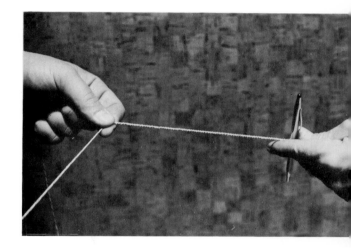

5) Walk toward your helper, pushing the pencil between the two parts of the twisted loop, forcing the twists down the line toward your helper. Eventually you will have forced the twists into a very tight, compact twisted section only a few inches long.

6) Instruct your helper to grasp the tag end of the line with his left hand and exert fairly strong tension on this end. While you continue to force the twists toward him, he now slips the grip of his fingers up onto the single part of the line, away from the twisted section.

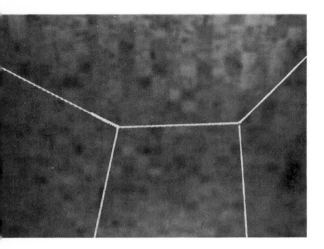

7) At this point the twisted section will start to untwist and the tag end of line will spin onto the twisted section in the manner of a rope whipping. The helper carefully guides the end of the line as it rolls onto the twisted part, working toward the loop end. You continue to apply twist pressure by pushing the pencil forward.

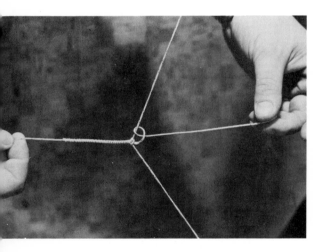

8) About half of the twists will be lost in the whipping process, but the final Bimini Twist will be a couple of inches long, flexible, but very tightly twisted and whipped. Clinch the tag end by taking a couple of half hitches through the open parts of the double line loop. Cut the end short and apply a safety whipping over the half hitches and tag end, using waxed dental floss. The double line should be tied together every two feet with a little dental floss.

The completed Bimini Twist looks a lot like the Albright Special. It is slip and cut proof, flexible, renders easily through rod guides, is not bulky when stored on the reel, and will maintain 100 per cent of the original line strength. It's not easy to tie the first time, so you will be wise to practice with old line before trying it on a good fishing line.

26 / Roosters Crow at Dawn

"GUESS I'D BETTER PUT ON A LIVELIER bait," I said and started to reel in. It was just after sunup. Birds were circling and diving, the boat crew was yelling. A school of roosterfish was boiling off the stern, my fishing partner was hooked up fighting a big one, and I felt left out.

As my bait surfaced alongside I reached out to grab the leader. A roosterfish rocketed up from below, rose clear of the water, missed the bait, and came close to getting my fingers instead. It thudded against the hull as it fell back into the water. Virginia Bonney yelled, "Better keep your hands inside the boat!"

I put on a fresh bait, lowered it over the side and threw the reel on open bail. Out ran the live bait, taking my light line with it. A few seconds later I had a hookup. Line started to peel from the reel. I let the fish go a bit, then engaged the reel bail and struck once strongly with the rod—and nearly got yanked overboard.

That was the beginning of a day of fishing such as many anglers only dream about. Almost every bait produced a strike; most strikes were hookups. The place was Rancho Buena Vista, some three hours' drive south of La Paz, close to the tip of the long Mexican peninsula of Baja California. Virginia Bonney, my fishing partner, was the wife of the Rancho's manager and a highly skilled light tackle anglerette.

The roosterfish circling the boat were all 40 and 50-pounders. We hooked and fought at least twenty that day, cutting loose all but five which we kept for the kitchen at the resort. Roosterfish are superb eating.

Best of all, we got them on light tackle. Virginia is a spinning enthusiast, as am I. She had a Tru-Line C4X-2 rod and Quick spinning reel. I fished a Mitchell 402 on a custom built Conlon rod that Garcia had made to my specifications. Its action is similar to their standard 2551 rod, but it breaks down into four 20-inch sections to fit in a suitcase. Both our reels were loaded with 15-lb. monofilament line.

My favorite roosterfishing ports are on the Baja peninsula: Mulege, Loreto, La Paz, Rancho Buena Vista, and Cabo San Lucas. I've also run into roosters while fishing off the Mexican mainland at Mazatlan and Acapulco. Usually the first schools appear in October, growing in numbers during winter and hitting a peak in January and February. The run begins to slack off by April, although the fish can be encountered to some extent all summer.

The roosterfish is an ugly brute. His thick, heavy body is broad-shouldered and he gets tremendous drive from his powerful tail. Round-headed, snub-nosed, with powerful jaws and a mean disposition, the rooster positively seems to enjoy a good fight. And that includes other fish, seals, people, anything or anybody who gets in his way.

His most distinctive feature is the giant "cockscomb" of a dorsal fin made up of long, stiff, sharp spines that emerge from the back. The quills are like those of a porcupine, but larger, and they don't break clear of the body. As big around at the base as a pencil, they can be folded down into a narrow slot that runs the length of the fish's back. Many billfish can do the same with their dorsal fins. When the roosterfish fights, the quills spring erect.

For fighting qualities, I rate roosters above any other fish. I believe they have at least twice the power of a Pacific albacore of the same size, which may approach 80 lbs. I've seen roosters break lines used on marlin up to 200 lbs. in weight, and roosters never stop fighting.

Many a big one is lost right at the boat when he makes his final rush, catching the tired angler unaware. To anyone getting ready for his first go at roosterfish, I recommend conventional marlin or light tuna tackle in the 50-lb. line class. The first few times you tangle with roosters you'll have a bad time. You can go to progressively lighter tackle as you learn his ways.

Don't be misled by my earlier mention of live bait fishing. At most Mexican ports, excepting Rancho Buena Vista, you'll fish by trolling artificial lures. At the Rancho, owner Gene Walters a while ago decided to give live bait fishing, as practiced in Southern California, a try. The best bait is a plankton-feeding small fish called a grunt, about nine inches long and weighing one-half pound. It looks like a small striped bass or a very fat herring. Long-lived, it has lots of action and stays lively on the hook for quite a while.

Grunts are natural forage for game fish in these waters. Roosterfish find them delicious. You can keep them alive in a standard live bait tank with an electric pump. Lacking such a tank, a plastic GI can will do, provided you change the water frequently with a bucket to provide oxygen and keep the water temperature at the normal sea value.

The way to locate roosterfish is to cruise along the shore watching for active sea birds. The angling is seldom done more than a half mile from shore and frequently takes place right in the breakers. Sea gulls, petrels, pelicans, or man-o'-war birds obviously fishing for bait are a sure sign of roosterfish beneath the bait.

When you find a school of bait being worked over by the birds above and large fish below, approach slowly and without noise. You can't scare the roosters, but a noisy approach may scatter the bait on which the big fish are feeding. The trick is to get up-wind of the feeding fish, kill the engine, and drift the boat close to the school without alarming it.

Every baited line should get a strike as you get into the fish, but by the time you bring your fish to gaff or release them, the school may have moved elsewhere. That's why a fast boat is preferred. Unfortunately, many of the Mexican charter boats are slow, although some of the better resorts are now providing fast open boats of the United States type, equipped with inboard, inboard-outboard, or big outboard motors.

Roosterfish will strike a variety of lures. I've had good results with the chrome and fluorescent-red Hot Shot Wobbler. The smaller Knucklehead models have been quite good. Matadors and Outlaw lures are productive, as are ordinary albacore trolling feather lures tied on a pearlescent head. Best color combinations seem to be pink-and-white, yellow-and-green, and blue-and-white.

The trolling technique bears similarity to the bait fishing system. You run to the vicinity of the working birds, slow down, and try to circle the school with your lines. Trolling speeds are fast, six knots and up. A smart skipper experiments with speed to find exactly the velocity that a particular group of fish may prefer. If the lures skip on the surface, this is fine. Roosters love skipping lures.

No one can set rules of behavior for roosterfish. I've hooked them among

Tall, stiff dorsal spines mark a big roosterfish caught on spinning gear by Virginia Bonney. These fish weigh up to 50 lbs. and taking them on line testing under 20 lbs. is a real test of fishing skill. Scene is off Baja California in the Sea of Cortez. An excellent food fish, the rooster is an inhabitant of shallow water near shore, prowling in schools for food.

Best bait is a Baja grunt. The hook is inserted through the back behind the head, not deep enough to injure the spine. The boat drifts downwind into the area where the roosterfish are feeding, avoiding any commotion.

roving bands of yellowtail and as strays with no other fish around. I've even caught roosters while casting from the shore. This is probably the most thrilling surf fishing you can find on light tackle. Even a 20-lb. rooster will give you more of a fight than a 50 or 60-lb. striped bass on the same tackle.

Perhaps the greatest thing about any kind of angling in Baja California waters is that you don't have to visit a rough fishing camp if you don't want to. Fine resort hotels are available. The towns are charming and the people friendly. You can drive to La Paz and other Baja towns, but the easiest and quickest way is by air. Several California travel agencies handle all arrangements from air reservations to rooms and charter boat bookings.

In recent years, the appearance of large, powerful party and private sport fishing boats in Southern California ports has opened adventurous travel-by-water fishing expeditions to Baja and other Mexican areas. Many of these boats carry Boston Whalers or other small craft on deck for the express purpose of fishing roosterfish and other game species under the best possible light tackle conditions.

Although the best roosterfishing usually is early in the morning when the fish are very active and have not been worked over by anglers, they do feed and move all day. There's only one drawback to roosterfishing, as I see it, and this is a relatively minor one. Roosters may spoil you for other kinds of fish, once you've learned to handle them on light tackle.

The only cure is to plan future trips to Baja for more of the same, for in this case the disease is its own cure.

27 / Rigging the Mullet Bait

THE MULLET BAIT IS A SWIMMING RATHER than a skipping bait. It achieves its distinctive, very natural swimming action a foot or two under the surface at trolling speeds of three to five knots. At faster speeds, the mullet will skip, but erratically.

The swimming mullet is basic to sailfishing, trolling for marlin, swordfish, game sharks, and large bluefin tuna. Important to the success of the bait is removal of the backbone, accomplished by means of a hollow coring tool. You can buy a backbone corer at almost any tackle shop, or you can make your own by taking a foot-long piece of three-eighths-inch aluminum tubing and, with a triangular file, cutting a set of sharp teeth into the edge of one end. The other end can be wrapped with friction tape or fitted with a rubber or plastic handle.

Mullet keep best frozen whole and are thawed out before rigging. After rigging, they can be kept on chopped ice or can be re-frozen provided they are used within a week or so of the time of the second freezing. They are fairly durable baits, but you'll use up a number each day due to attacks by barracuda, sharks, big jacks, and the like. They can be trolled from outriggers or flat-lines.

Tools needed include pliers, knife, coring tool, darning needle, twine, hooks, egg sinkers, leader material. Hooks should be good sized, from 7/0 to 10/0 depending on bait size.

1. After thawing the mullet, make a triangular cut in top of bait's head, then remove the backbone by using the hollow coring tool as illustrated.

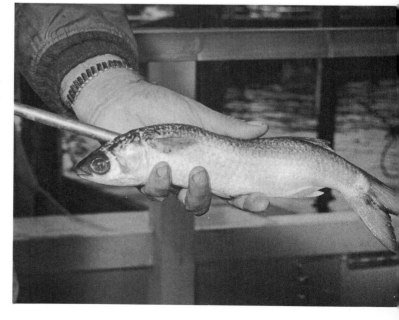

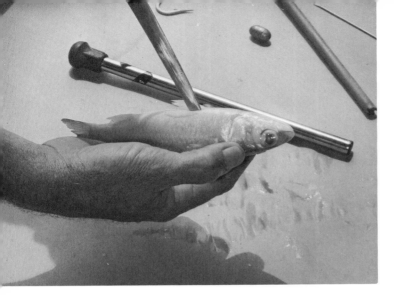

2. Make a fore-and-aft slit in bait's belly at the proper location to place the eye of the hook at a position exactly between the eyes of the bait.

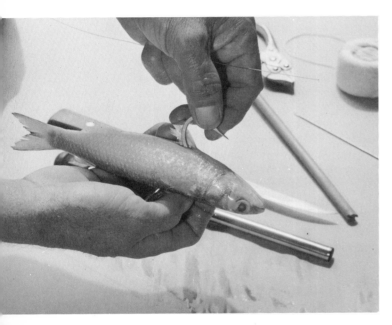

3. Gently squeeze the bait's intestines out of the stomach via the slit, then thrust shaft of hook into body so hook eye comes to the proper spot.

4. Cut 15 foot leader from #7 to #10 wire, make a small loop in one end, coil leader leaving two foot working end. Select suitable egg sinker.

5. Sinker can weigh ½ to several ounces. Two to three ounces is average. Slip sinker onto end of leader wire and locate wire end under head.

6. Push end of the wire up through bait's head and through the eye of the hook inside the mullet's head. Hook is secured in position by the wire.

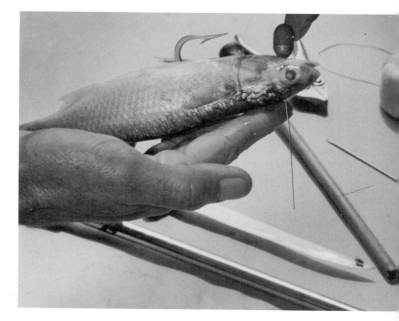

7. Bend end of wire forward to meet main part of leader, positioning sinker under bait's chin as illustrated. Marry wires with haywire twist.

171

8. *After finishing leader twists, sew gills closed with needle and twine. Also send twine through head to anchor sinker under head so it can't slip.*

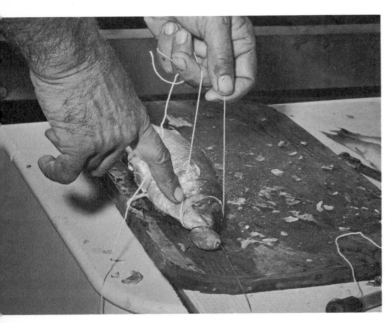

9. *Take two turns of twine around head, mouth and gills before tying off twine ends. This is to keep head from pulling apart while being towed.*

10. *Variation of the mullet bait has sinker placed over rather than under the nose, causing it to dive more deeply, sometimes used on wire line.*

28 / Rigging the Balao Bait

ALTHOUGH SOME PACIFIC SPECIES OF balao reach a length of two feet, most balao are under a foot long. Swimming in fast-moving, close-packed schools near the sea surface, these agile little fish form a very important part of the food of sailfish, marlin, dolphin, wahoo, tuna, bonito, and other oceanic game fish. White marlin and sails, especially, dote on balao, as do dolphin.

Most anglers buy balao from bait dealers, and it pays to inspect the baits for freshness. Make sure the balao's eye is clear, not milky or muddy-looking. Reject any balao that do not have distinct dark bluish or greenish color on the back, or show signs of freezer burn or dehydration, which usually affects the fins and tail first.

Balao keep well frozen, but should be protected from dehydration by wrapping in plastic or metal foil. They also keep for several days on plain ice. The modern way to rig balao is to use a light (#4 or #5) wire leader about two feet long, the outer end of which terminates in an eye. Wire as heavy as #8 or #9 can be used with big balao if small blue marlin are around.

The rest of the leader is monofilament, at the end of which is a stainless steel snap swivel. The mono should be 40 to 60-lb. test for sailfish, 80 for white marlin, and correspondingly heavier for bigger fish. Balao troll equally well from outriggers and flat-lines and are sometimes fished deep with wire line or underwater outriggers (described in Chapter 34).

Equipment needed for rigging the balao bait includes O'Shaughnessy hooks in 6/0 to 8/0 size, leader wire, thin soft copper binding wire, pliers. For tournament fishing with lines of 12 or 20-lb. test, the hooks may be as small as 4/0. The "Masters," fished out of Palm Beach each winter, stipulates barbless hooks so sailfish may be released unharmed.

1. Wire hook to leader leaving a tag end ½″ long. Tag end is used to anchor bill-wrapping wire.

2. *Position hook and leader alongside balao with wire tag end pointing up just forward of eye.*

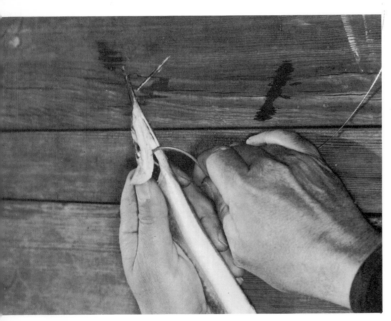

3. *Point of hook is started into bait's body via gill cover opening, is pushed into body cavity.*

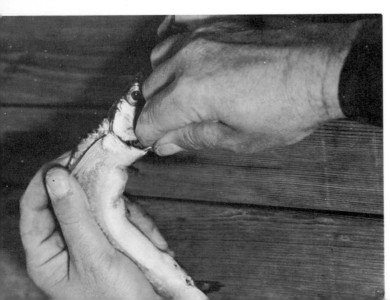

4. *Body of bait is bent around bend of hook, point is aimed to emerge at position shown in Fig. 2.*

5. *Exit hole of hook is enlarged with knife point so hook can move freely inside body of the bait.*

6. *Tag end of leader is pushed up through lower and upper jaws, skewering them together from below.*

7. *Break off "bill" of bait (lower jaw) about one inch beyond point of upper jaw, as shown here.*

8. *Lay leader splice along centerline of lower jaw and at the same time position the hook properly.*

9. *With tag end of leader skewering the jaws, bind jaws together with copper wire in a smooth wrap.*

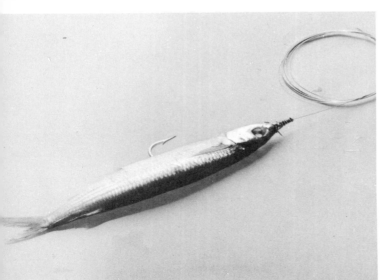

10. *Finished balao bait is lifelike, with wire of leader projecting smoothly from tapering jaws.*

29 / Rigging the Trolling Squid

SQUIDS ARE AMONG THE MOST WIDESPREAD and available of all forage fish in the oceans of the world. Giant squids up to 40 and 50 feet long exist in some seas and are food for sperm whales, great sharks, and other large predators. The squids of our interest here are smaller, 8 to 24 inches in length. They are usually obtained from commercial fishing sources, although it is sometimes possible for anglers to jig their own squid at night in summer, beside oceanside harbor docks with clean water.

The squid is not a very durable bait, either in terms of how long it can be towed and retain fish appeal, or how long it can be kept on ice. Fresh-frozen squids can be kept for weeks provided they are not thawed, then re-frozen. The best trolling baits are made from fresh, whole squids that have been refrigerated, but not frozen.

Squids as small as 7 or 8 inches long are sometimes used for white marlin and sailfish. Squids as long as two feet have been used successfully for large swordfish, big blue marlin, and sharks. The best general purpose squids for outrigger trolling are from 12 to 16 inches long, including length of head, but not counting length of the arms.

Hooks should be fairly large, 8/o to as much as 13/o, depending on size of bait. Leader can be wire, monofilament, or cable. You'll need a knife, long darning needle, twine, and the usual pliers to make squid baits in either of the two methods shown in the following photos.

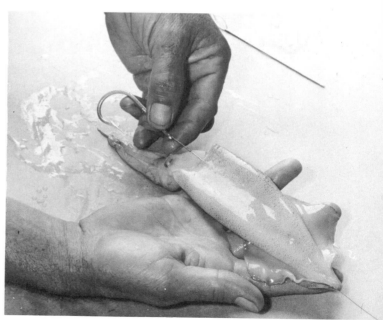

Hook-in-head squid bait
1. Hook-in-head bait starts by inserting the wire of short leader through envelope of squid imbedding hook in the squid's head while wire of leader projects out through bait's pointed tail.

2. *Using a heavy needle and store twine, sew the body of the squid securely around the leader in the manner indicated, using half-hitches clear through the body of the bait to make it flat.*

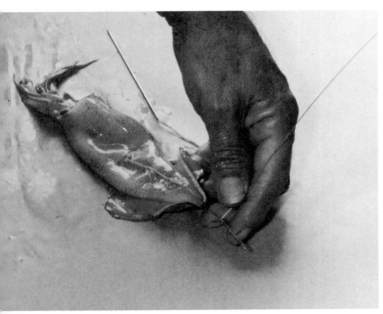

3. *Employing the haywire twist, make an eye in the end of the leader wire so that the twists will come exactly at the bait's tail point when the bait is laid out in a naturally flat position.*

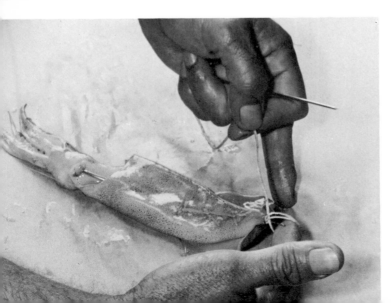

4. *Half-hitch the sewing twine onto the twisted eye of the leader to hold bait in position and keep it from slipping down the leader when it is being towed from an outrigger in rough sea.*

5. Tie squid head to body in natural position with a loop of the sewing twine. This will prevent head from tearing loose from body in trolling. Natural trolling position of bait is tail first.

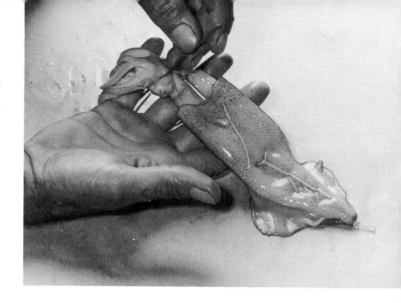

6. Attach monofilament, wire, or cable leader to the wire leader eye with stainless steel snap swivel. Wire should test at least 180 lbs. and mono should be of at least 200-lb. test class.

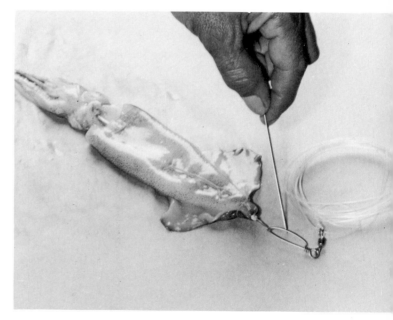

Hook-in-body squid bait

7. The hook-in-body bait is started by inserting end of leader through the squid belly at point indicated, then out through the bait's pointed tail, as was done in the hook-in-head bait rig.

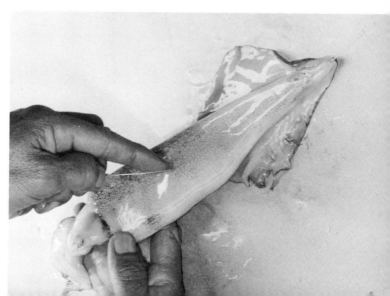

8. *Hook is worked in through slit in belly, allowing shank of hook to be buried, but point and bend of hook to remain outside. Slot is made larger with knife point to allow hook to move.*

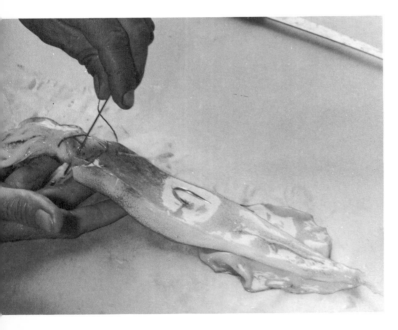

9. *Leader is sewed firmly in place with stitches as in first squid rig. Head is sewed secure with loop of twine. Eye is made in leader end as before, keeping hook properly positioned.*

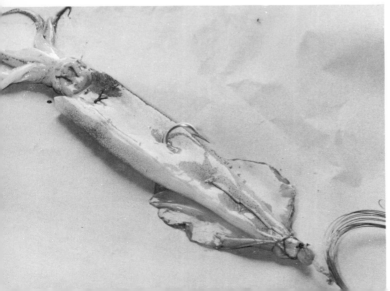

10. *Twine is secured to leader eye twist with half-hitches as before and tip of tail is wrapped with twine to make a smoothly pointed taper as profile of bait blends into thin leader wire.*

30 / Rigging the Strip Bait

THE STRIP BAIT IS ONE OF THE SIMPLEST, yet oldest and most effective of all off-shore baits. Albacore, dolphin, tuna, sailfish, marlin, swordfish, and sharks all go for strip baits, as do kingfish, barracuda, amberjacks, and a host of other game fish.

Strip baits can be made from a wide variety of basic materials. Belly strips from tuna, bonito, and dolphin are very good. So are thin strips of prepared pork rind. A large natural squid will provide several top grade strips. No tools other than a knife, pliers, twine, hook and leader material are needed. Strips are usually made up on the spot for each day's requirements, although some anglers keep a supply of pork rind or salted squid

handy for when other baits run out.

Pork rind and squid require little work other than careful shaping. Strips from fleshy fish must be dressed with a sharp filet knife to remove most of the meat. Don't use heavy hooks with strip baits. Eagle Claw or O'Shaughnessy models of from 4/0 to 6/0 are good for sails and similar sized fish, and 8/0 hooks will suffice for larger game. Strips are most effective on tackle of 50-lb. line class and under.

Strips work equally well from outriggers or flat-lines. On getting a strike, try to set the hook after only a minimum drop-back. Many fish hook themselves. Well-made strips will troll all day without losing their fish appeal.

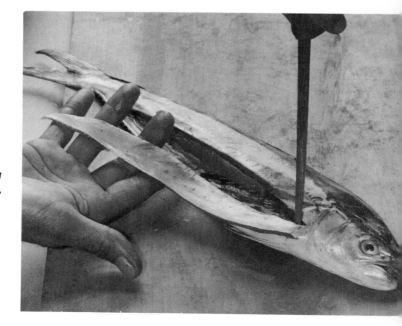

1. Using sharp knife, slice long strip from side of fish's belly, then trim meat close to skin.

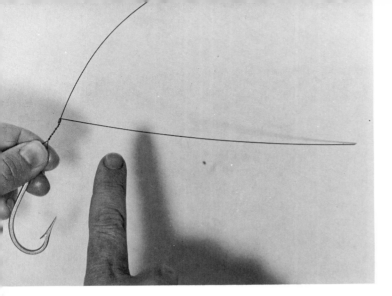

2. *Bend hook to end of leader wire in usual way. Make end four inches long to form safety snap.*

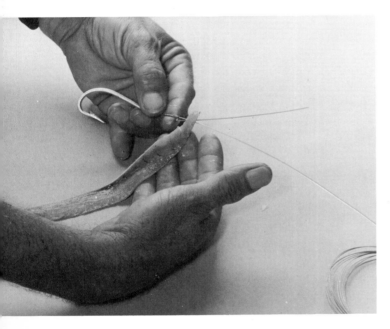

3. *Lay hook and leader beside strip to locate hook hole. Point of strip should equal leader twist.*

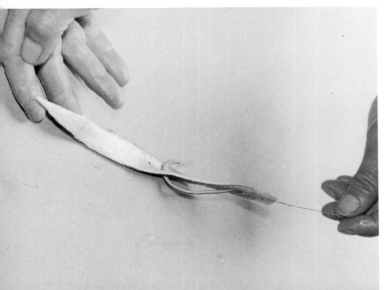

4. *Push barb through at proper spot. Impale end of strip on safety snap, bind end to leader.*

5. Sew leader snugly to forward end of strip, wrapping twine around strip nose to streamline it.

6. Adjust length of hook slot so hook is free to "work" in hole, letting strip flutter in use.

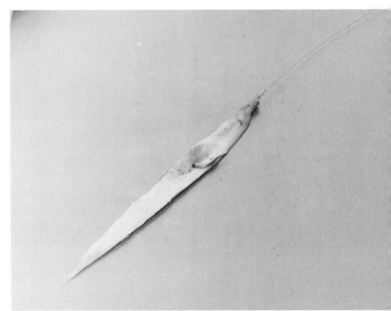

It may not be the prettiest bait in the world, but the black eel rigged for offshore surface trolling is a real killer for white marlin, big dolphin, large school tuna, small to medium swordfish, mako sharks, and many other game fish. The primary advantages of the eel are good supply, durability when trolled, ease of rigging, and longevity when stored on ice or salt brine.

The best surface trolling eels are medium sized, from 12 to 16 inches long, and thin. Don't attempt to rig fat eels. They don't troll well and are heavy. Live eels can be killed easily by placing them in a bucket and covering them with coarse Kosher salt. Rubbing with the salt will then remove the objectionable skin slime, after which they can be rigged or stored frozen for future use.

Eels keep for a week or ten days when placed in a Saran food bag along with a sprinkling of salt, and then packed in shaved ice. They will keep indefinitely without freezing if placed in a glass jar containing a saturated salt solution to which a little benzoate of soda has been added.

You'll need leader material of stainless wire in sizes #7 to #10 (for sails and "whites" and fish up to swordfish), ringed-eye O'Shaughnessy hooks in sizes 6/0 to 8/0, small brass swivels, eel-rigging needle, Nylon or Teflon-covered leader material, crimp sleeves and crimping pliers, darning needle, and heavy black mending thread.

31 / Rigging the Trolling Eel

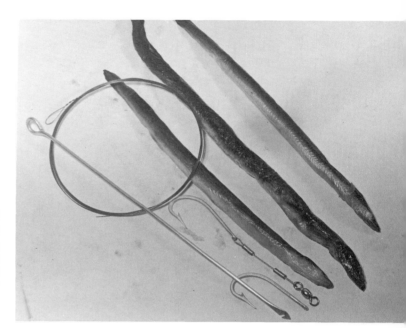

1. *The rigging needle is made from a piece of brass welding rod. End is hammered flat, then dressed to a point with file, sharpened, and slot is cut in pointed head to receive leader swivel or loop.*

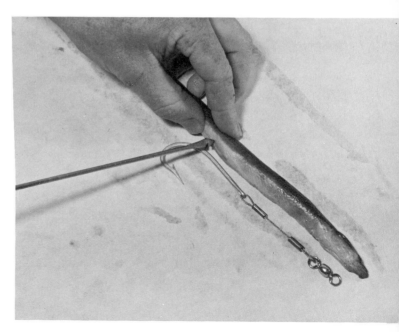

2. *Rig hook and swivel on piece of coated leader as shown, making length half the length of eel. Put rigged hook beside eel and puncture eel's belly at the spot where hook will protrude from belly.*

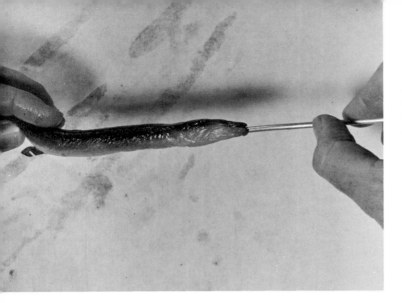

3. *Push needle through mouth and out through belly cut. Slot is angled to eye of the brass swivel.*

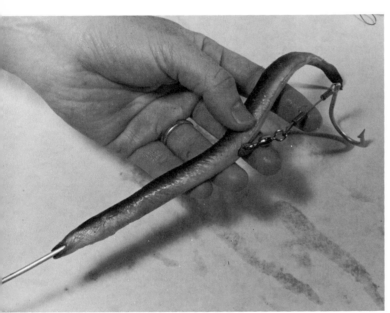

4. *Place eye of swivel in slot of needle. Haul the swivel, wire, and hook shank inside body of eel.*

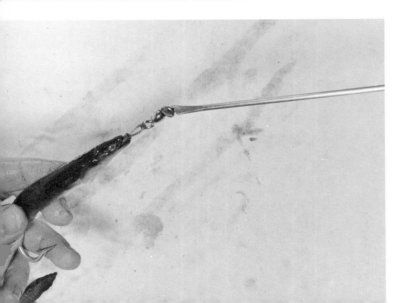

5. *Swivel has been hauled through with the needle. Swivel eye should come just clear of eel's mouth.*

6. Pass end of the fishing leader through the eye of the swivel and make it fast using haywire twist.

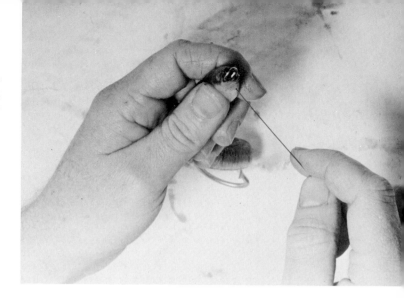

7. Bind head of eel securely to swivel with twine. Darning needle is handy for sewing rigged eels.

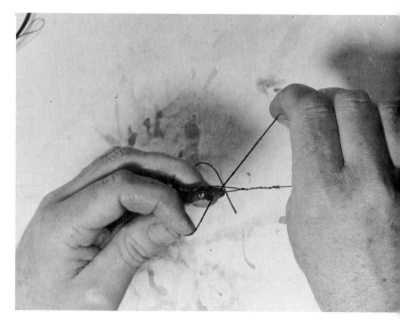

8. Hook should always be just forward of halfway point of eel's body for best trolling action.

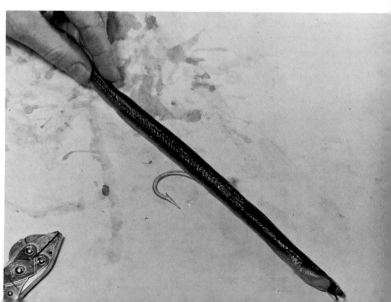

Russell Tinsley admires a prime kingfish caught in the Gulf of Mexico by his light tackle method. Hundreds of small boats leave the Texas beaches each good summer day when schools of scrappy kingfish arrive within range.

32 / New Look for Kingfish

IT WAS ONE OF THOSE MAGIC MOMENTS of fishing that a man never forgets. I'd allowed the heavy silver spoon to sink almost to the bottom of the Gulf of Mexico. Then, with rapid stop-and-go jerks, I brought it back toward the surface. On the fifth pull something swift and very much alive tried to take the rod and reel out of my hands. The jolt shot through my body from shoulders to hips as a freshly hooked kingfish headed pell-mell toward the open Gulf.

Match a 20-lb. king against tackle better suited to black bass on an inland lake and you have the makings of classic sport fishing. My seven-foot, medium action glass rod and fresh water spinning reel loaded with 10-lb. test monofilament had seen more action among the lily pads than on salt water. For a while I was sure the king was going to strip my reel, but finally it paused for breath and from then on things went my way. At least they did as long as I was able to steer clear of the lines of Johnny and Billy Disch, both of whom were also battling kings.

A few minutes later I had the long, silvery fish alongside the outboard-powered fishing skiff. Bob Hill raked it in with the gaff. Billy and Johnny were still struggling with theirs. As I dumped my fish into the GI can already half full of kingfish, I was struck by the contradiction of kingfishing as we were doing it and the way it is usually done from big boats with tackle heavy enough for tuna or marlin.

Kingfishing off the Texas coast has come a long way in recent years. Untold thousands are still caught on heavy tackle and such natural baits as balao, shrimp, mullet, ribbonfish, and even strips cut from the bellies of other kingfish. But hundreds of anglers have learned that it's possible to catch almost as many kings on "hardware" as on bait, and it's twice as much fun, especially from small, beach-launched outboard boats such as we were using this day.

The technique is simple. Instead of trolling or drifting with baited hooks, the light tackle angler casts artificial lures as he would for snook, tarpon, or big bass in inland waters. Trolling puts the kingfish at a disadvantage. The forward motion of the boat plus the heavy tackle usually employed quickly overpowers the fish. Drift fishing boats use heavy tackle because of the necessity to keep tangles down to a minimum with all those passengers on board. But the light tackle small boat kingfisherman has a ball!

On light equipment the kingfish really shows his best. The first run is enough to stop your biological clock. With many species of game fish, bass included, a slow lure retrieve gets results. Not with kingfish. The king loves a fast-moving lure and the faster your retrieve, the more action you get. It's physically impossible to reel a lure away from a determined kingfish and at top reeling speed, when you get the strike, it's like being struck by a small torpedo.

Shock waves race up the line, but this is only the start. Once hooked, the king takes off in a sizzling run that would make a bonefish take notice. Some kings go flat and straight just under the surface. Some dive, speeding up until they find bottom. A few take to the air. The fisherman who says kingfish are no real sport obviously has never fished them the Texas way.

Along much of the Florida and Gulf coastline, the king is known as a "tourist fish." This is in no way disrespectful to tourists. It merely implies that, among other fish, the king is considered quite cooperative. Kings are abundant throughout sub-tropical American waters. They roam in large schools and where you hook one you almost surely will hook more. This makes fishing for them supercharged sport. The only major problem is finding a good school.

Like the bonefish, the king is primarily a sprinter, not a born jumper. He is shaped like a surface-to-air missile. Streamlining is nigh perfect. Studies have shown that the kingfish never stops swimming. It must forever move forward through the water in order to drive oxygen-bearing water over its gills. It migrates for great distances and schools may move many miles overnight.

Actually, not much is known about the kingfish's life cycle. Some marine biologists have pointed to the waters off Puerto Rico as a major spawning area in late winter. The fish are definitely plentiful in the Florida and Gulf region all year. The peak time off the Texas coast is in summer.

Despite increasing fishing pressure from sport and commercial fishermen, no inroads seem to have been made into the general kingfish population. The fish that we have off Texas in summer probably are the same ones that give Florida a big play in September, October, and November.

The first step in this condensed course on how to catch kingfish on artificial lures is learning how to find the fish. This is elementary in theory, but often complicated in fact. One growingly popular method is to use an electronic sounder to locate both the huge schools of fish and the deep reefs over which they like to feed.

Small boats often cruise about, looking for concentrations of larger boats. Recently, the little fellows have adopted big-boat tactics. Several small boats that are equipped with sounders and citizen's band radio fan out from the starting point on a pre-arranged search plan, their sounders working. As soon as one locates a school, he calls the others by CB radio and all hands enjoy good fishing.

Along the Texas coast (and much of the Gulf off Louisiana, also) the offshore oil pumping stations have kings schooling around them feeding on bait fish that gather around the barnacle-encrusted pilings. Natural rocky reefs also seem to be attractive to kings. Very recently, the new artificial reefs being created by sportsmen off Galveston, Freeport, Port Arkansas, and Port Isabel have started to attract kingfish.

Still another good kingfish region is the unmistakable cleavage line between the green inshore water and the blue offshore water. This current rip, as it is sometimes called, appears to trap and hold the bait fish that the kingfish love. This is true of species other than kings. Tuna, marlin, dolphin, and sharks all seem to like the "edge of the blue water."

If all else fails, there is always the tried-and-true trolling search method that the charter boats use. A couple of balao baits and a couple of heavy feathers are trolled in the wake. When kingfish strikes are had, overboard goes a small flag buoy or similar marker and the casting begins. Frequently, when fish-catching action starts, widely scattered kingfish appear to gang up on the scene of the sounds and commotion in the water.

Teeth of a kingfish can inflict a bad wound on arm or leg. Careful anglers do not let freshly caught kingfish thrash around underfoot, but stow them in plastic garbage cans, potato sacks, or portable, insulated ice chests.

Back at the beach, fishermen lay out the catch for cleaning. Availability of trailer-borne outboard boats that can be launched directly from a beach has opened deep sea game fishing to hundreds of thousands of sport anglers.

Kings usually swim fairly deep, so once they have been located, the idea is to go right down after them with lures that sink quickly. It pays to know the sinking-time of any given, productive line. Thus, by "counting down" as the lure sinks, you can stop it for the retrieve at any proven or suspected kingfish depth.

My pet lures are heavy silver spoons and ball-headed feather jigs in white and yellow. The weight of the lure may vary from one to two or three ounces. The best line is monofilament, which cuts through the water with little resistance, putting the bait down quickly. A short solid wire or braided leader two feet long will protect the line from the kings' very sharp teeth. If you use a metal swivel or connector between line and leader, spray the swivel with dull black paint, otherwise a hungry king may hit it, parting your line and costing you a valuable lure.

With respect to rods and reels, a wide variety of light tackle is used by Texas kingfishermen. Bait casting reels have hardly enough capacity of line to hold really big kings, but any good conventional or spinning reel that can load at least 250 yards of 15-lb. mono or 300 or more yards of 10-lb. line will handle even the big ones. The reel must have a really good drag that won't burn out or sieze up under extremely heavy fishing pressure.

Once the lure has sunk to the bottom, bring it back with a swift lift of the rod, reeling as fast as you can. The faster, the better, and a reel with a high gear ratio is preferred for this kind of fishing.

Some anglers frown on light tackle for kings. They cite the instances when very big kings, of 35 to 50 lbs., have stripped "button thread" tackle in seconds. I'll admit that this sometimes happens. But that doesn't stop me from fishing for these fine fish with the tackle I like to use, and I've seen kings of over 35 lbs. beaten by good anglers with bass fishing tackle.

Before hauling a kingfish into the boat, it pays to club the fish into submission. A wildly thrashing king in the cockpit of a small boat can inflict dangerous slashes with its razor-sharp teeth. Many careless anglers have scars to verify this point.

Personally, I'm happy to see this new look in kingfishing. I've long been one of the king's most ardent admirers. While I don't care much for the fish on the table (which may shock many fish-eaters), I love its fighting ability on the end of a fishing line. Now, with the new lighter tackle I'm catching a few less fish than I used to, but having more fun with the fish I do take.

33 / So You Want to Go Pro

EVERY PROFESSIONAL SPORT FISHING captain at some time has had to answer the question, "Say, Cap, how does a guy become a charter boat skipper?"

Sometimes the questioner is a commercial fisherman who would like to supplement his income during off seasons. More often it is a small boat owner who is anxious to cut down the expense of fishing without losing any of the fun, or a young man with a boring shore job who has been freshly bitten by the glamour of deep sea sport fishing. In either case the answer is usually gruff and to the point.

"Get a mate's job on a good charter boat and learn the business first!"

This is excellent advice. Landlubbers are inclined to regard sport fishing boat skippers as glamorous characters who come and go as they please, fishing Florida or Baja California in the winter and the Pacific or Atlantic northern fishing areas in summer. Their distinctive boats, charging out of an ocean inlet or emerging silently from an offshore fogbank, have a purposeful air found in no other craft except men-of-war.

Actually, professional sport fishing is a tough, demanding business that is not immune to problems that plague service industries ashore. These problems are compounded by those notoriously fickle elements, the fish and the weather. Before chucking that steady shore job and mortgaging the family homestead to buy a flashy fishing cruiser, a would-be pro is wise to find out how much a boat and its equipment costs, how much take-home pay charter skippers actually make, the legal and professional hurdles they must surmount, and what future, if any, professional sport fishing offers.

Immediately after World War II, when most now-senior charter skippers got their start, a man handy with tools could convert an old cabin cruiser or surplus government small craft into a serviceable sport fishing boat at a cost of only a few thousand dollars. A brand new 35-footer with single screw, specifically laid out for fishing, could be bought for less than $10,000. Boats rarely ventured more than 20 or 30 miles offshore and a speed of ten knots was quite enough. Things are different now.

The pleasure boat boom that started in the early 1950's brought into the boat market many wooden and fiberglass hulls that could perform rings around the older charter boats. With better boats and rising competition, enterprising skippers pushed their working limits as far as 50 or 60 miles to sea. Fishing customers became fed up with lengthy boat rides to and from the fishing grounds. Fishing being equal, the faster boats sailed more frequently.

A 35-footer built to present day standards should be twin screw and capable of holding at least a 16-knot speed in any reasonable weather. Such a boat, with chairs, outriggers, bridge, and tower may cost as much as $50,000 brand new, or between $30,000 and $35,000 in good, used condition.

Many forms of sport fishing require

adequate electronic equipment. The three most basic instruments, radiotelephone, radio direction finder, and sounding machine, will total at least $1,200. A loran navigator is worth about $1,300. If fog is a real problem, a small radar unit may account for another $3,000. It is easy to see that a modern twin screw charter fishing boat, fully equipped for inshore and offshore fishing, represents a hefty investment even if the hull and motors are not new.

People who see charter skippers raking in $100 to $150 a day all season long are inclined to exclaim, "What a nice way to get rich quick!"

It would be nice, if all of the money stayed in the skipper's pocket. Unfortunately, a great deal doesn't. Suppose that an energetic young man with some fishing skill got hold of a 35-footer such as we have been talking about, and had a berth at a port that could be depended on to provide him with 120 trips during a typical season, paying $125 per trip. His gross would be $15,000. How much would he keep for his own net profit? Typical expenses add up this way:

Mate's wages	$2,000
Bait, ice, tackle	1,500
Dockage, advertising	500
Fuel	2,500
Insurance (marine, P&I)	1,000
Upkeep and storage	1,500
Total expense	$9,000

This leaves him $6,000 or 40 per cent of his gross income from which he must deduct his personal federal and state income taxes and Social Security, plus his legal share of his mate's Social Security and related taxes. From this he must also deduct any mortgage or loan pay-

Striper, *formerly owned by Capt. Joe Eldredge, is typical of the fast, well-equipped boats that now dominate the American charter fishing picture.*

ments charged against the boat. If he works 2,000 hours during the season and his tax bite is roughly $1,000, he winds up with $5,000 before mortgage payments, or $2.50 per hour for his efforts.

The pros make ends meet by being their own mechanics and shipwrights, by mending their own tackle, by going commercial fishing when parties are slow, by selling fish left behind by customers, and by eliminating every possible source of waste in their operations.

Diesel power operates at 25 per cent of the fuel cost of equal gasoline power, so a great many charter men have switched to diesel. But most of the pros make ends meet because they have gotten over the hump of acquiring a steady, faithful clientele. They scan the Tide and Current Tables months in advance and assign good dates to steady customers well before expected fish runs. They run clean, comfortable, well-equipped boats and they employ experienced, congenial mates.

Above all, they produce fish consistently, come good weather or bad. The ability to produce fish consistently is not acquired overnight. It develops from years of experience coupled with deep

insight into fish behavior. It requires that the skipper be able to teach his customers new fishing techniques and to exercise leadership over them when it comes to making basic fishing policy decisions.

A Motor Boat Operator's Permit is required to operate boats carrying six or less passengers for hire. Years ago almost any duffer could get one, but present examinations are quite strict and working experience must be proved before the examination may be taken.

To operate boats carrying more than six passengers for hire, one must pass an even more stringent Ocean Operator's License examination. This entitles one to operate vessels of not over 100 gross tons within certain geographic limits. Open party boats, which carry passengers at so many dollars per head up to the legal limit, require Ocean Operator's tickets for their masters.

Boats carrying more than six passengers for hire must also have a radio telephone of a certain power and an operator with a Third Class Radiotelephone Operator's License. This may be the skipper if he is so licensed.

Not only must the skipper be licensed

There is money in running a big party boat, but the initial investment is quite high, up to $150,000 in some instances, and the competition among head boats, as party boats are called, eliminates all who can't catch fish.

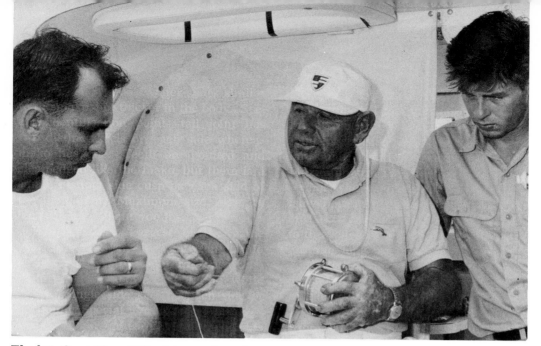

The late Capt. Tom Gifford (center), with 50 years of charter fishing on his record, had a profound effect on the techniques and standards of professional sport fishing. Here he gives tackle tips to two young skippers.

to operate boats carrying passengers for hire, his boat also must be inspected and awarded a document to do this work. Boats carrying more than six passengers for hire come under a particular section of Coast Guard rules and inspection. Those licensed to carry six or less are documented through a different branch of the Customs Service. A man planning to have a boat documented for party or charter boat work is wise to seek the guidance of a qualified Customs House broker.

Penalties for carrying passengers for hire without a valid operator's license or boat's document are quite severe. Interpretation of the law is very strict. It's not even legal for friends to share the cost of a private boat's fuel, bait, and other expenses.

In at least two United States East Coast areas and in parts of the Canadian Maritime Provinces, there are moves afoot to encourage owners of small commercial fishing boats to break into the party boat business as a source of added income. How can such commercial fishermen expect to make out? This is a

tough question to answer. Modern sport fishermen have become accustomed to almost yacht-like comfort on sport fishing craft and expect to have top quality tackle provided. They usually know quite accurately where the best-equipped boats and most productive skippers are located.

Some people may object to calling sport fishing a "business," but an analysis of the professional end of sport fishing shows that here is an important segment of the nation's maritime industry. A survey conducted by this writer in 1964 for the National Party Boat Owners Alliance, Inc., indicated that at that time there were at least 5,000 open party boats in the country and at least an additional 5,000 charter fishing boats licensed to carry passengers for hire.

Bringing values up to present levels, the average value of a charter boat in operation is now about $20,000, and the average value of a typical party boat is about $60,000. This means that 5,000 charter boats have a total value of about $100,000,000 and 5,000 party boats are worth $300,000,000.

These boats are said to carry at least

Behind every successful charter boat skipper stands a capable, congenial mate. Professional mates like John Potts, of Montauk, shown gaffing small barracuda in the Bahamas, coach the passengers in effective use of tackle.

15,000,000 passengers per year for a gross business of about $250,000,000. They produce about 300,000,000 lbs. of edible fish each year, which the customers take home to consume, while providing employment and income to at least 22,000 persons. In any man's language this adds up to a fairly large business.

Oddly enough, no government agency has ever taken a direct survey of this large and very active segment of the United States' maritime economy. Relatively little is known about its impact on boatbuilding and repair, marine motor sales, fishing tackle sales, insurance, sales and use of electronic components, and the effect of its massive catch on local populations of fish.

More boats on the water mean stiffer competition for fish. The cost of tackle, motors, bait, and services keeps going up faster than the price that people are willing to pay for being taken out fishing. The number of charter and party boats in service has not materially increased since 1960, but the number of private sport fishing boats has doubled since then.

All this points to the fact that being a charter or party boat skipper is not a business for a man who wants to make a lot of money.

But for a man with a different goal than money, the life has great appeal. In few other ways of making a living can a man be the captain of his own stout little ship, master of his own soul. Knowing danger, these men are quietly courageous. Tested by the frequent frustrations of competitive fishing, they are patient and resourceful. Living on the sea and among its creatures, they have love and respect for the wild, free, elusive fish that they pursue.

It is probably recognition of this freedom and these qualities that attracts many men and a very few women to professional fishing. It's a tough business, but a clean one. If you still harbor a yen to give it a try after having a look at what goes on behind the glamour of fast boats and big fish, then remember the advice: get a mate's job on a good boat and learn the business.

FRANK T. MOSS

34 / Target — A Record Striper

WHEN GUS PIAZZA OF NEW YORK'S FULTON Fish Market opened the box of fish from a Maryland commercial shipper, he let out a whoop. Inside was a striper bigger than any he had ever seen. Hung on a scale, the huge fish weighed a stunning 81 lbs., 8 lbs. over the record set by Charles Church at Quick's Hole, Massachusetts, way back in 1913.

To save the noble fish from becoming steaks on some seafood restaurant's menu, Gus bought it from his employers and later turned it over to the F. & M. Schaefer Brewing Company which had it mounted. Since then the mighty striper has been displayed at many sporting shows, tangible evidence that record-breaking stripers still swim in Atlantic (and possibly Pacific) waters.

The search for a new all-tackle record striper has been going on for many years. Thousands of dedicated anglers have sworn to strike their hooks into the first 75-lb. striper to be caught with rod and reel. When that striper is caught, the uproar among fishermen will sound like a hurricane.

What are the chances of connecting with a record striper? Admittedly, they are small for any individual fisherman. But experience has shown that those who fish for very big bass and nothing else, at times and places where they abound and with the proper tackle and methods, usually find the odds stacked more in their favor. Massachusetts fisherman Charles Cinto can verify this statement. His celebrated 73-pounder, caught off Cuttyhunk

in the summer of 1967, missed acceptance by the International Game Fish Association as a tie for all-tackle striper honors because Cinto took the fish with wire line and a gang-hooked plug, tackle not sanctioned by IGFA rules. But it was still a record-tying striped bass where weight alone is concerned.

With this example in mind, let us take a careful look first at places that have produced the majority of really big stripers in recent years, and then at tackle and fishing techniques that are appropriate for trophy stripers, yet "legitimate" in the eyes of the IGFA.

The geographical target for super stripers on the Atlantic seaboard is the coastal range from northern New Jersey to Cape Cod. This large target has a number of bull's-eyes, any of which could produce a new record striper. At least ten eastern locations merit special mention: Sandy Hook; the Long Island South Shore; Long Island Sound; Montauk Point; the Rhode Island shore from Watch Hill around Point Judith to Jamestown; Cuttyhunk Island; Martha's Vineyard; Cape Cod Canal; Cape Cod Bay; and Cape Cod outer beaches.

On the West Coast, where efforts are now being mounted to capitalize on the big stripers there, the Oregon coast is considered prime territory with Coos Bay and the Umpqua, Rogue, Coquille, and Alsea Rivers named as producers of trophy bass.

In naming these locations I realize that many places have been overlooked where bass of over 60 lbs. have been caught.

My purpose is not to slight these worthy places, but to pinpoint the bull's-eyes where the largest concentrations of very big stripers have been found.

Records show that the majority of stripers weighing over 6o lbs. have been caught from boats. The boat fisherman has vastly more mobility than the surf caster and better opportunities to reach the places where kingsize stripers live. So, if your ultimate aim is a new record, national, regional or personal, it will pay to sharpen your boat fishing skills.

These skills fall into three categories: casting, trolling, and live-bait fishing. In addition there are the subtle skills of learning to "read" the water, observing signs of nature that reveal the presence of bait or stripers, and working out the delicate equations of tackle, lures, and fishing techniques. Let us start with that enjoyable sport, boat casting.

The boat caster prefers this style of fishing because it is so tremendously thrilling to watch the big fish rise to and smash a cleverly-worked lure on the surface of the water. The caster's primary aim is to find bass water that is relatively undisturbed, either by boats or roistering fish. Much has been written about seeking out fish that are in a so-called feeding frenzy.

The experienced striper man knows that for every instance of feeding frenzy encountered, he finds at least twenty other instances of fish striking when no one would guess from surface appearances that fish were present in the water. But big stripers habitually take up residence in definite hospitable locations, and the fisherman who understands them knows that in any local population of such fish there will often be a few that can be teased into rising to and smashing a cleverly presented surface or sub-surface lure. Such action may break the record.

A noisy approach upsets the fish and puts them on guard. The careful angler approaches known abodes of big bass as quietly as possible. He places the boat in a position, for the all-important first drift, where wind and tide will enable him to cast to and work over the largest possible portion of the good area. As a rule, dark days and dark water call for light-colored lures while the reverse is true for bright days and clear water.

The action of the plug or casting jig must be realistic to the natural bait it is designed to represent, and to the existing water conditions. On a rough day a popping plug should be worked with snap and energy. The same is true in murky water, where bass must find their food by sensing the vibrations it makes in the water. On the other hand, a slow, lazy, sub-surface swimming plug may entice deep-hiding bass when the surface is calm and the water clear.

The mighty 68½-pounder that Ralph Gray caught off the outer Cape Cod beach back in 1958 took a surface swimming plug fished from an aluminum outboard skiff. Along the Cape shoreline huge bass lie in schools in summer in the deep holes between the shore surf and the outer bar. Sow and Pigs Reef off Cuttyhunk Island is another magnificent casting area.

Boat casters catch big fish in the tide rips of the Devil's Bridge off Gay Head, Martha's Vineyard, along the south shore of Block Island, and along the equally precipitous south shore of Montauk Point. The Rhode Island shore has many excellent casting locations. Top spots are Point Judith, the inlets between Matunuck and Watch Hill, and the Gangway Rock area between Watch Hill and Fishers Island.

Imagine Gus Piazza's amazement when he hauled this 82-lb. striper from a commercial shipment. The all-time 73-lb. game fishing record may soon be broken.

Casters have dug many very large stripers out of the waters near Long Island's lengthy inlet jetties. This is sand beach country, not much different from the Cape Cod outer beach. Throughout this wide area, morning and evening twilight periods are best. Many anglers now prefer to fish nights because of the interference from fishing and non-fishing boats during daylight hours. Unfortunately, so many trolling boats congregate at popular striper spots like Sandy Hook, Montauk Point, and Race Point on Cape Cod as to force casters to take up trolling in self defense.

It is an axiom of striper trolling that the big fish like big lures presented down deep. The advent of Monel wire line and leadcore line gave trollers new weapons for connecting with these deep stripers. But, as has been pointed out, any form of wire automatically disqualifies a fish from IGFA recognition. Therefore, many record-conscious anglers are going back to that old pre-wire standby, the underwater outrigger.

A simple underwater outrigger can be made from an old iron sash weight, a five pound lead gooseneck drail, or a modern trolling planer, to the rear end of which is wired a snap-jaw clothes pin to act as a line-holder. The weight or planer is suspended from a separate line, adding no weight to the fishing line itself. In action, the underwater outrigger works as follows.

A lure such as an eelskin, spoon, nylon or feathered jig with pork rind strip, or a trolling plug is attached to the leader of the fishing line and is dropped back 20 to 30 feet behind the slowly moving boat. The fishing line is then clipped into the jaws of the clothes pin and both weight and fishing line are lowered into the water to the proper depth. When a fish strikes the lure, the line is yanked clear of the clothes pin, the fisherman fights the fish unencumbered by extra weight, and the outrigger is hauled in for further use.

Great Lakes trollers who have to dig very deep for coho salmon have taken to using underwater outriggers rigged on short outrigger poles made of fiberglass or metal tubing. The weight or planer line is usually 80-lb. test mono that is stored on a fair-sized salt water star drag fishing reel attached directly to the outrigger pole shaft. The mono is marked to indicate length of line paid out, and, after a strike, is reeled in for further use as you would reel in a fish.

Successful deep trolling practically demands the use of a flashing or recording sounding machine. As a rule of thumb, try to troll your deep lures at a depth of at least three-quarters of the total depth of water. Where there is a thermocline, put the lures six feet under the thermocline.

McClane's Standard Fishing Encyclopedia defines a thermocline as: "A biological and physical term to describe the intermediate layer of water in a lake where temperature changes rapidly." Fish that prefer cold water are usually found below a lake's thermocline. Those that prefer warm water will be found above the boundary layer. Under certain circumstances, thermoclines are found in ocean waters. The presence of a thermocline can be established by using a depth-recording thermometer or a remote-reading thermocouple with a color-coded wire that indicates the depth in feet or fathoms. Both instruments are commercially available.

Trolling with underwater outriggers is best done in open water where there is room to make slow, easy turns. Short, quick turns may cause the weights or lures to foul on the bottom. You must be quick to haul in some outrigger and fishing line as the boat comes up on a bar or shoal. Conversely, you must be ready to drop back line to probe deep channels

Cape Cod striper fishermen pioneered the art of drifting live mackerel for record stripers. Mackerel are kept in the GI can in the boat and are fished on bare monofilament line in the deep slough between barrier bar and shore.

Planer rigged as an underwater outrigger is hung from a separate heavy line. Fishing line, held by a clothes pin clip, is released when a striper or other fish hits the trolled lure. Planer is then hauled in for re-use.

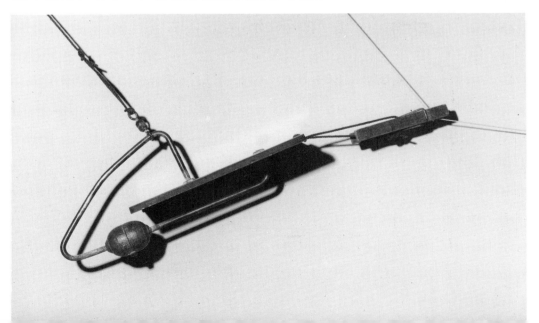

and holes where large fish may be resting.

When a heavy fish strikes, it is necessary to keep the boat moving forward until the outrigger lines can be hauled in. Otherwise, if the boat is stopped suddenly, the other deep lines may hook onto the bottom and you'll be in an awful mess. Underwater outriggers require constant care and work, but they will produce big stripers if they are rigged and used properly.

Where water depths don't exceed 20 or 25 feet, you can often troll deep enough by using elongated lead trolling sinkers placed between fishing line and lure leader. The sinkers have to be of at least four ounces weight to achieve worthwhile depth with lines of more than 20-lb. class. The weight limit that can be used directly on a trolling line without excessive personal discomfort is about a pound.

A 1-lb. trolling sinker at the end of 100 feet of 50-lb. class mono line will achieve a trolling depth of 8 to 12 feet at the normal higher and lower range of striper trolling speeds. This is just about what you could expect from 100 feet of .024-inch solid Monel wire testing about 45 lbs. breaking strain. Of course, the wire used would weigh very much less and have less drag resistance than the heavy trolling sinker, but we are looking for ways to troll deep within IGFA rules, not for maximum fishing comfort.

An alternative is to use trolling lures with built-in deep-digging action. There are many bevel-head jigs and special diving plugs that achieve depth by the dynamic action of being towed rather than through weight. Some of these are proven big bass killers. To use diving lures successfully, you must "calibrate" the lure by deliberately dragging bottom with it in water of a known depth. Then, by adjusting line length and boat speed, you can arrive at combinations that will place the lure at almost any reasonable

trolling depth within the range of your tackle.

So far we have discussed boat-handling functions without saying much about personal fishing skill. This is because in deep trolling, the arts of boat handling and tackle rigging are extremely important to over-all success. Now let's examine an entirely different kind of fishing— live-bait angling.

In the old days, bass experts used whole chicken lobsters and lobster tails to bait big stripers. Modern anglers prefer to eat their lobsters, having found that live mackerel, herring, alewives, and black eels make very excellent live bait. Tackle is relatively simple. A fairly supple rod is used, one that will match well to 20, 30, or 40-lb. test mono or Dacron line. A live-bait tank is needed, and a plain plastic GI can will do quite well. A 4/0 or 5/0 Eagle Claw hook is tied directly to the end of the line, sans leader. The live bait is hooked gently through the meat of the back or the lips and is eased overboard where big bass are known to congregate down deep. Some anglers place a split cork on the line far enough above the bait to keep the bait off the bottom. Others depend on an educated thumb.

The mackerel usually signals the approach of a big bass by a burst of frantic swimming. When the angler feels the bait being picked up, he allows line to pay out on free spool so the striper can carry the mackerel away and eat it undisturbed by line tension. Finally the angler strikes hard and the fireworks begin.

Stripers up to the 65-lb. mark have been taken on live mackerel in the Cape Cod area. In Cape Cod Canal, boat and shore fishermen alike have nailed huge stripers by fishing with live herring or alewives during the spring runs of these bait species. Live eels fished deep are very effective along the Rhode Island shore and at Montauk Point. This observer would not be surprised if the next all-tackle record striper were to fall to live bait along the Long Island-New England coast, or possibly in Oregon waters.

It takes skill and persistance to catch big stripers, and it also takes a measure of luck. Witness what happened to Carmen DePalma of Milltown, New Jersey, when he fished at Sandy Hook State Park for bass with two buddies. When the worms were used up, Carmen refused to quit fishing and switched to a big sea clam for bait. His friends scoffed, but soon he had a tremendous strike. Forty-five minutes later, he brought in a magnificent 63-lb. striper, a fish that set a new New Jersey state record.

The point here is that whenever there's a good chance of connecting with a potential record striper, you must be prepared for just such a fish. If Carmen DePalma had given up when the worms ran out, or if he had horsed the fish and broken the line during the long fight, all the good luck charms in the world would have done him no good.

That's the wonderful thing about stripers—we catch big ones, but we know that there's always a bigger one in the water, and we may get him if we are skillful, patient, and lucky enough.

Veteran Cape Cod striped bass angler Jerry Kissell took this huge bass on a live mackerel fished off the beach just east of Provincetown. Live bait is effective on big bass from Maine to Hatteras and also in the Pacific.

Elliot Fishman caught this 845-lb. world record Atlantic blue marlin with 130-lb. IGFA line class tackle at St. Thomas in the Virgin Islands in 1968.

FRANK T. MOSS

35 / Registering Record Fish

WHETHER AN ANGLER'S FISHING IS motivated by enjoyment of congenial company, a desire to eat the delicious catch, or a yen to experience the solitude of nature, all fishermen share the ambition to catch a record fish. How can you tell whether a fish is a potential record? How does one go about registering a potential record for official recognition?

Taking the first question first, there are three organizations that publish lists of recognized salt water records. The International Game Fish Association sets standards for and keeps records of approximately 49 species of salt water game fish caught on conventional (revolving spool) or spinning tackle. From time to time the IGFA amends its lists of species, and the full count of recognized species may be different from that given here.

The Salt Water Fly Rodders of America is an organization that performs the same function for a more limited number of salt water species taken on fly rod equipment. The International Spin Fishing Association does the same for fresh and salt water species caught exclusively on spinning tackle.

Naturally, to be meaningful, records have to be caught according to accepted standards of tackle and fishing behavior. Records are subdivided into various tackle classes, usually by the maximum breaking strain of the line, or, in the special case of fly tackle, by the maximum breaking strain of the leader tippet. The IGFA also subdivides its records into three major categories: All-tackle catches for men and women, men's and women's combined catches under the six accepted line classes, records for women only under the six accepted line classes.

This unusual category subdivision was established in earlier days when female participation in sport fishing was not as extensive as it is now. Recently there has been agitation to ask the IGFA to restructure its major categories to reflect catches under all-tackle, men's, and women's categories, eliminating the sometimes confusing men's-and-women's division.

The six line classifications under which records are kept are the following test strengths in pounds: 12, 20, 30, 50, 80, and 130.

Fish caught on line heavier than 130-lb. test, but not exceeding 180-lb. test, are recognized under a special 180-lb. test division, but records in this class are not listed except in the all-tackle class.

The International Game Fish Association was formed in 1939 as a result of much pressure to create a responsible organization that could bring order out of the chaotic condition of world salt water records and standardize rules for accepted fishing tackle and fishing behavior. The IGFA does not sponsor tournaments, engage in commercial enterprises, lend its name to commercial promotion, or attempt to influence legislation. It does act at times in an advisory capacity and from the start has been deeply instrumental in supporting programs of marine science directly connected with the study of various game fish species.

Membership in the IGFA is not open

to individuals, but is made up of member fishing clubs and associations in the United States and throughout the world. Proposed rules changes are voted on at regular intervals by member organizations and the IGFA has sometimes been accused of being glacially slow in making hoped-for rules and tackle changes.

Actually, the IGFA keeps a constant finger on the pulse of tackle developments in sport fishing, and when a majority vote of member clubs indicates a change should be made, that change is incorporated into the rules.

One great benefit of the grinding-slowly process is that recognized rules of tackle and fishing behavior are stable and do not change capriciously on short notice. This is of tremendous advantage to tournament directors and others who use IGFA tackle and fishing rules as standard procedure in running their fishing tournaments.

Record-conscious anglers should write to the IGFA, at the address given at the end of this chapter, requesting a copy of tackle and fishing rules and also existing records. The important points for fishermen to remember about IGFA rules are basically as follows:

1) The leader and double line on all weights of tackle up to and including 50-lb. test line shall be limited to 15 feet of leader and 15 feet of double line. For heavier tackle, the double line and leader may not exceed 30 feet respectively.

2) Rods must conform with sporting ethics. Tip length should not be less than five feet.

3) No more than two single hooks may be attached to the leader. These must be at least a shank's length apart. No free-swinging hook is allowed. *Casting plugs* are permitted with not more than two treble hooks attached to the plug.

4) The use of **any float other** than a **small cork, balloon, or bladder** is procibited. Such a float may be attached to the line or leader solely for regulating depth.

5) Use of a plug for trolling is permissible only if the plug has no more than two single hooks. In this case, a photograph of the plug, fish, rod and reel must be submitted with the application. Plugs with gang hooks are not permitted.

6) A detatchable or flying gaff shall not exceed eight feet in length, and the safety rope attached to the gaff head may not exceed 30 feet in length.

7) The angler must hook, fight, and bring the fish to gaff unaided by any other person.

8) Fishing line containing metal, in whole or in part, is not permitted.

9) The following acts will disqualify a catch:

a) Failure to comply with existing rules or tackle specifications.

b) Acts of any person other than the angler in adjusting the drag or touching any part of the tackle during the playing of the fish, or giving aid other than taking the leader for the purpose of gaffing, or in replacing or adjusting the fishing harness. (Only one person is allowed to hold the leader, but there is no restriction regarding the use of a gaffer in addition to the person holding the leader.)

c) A broken rod.

d) Handlining, or using a handline rope attached to line or leader for the purpose of holding or lifting a fish.

e) Shooting, harpooning, or lancing a fish, including sharks, at any stage of the catch.

f) Mutilation of the catch by sharks or any other means.

The IGFA designates official representatives in many fishing localities and will supply a list of such names on request. If you catch a fish that you suspect may be a new all-tackle or line-class record, the correct procedure is to obtain an official IGFA record entry form and fill in all

Under leadership of men like William K. Carpenter, the International Game Fish Association has become the main arbiter of salt water fishing rules, tackle characteristics, and records. A dedicated fisherman, Mr. Carpenter has participated in many programs of marine research devoted to game fish study and management. The IGFA makes funds, boats, and manpower available to institutions of oceanic research.

particulars. If such a form is not immediately available, obtain the following information about the fish and get a signed statement from witnesses that the information is correct:

> Length
> Girth
> Weight (on a legally tested scale)
> Species
> Location of catch
> Tackle, lure, or bait used
> Class of line
> Length and type of leader
> Arrangement of hooks
> Picture of the fish clearly showing all fins, tail, major parts
> 30-foot sample of line for testing

Essentially the same information is required by the Salt Water Fly Rodders of America and the International Spin Fishing Association. It would be good to write to the offices of these organizations requesting latest record lists, tackle and fishing rules, and conditions of membership. While membership in the IGFA is possible only through being a member of an affiliated club, both the Salt Water Fly Rodders and the International Spin Fishing Association accept individual members. Membership in either or both organizations brings special benefits not available to non-members.

International Game Fish Association
Holiday Inn Arcade
3000 E. Las Olas Blvd.
Fort Lauderdale, Florida 33316, U.S.A.

Salt Water Fly Rodders of America
Box 304
Cape May Court House, New Jersey
    08210, U.S.A.

International Spin Fishing Association
Box 81
Downey, California 90241, U.S.A.

Introduced into Pacific waters before the turn of the present century, the striped bass is now one of the most important of western marine game fish. This school striper was caught on a plug designed to imitate forage fish.

36 / Pacific Striper Trolling

WHEN SCHOOL STRIPERS FIRST RETURN in early spring to the river delta area of central California from their annual spawning run, the bass pour into the quiet, shallow waters of Suisun, San Pablo, Richardson, and San Francisco Bays. Here, in the bait-infested waters of these bays, the bass feed until they have replenished the fat they had before spawning. With open jaws and ravenous appetites, these stripers roam the bays in schools in search of food. This is the one time of year when the stripers are most vulnerable to anglers. Using plug, fly, spoon, or bait, striped bass anglers will find the bass cooperative.

But what about later in the summer and fall when most of the bass have fattened and scattered? No longer do they boil the surface or display their whereabouts so obviously. In summer, the bait fish work their way out of the bays, and the bass must now hunt for their food along the bottom. This is the time of year when most Western bass anglers take to trolling.

Trolling during the late summer and early fall is the most effective method of fishing for Pacific stripers at this time of year. Western fishermen have worked out techniques for bass trolling that have proven to be deadly, and I see no reason why these same techniques might not be used to good advantage on the East Coast. A few Western anglers attempt to label trolling as an unsportsmanlike way to catch bass. I for one do not agree. I find little distinction between fly, spin, bait-fishing, or trolling. Each is a form of angling that requires a good deal of patience, skill and finesse.

I do know that trolling is one of the best methods of locating bass when the fish are not feeding on the surface, and trolling to locate fish is something I often do even when fly fishing. I've found that I can locate fish faster by trolling because I can cover a greater area in a short amount of time. Western bass trollers have developed trolling techniques that are as sophisticated and as highly effective as fly fishing, or, for that matter, any other form of striped bass angling.

It is fairly easy to locate school bass by setting up a trolling pattern. A trolling pattern is simply a direction or a set of directions you choose to troll to cover an area. This seems to be much more effective than just trolling any place and every place in the hopes of hitting either a school or a stray fish. A pattern may be crisscross or zigzag, or simply one which carries you back and forth across an area. You should first size up the area you intend to troll, then lay out a visual map or itinerary of the courses you will follow to try to hit a school of fish.

Once you hit a fish by trolling, you should immediately turn and troll back through the area to prove it out. If you get one, two, or three hits in the same general area, you can justifiably conclude that you have located a school. Then you will probably limit quickly by keeping over the school.

Striped bass trollers who work the San

Francisco and adjoining bays of central California use a technique that is unique and highly effective. Two baits are trolled behind a device known as a spreader leader. The spreader leader is simply a Y-shaped piece of spring wire looking very much like a turkey's breastbone. The two legs of the spreader are approximately ten inches in length. Each of the two legs is equipped with a leader, snap, and swivel. The leader of one leg is six feet in length, and the leader of the other leg is three feet.

The spreader keeps the two leaders away from each other, so they will not become tangled when trolled through the water. The usual manner of setting up a spreader rig for striper trolling is to attach a two, three, or four-ounce feathered or nylon jig to the shorter leader. Then a spoon, plug, or spinner is attached to the longer leader. Spoons are usually more effective when they are trimmed with a trolling feather or a piece of pork rind, either natural or yellow in color.

When trolling in shallow areas under this setup, no additional weight is needed. Usually the weight of the jig is sufficient. When trolling over deep water or water with swift currents, however, an additional weight may be necessary. In this case, a torpedo sinker of desirable weight can be snapped onto the forward end of the spreader.

There are more advantages to using a spreader leader than just being able to troll two baits through the water on one rod. By placing a heavy lead core or leadhead jig on one of the spreader's leaders and a floating plug on the other, you'll be able to fish two different depths. The lead jig will hug the bottom, while the floating plug will work as close to the surface as the leader allows. The slower you troll, the farther apart the lures will be. Whatever bait is taken should indicate at what depth the school is lying.

You can place any combination of lures on these spreader leaders to obtain whatever action or depth you wish. To understand the combinations and to see how each differs from the other, I have broken the baits down into three separate categories: spoons, jigs, and plugs.

Spoons. Chrome spoons that produce a slow side-to-side wobbling effect are deadly effective trolling lures for school bass. Usually the hook of the spoon is concealed with a spray of feathers. Yellow or white are the most productive colors. To add an even greater attraction to the spoon, most Western bass trollers attach a strip of pork rind. Again, yellow or white pork rind brings the best results.

If you are getting a lot of hits but few solid takes with this combination, then you may assume that the bass are striking short. A trailing hook placed at the tip of the pork rind will cure the bass of short strikes. You may find that you will have to vary the size of the spoon or length of the spoon to obtain maximum results. This substantiates the importance of closely matching the length of the baitfish the bass happen to be feeding upon that particular day.

Gold, copper, or brass-plated spoons do not seem to be as effective as chrome or white-painted spoons. When using spoons, or for that matter any wobbling or action lure, first place the lure in the water alongside your boat. Then set the speed of your motor to the point where your lure produces the best action.

Jigs. If you are using a weighted or bug-eyed jig (most popular in Western waters), you'll not need any additional weight. The jig itself will serve as weight enough. To attain greater depths, I've always found it advantageous to go to a heavier jig, rather than to use a light jig and add a trolling sinker. Hair or bucktail jigs generally seem to produce better than feathered jigs, at least this is so in the bays of central California. Again, white or yellow are the two colors most

Lures that catch Pacific stripers (above) are (left to right) metal casting jigs and spoons, surface and diving plugs, bucktail trolling jigs. Wire bridles are used for trolling two separate jigs, spoons, or plugs, dropper style. Typical San Francisco Bay bass trolling outfit (below) consists of a light rod matched to 20 or 30-lb. test line, and a light star drag trolling reel. Lures on spreader have leaders of unequal length made up of 60-lb. mono.

used by Western bass trollers. I find the combination of a bug-eye jig and a chrome, feathered spoon, used with a spreader leader, to be deadly in San Francisco Bay.

Pork rind is a good persuader on bucktail jigs. Most jigs are manufactured so that the hook will ride pointing up when the jig is trolled through the water. This allows you to bounce the bottom without snagging. When a jig is trolled across a muddy or sandy bottom it leaves a trail of dirty water behind it. For some reason this seems to arouse the curiosity of school bass. I have done this often in the shallow flats of San Francisco Bay, and on numerous occasions I have watched an entire school of bass follow this dirty trail behind the boat.

If you are trolling in an area where the bottom is lined with big rocks, you may want to try slowing down your troll so that the jig can hop and skip from boulder to boulder and drop down into the deeper holes between. Many a time this technique has produced for me when a fast troll over the rocky area would not.

Plugs. There are thousands of plugs on the market today, most of which would probably take a striped bass at one time or another, purely because of the bass's unpredictable nature. Only a few plugs, however, have proven their ability to attract striped bass consistently in the waters of the West Coast. Western bass trollers seem to prefer regular five-eighths-ounce fresh water bass plugs over larger plugs originally designed for bass. I personally find that these smaller plugs promote more strikes than the larger plugs. Bass anglers trolling plugs on the East Coast may also find that this is so.

Again the color white predominates in most of the more productive trolling plugs used for bass. Perhaps the most widely used is the plug that has a red head and a white body. Both solid and jointed plugs are used for trolling. I find that the solid plugs produce as much as or more action than the jointed or two-piece plugs. I prefer plugs with treble rather than double or single hooks and have equipped most of my fresh water plugs with sturdy nickel plated hooks for striper trolling.

The flat plug or perch-bodied plug in recent years has played an important role in striped bass trolling in the waters of central California's bays and sloughs. I attribute this to the fact that our bays and sloughs are infested with a small, flat fish called shiner perch. These shiner perch, having broad, flat bodies seldom over three inches in length, are an excellent food source for migrating school stripers. Live bait drifters use shiner perch with terrific results. There were many perch-bodied black bass plugs of this design on the market. When they first became popular, these plugs were quickly adapted for salt water and soon became the only thing for bass trolling or casting in San Francisco Bay, where shiner perch are abundant.

Now the new flap-tail or propeller-equipped surface plugs and long, slender plugs seem to be the rage. All produce well for trollers who can locate school fish and determine what they are feeding on.

I do not believe that there is any such thing as a "perfect" trolling speed for bass. There are just too many circumstances to be considered. I like to troll at a speed where my lures produce the best action. Some plugs work best while trolled slowly, others work best at a fast clip. As a general rule, a fast troll has just as much effect on bass as a slow one. I base this statement on the fact that the majority of striped bass trollers in the bays of central California use either inboard or large outboard craft. These larger boats will not idle down as slowly as small outboards. Yet, anglers working from the larger, faster trolling boats pick up a lot of fish where the small skiff fishermen often do not.

I have taken fish trolling with my 9½ h.p. motor and my cartop boat at speeds under three knots, and I've been passed by larger craft trolling alongside at speeds of up to six or seven knots. Yet, upon docking, I often find that these anglers have as many bass as I do. There really isn't any "best" speed for trolling, nor for that matter can one set any certainties on a fish as unpredictable as the striped bass. But that in itself is what makes these fish such a great challenge.

The delta region of San Francisco Bay is a popular fishing ground for boats like this Uniflite cruiser. Stripers breed in many western coastal rivers.

FRANK T. MOSS

37 / Conservation and Sport Fishing

AMERICANS ARE RAPIDLY BECOMING aware of the threats of pollution, over-fishing, and mismanagement of land and water resources to our way of life. Few non-scientists are more aware of these dangers to our environment than are sport fishermen. This awareness comes from close personal contact with the sea, with fish, and with the outdoors.

Two questions frequently asked by concerned sport fishermen are: "What are the real problems?" and "What can we do about them?"

Before we look at the problems it would be wise to discuss what is meant by "conservation." The word now has many more meanings than it did when Theodore Roosevelt defined it as "use without abuse" of our natural resources. For example, some sportsmen seem to feel that conservation means preventing commercial fishermen from harvesting fish that the sportsmen think of as their own.

Other sportsmen deplore this narrow interpretation, pointing out that very often both commercial and sport fishermen suffer equally when fish or habitat are destroyed. People who are oriented toward the commercial fishing industry usually define conservation as being that type of fisheries management that makes it possible to obtain the maximum sustained yield that a population of fish is capable of producing.

Sport fishermen, on the other hand, generally agree that conservation means protecting the fish and their habitat from activities that would reduce the quality as well as the quantity of the fish available for harvest or place their future reproduction and state of well-being in jeopardy.

These differences of definition have been a bone of contention for many years, but right now sport fishermen have too much to lose to waste time, money, energy, and political leverage sniping at domestic commercial fishermen over matters that don't amount to much. Let us therefore delay a final definition of "conservation" until we have examined the very real dangers that confront sport and commercial fishermen together, and also the other dangers that sport fishermen must face for themselves. Three of the former are:

Pollution of our inland, coastal, and high seas waters to the degree that many formerly abundant species are "commercially extinct," and that many other valuable species are showing signs of weakening in quality and abundance.

What is it like to be a fish? Imagine yourself able to float weightlessly in water which you could not feel because your body is at the same temperature as the surrounding liquid. You don't need ears because your entire body is sensitive to sound and vibration. The air above is "outer space."

217

This juvenile sailfish, three inches long, was taken in a plankton tow by scientists of the University of Miami. From this tiny beginning, a sailfish grows to a length of seven feet and weight of 50 lbs. in only three years.

Loss of wetlands, those fish nurseries along our coasts that are absolutely essential to the continuation of many important sport, food, and industrial fish.

Overkill of fish and tearing-up of ocean bottom on the continental shelves off our shores by huge and continuously growing fleets of foreign factory ships.

These three problems have been given wide publicity, and thoughtful sport fishermen usually agree that they have as much to lose as their commercial cousins if workable solutions to these problems are not found. But sport fishermen also have a lot of new problems that are peculiarly their own.

One is the manner in which Atlantic salmon are being taken in increasing quantities by commercial netters and long-liners working off Greenland. Fortunately, the Danish government has agreed to phase out its high-seas salmon fishery by 1976, and Canada banned commercial taking of Atlantic salmon in 1972.

Another is the probability that national tuna catch quotas will soon have to be imposed on all nations harvesting Atlantic tuna. Back in 1966, the first international

Tagging of game fish is carried out by a number of institutions. A striped marlin is about to receive a dart tag from biologist of the Tiburon Marine Laboratory in California as part of an international billfish study effort.

Atlantic Tuna Convention was held at Rio de Janeiro, Brazil. By good fortune (and not without considerable political arm-twisting) two able sport fisheries representatives were assigned to the official United States delegation.

These men, Richard Stroud of the Sport Fishing Institute of Washington, D.C., and Alan Schwartz of the Bureau of Sport Fisheries and Wildlife, were able to persuade the convention that the United States sport fishery has a large and long-standing interest in the harvest of Atlantic and Pacific tuna.

They also convinced the convention to include the various species of billfish in the pelagic fish research programs being planned. The significance of official sport fishermen's representation to this international convention was not lost on the scientists and diplomats of other attending nations.

Closer to home we have many problems that weren't dreamed of just a few years ago. One is to resolve the question of whether the federal government or the various states should have ultimate management control over domestic migratory fish such as the anadromous striped bass.

Another is how to protect important fish-breeding rivers like the Hudson, the Delaware, the Roanoke, and many others from pollution and industrial encroachment of great danger to the fish. Still another is how to obtain the funds needed to get programs of sport fisheries research under way.

Should there be a salt water fishing license? If so, shall it be state or federal, and who will get to control and administer the money such licensing will provide? Are bag limits and open and closed seasons already needed to protect endangered populations of fish? Is it true that in some cases protective bag limits and seasons actually are detrimental to the fish?

The questions and problems could go on and on. Suffice it to say that there is plenty of work for those who stand up and ask, "What can we do?"

For one thing, we can refuse to be apologetic for being sport fishermen. There's nothing wrong with fishing for fun and for the table and the family freezer. Sport fishing catch estimates of the Bureau of Sport Fisheries and Wildlife, updated to 1970, indicate that on salt water alone sportsmen are catching more than 1.5 *billion* pounds of edible fish a year, equal to about 60 per cent of the entire commercial catch of food fish per year in the United States.

The trouble is that nobody hears much about the great American sport fishing effort. Hunters and gun buffs have the redoubtable National Rifle Association and golfers have their great professional and amateur golf associations. But there is no such thing as a national sport fishermen's association to carry the ball of legislative and fisheries management needs through the halls of Congress.

Fortunately, what is good for fish is also good for wilderness and wildlife, so sport fishermen have powerful allies in organizations such as The National Wildlife Federation, The National Audubon Society, The Sierra Club, Ducks Unlimited, and many others. Also, fortunately, sport fishermen are learning the value of organization when it comes to fighting pollution, unnecessary industrial encroachment on good fishing waters, and wasteful fishing practices, and helping programs of marine research of value to sport fishing.

Being against sin and pollution and for motherhood and good, clean fishing waters is great, you say at this point, but what can plain ordinary citizens who fish for fun *do*?

They can do plenty, and here are some concrete suggestions.

The New York Power Squadron in 1965 instituted a series of winter classes in sport fishing techniques. Well-known professional guides from Montauk and other fishing ports donated time, demonstrations, and lectures. The classes were so successful that other Power Squadron districts have adopted them as prime wintertime educational projects for members and prospective members.

The Salt Water Fly Rodders Association of America, with headquarters in New Jersey, sponsors a series of fly fishing seminars through various chapters located near good fishing areas. Besides tackle rigging and technical advice from experts, the Association has undertaken the recognition of official salt water fly rod catch records.

United Mobile Sportfishermen, Inc., a federation of surf fishermen's clubs, undertakes through its member clubs the restoration of sand dunes in areas used by their fishermen, and requires of its members a high standard of group and individual fishing conduct. A UMS fishing team in 1968 took part in a joint United States-Canadian striped bass tagging venture in Nova Scotia, New Brunswick, and Prince Edward Island.

The Hatteras Marlin Club is only one of many such clubs that annually tags and releases numbers of billfish and tuna, working in cooperation with biologist Frank J. Mather III of the Woods Hole Oceanographic Institution, Woods Hole, Massachusetts.

The American Littoral Society is a lively group of fishermen, students, scientists, skin divers, boat owners, and others who have set up a sort of early-warning system to report instances of accidental or intentional pollution of the New York-New Jersey region. Education-oriented, the Society puts on an annual spring oceanographic teach-in that attracts standing-room-only crowds to Hunter College in New York to listen to such deep sea luminaries as Phillipe Cousteau, Scott Carpenter, Dr. Lionel A. Walford, Dr. Eugenie Clark, and Elgin Ciampi.

By contrast, the Hudson River Fishermen's Association has made the salvation of that grand stream from assorted highway builders, power corporations, and sewage-spouting municipalities a national crusade.

Quite necessarily we look at the idea of conservation from the rather specialized viewpoint of sport fishermen. But what affects fish and fishing also affects people. We breathe in the same oxygen, drink and bathe in the same water, and suffer from the same poisons and pollutants. From this viewpoint we might regard conservation not so much as an abstract idea as a very concrete plan of action to curb the abuses that are bad for men and for fish.

Ten major points make up the plan sport fishermen should work collectively and individually to put into action:

Biologist John Casey of Narragansett Marine Laboratory examines results of a plankton tow made off Montauk Point. The jar is filled with a rich mixture of fish eggs, larvae, and microscopic life, truly the lifeblood of the sea.

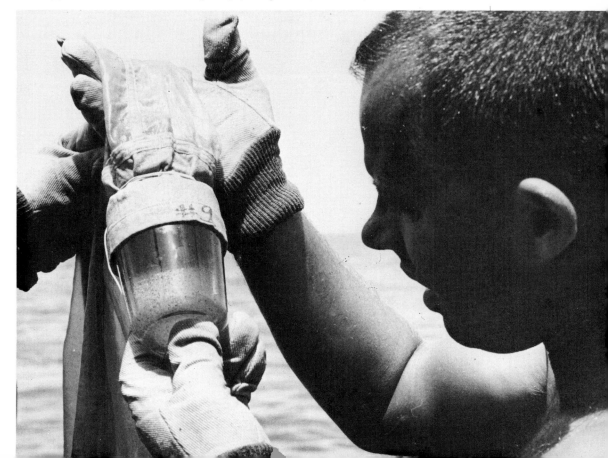

1) Bring under control the increasing floods of municipal, industrial, and agricultural pollution that are poisoning our waters.

2) Seek elimination of DDT and all other persistent pesticides that, because of their long life span, become cumulative in the food chains that support life.

3) Fight to prevent the loss of coastal and interior wetlands.

4) Establish controls over the commercial exploitation of underwater resources such as sand and gravel, oil, minerals, and commercial shellfish grounds, so that such exploitation will not ruin nearby fish or habitat.

5) Decide whether states or the federal government should have management control over domestic migratory fish.

6) Make sure that sport fishermen's interests in research and management are protected in the National Marine Fisheries Service, a branch of the Department of Commerce that now combines the former Bureau of Commercial Fisheries with the marine fisheries section of the former Bureau of Sport Fisheries and Wildlife.

7) Secure sport fishermen's representation at all major domestic and international fisheries conferences.

8) Help develop effective controls over foreign vessels fishing on the continental shelves off our shores.

9) Establish a means for obtaining sport fisheries catch and fishing effort data and make this information available to research agencies and the sport fishing industry.

10) Educate fishermen and the public in good conservation practices, sportsmanship, and an understanding of the need to preserve the relatively good fishing that we enjoy.

These are realistic goals. A good start has been made on some of them. Teddy Roosevelt's definition of "use without abuse" looks like a good one for modern sport fishermen. It covers a lot of territory, is not complicated, and doesn't beat about the bush. Sport fishermen taking it to heart will do well to protect it from corrupt and misleading interpretation.

38 / Sing Me the Blues

IT'S A GOOD THING THAT BLUEFISH DON'T grow as big as giant bluefin tuna. No tackle now in existence would hold them, and thousands of miles of our best swimming beaches would be unsafe for humans, or even plain ordinary sharks.

Professor Spencer Fullerton Baird, first head of the old United States Commission of Fish and Fisheries, cast academic restraint aside in 1871 when he denounced the bluefish as an "animated chopping machine." In the authoritative book, *Fishes of the Gulf of Maine*, Bigelow and Schroeder called *Pomatomus saltatrix* ". . . perhaps the most ferocious and bloodthirsty fish in the sea, leaving in its wake a trail of dead and wounded mackerel, menhaden, herring, alewives, and other species on which it preys."

Yet, taken on suitable tackle, the bluefish comes close to outclassing the redoubtable Atlantic salmon. If this sounds like heresy, then find out for yourself by hooking a 15-lb. blue on a regulation salmon fly rod and see if you can whip the fish before he strips all your backing or chews through the leader.

And they are fish not to be trusted. Marine biologists and outdoor writers expound on the sharp-toothed, cannibalistic fish. I doubt that many of them have suffered the indignity and pain of being bluefish-bit. I have, and it was no picnic.

Plugging for school bluefish in Long Island Sound off Mattituck, I landed a 2-pounder on a small Creek Chub popping plug. The fish had the tail hook deep in its gullet, the head hook swinging free. As I lifted the ornery little critter out of the dip net the loose barb caught lightly in the heel of my hand. In an effort to keep the barb from penetrating under the skin I raised my hand closer to the bluefish's mouth—and was promptly bitten on the index finger.

"Help!" I squawked to Jerry Dominy, my fishing buddy. "He bit off my finger!"

The damage wasn't quite that bad, but my finger bore a neat semi-circle of toothmarks for nearly three weeks If that bluefish had weighed 15 lbs. instead of 2, it probably would have had the finger. Just for the record, the father of Yale icthyologist Edward Migdalski did lose part of his right index finger to a bluefish estimated at 2 lbs.

Is it safe to fish for and handle these animated meat grinders? "Yes," says Jerry Dominy, succinctly. "It's like fishing for sharks. Just keep your fingers away from the biting end."

Francesca LaMonte, in *North American Game Fishes*, describes the range of the bluefish as "north to Nova Scotia; abundant from Florida to Penobscot Bay, Maine, but not taken in the Bay of Fundy or off the Nova Scotian side of the Gulf of St. Lawrence."

Robert H. Boyle has stated that the species is available off the east coast of South America, South Africa and Madagascar, the Malay Peninsula, the Black Sea, the Mediterranean, the Azores, Japan, and northwest Africa between Agadir and Dakar. I have personally caught bluefish in the Tasman Sea off New South Wales, Australia. To put it mildly, bluefish get around.

The International Game Fish Association lists the all-tackle bluefish record as a 24-lb., 3-oz. monster caught by M. A. da Silva Veloso at the Azores on August 27, 1953. Lest anyone think you have to leave the good old U.S.A. for super-sized bluefish, forget not the huge 24-lb. plus chopper caught by an angler at Montauk in 1968. The Montauk fish would have been a new all-tackle IGFA record if it had not been taken on wire line, material not recognized by the IGFA for record status fish.

Some authorities speak of 30-pounders off the African coast and Phil Mayer of New York reports seeing a 35-pounder at Casablanca, Morocco. But any bluefish over 16 lbs. is a mighty big blue, even though super-sized bluefish were the rule rather than the exception at many points along the East Coast during the last half of the 1960's.

In an effort to analyze coastal bluefishing methods, I interviewed charter boat skippers from Nantucket, Montauk, Barnegat, and Hatteras. It was difficult to establish that these successful professionals were all talking about the same species of fish. Their methods were as diverse as their opinions, yet all of them catch large quantities of bluefish with astonishing regularity. I gathered the impression that throughout their range the fish themselves are consistently inconsistent. Fish that will hit nothing but spoons and bright jigs in one area won't take anything except feather or nylon lures with a lot of yellow in another region.

I did discover that no matter where I went, the really successful fishermen invariably called morning and evening twilight the really magic hours for bluefish. Also, they like tide rips and swift currents. Over a period of time you'll catch many more blues where the tide runs strong than you will in quieter water.

Look for bluefish in water where an island interrupts tidal currents pouring out of a sound or bay into the ocean. You'll find them on the great inshore reefs like Sou'west Ledge off Block Island, and the famous Elbow and Shagwong Reef rips at Montauk. Or you'll find hordes of them congregated over deep offshore bottom rises, like Barnegat Ridge off the New Jersey shore.

Fish the channels and bars of inlets like Shinnecock and Moriches on Long Island, Oregon and Hatteras in North Carolina. Try the mouths of tidal creeks where they empty into bigger water, or the deep slough formed between an outer surf bar and a sandy ocean beach.

Bait fish and other food creatures are tumbled about in rough, swift water. Bluefish lie in ambush for the victims. They can often be located by sounders like the Raytheon Fathometer or the Lowrance fish Lo-K-Tor. Expect bigger bluefish to lie deep, snappers and small blues to show on the surface more readily. Bluefish respond to a wide variety of fishing techniques, the most productive of which we will explore shortly. If some of these techniques sound outlandish, don't give up without giving them a try. There may be wonderful bluefishing right in your own back yard, so to speak, fishing that no one capitalizes on because the fishing methods required are different from the methods that local people know from force of habit.

Take our thousands of square miles of salt water wetlands for example. In a little boat, even a rubber raft, you can drift along the edges of tidal channels between the islands of marsh grass, casting to baby and immature bluefish that are growing up rapidly in this protected water. Waters like this exist along Long Island's Great South Bay and Peconic Bay regions, New Jersey's Barnegat Bay, the

Of world-wide distribution, yet oddly missing from our West Coast, the trim bluefish is superlative both on the line and on the table. This six-pounder was caught from a large school ravaging menhaden on the Long Island shore.

vast wetland complexes of Delaware and Chesapeake Bays, Pamlico Sound, and inland sounds and bays all the way down to Florida.

Here you can use exactly the same one-handed spinning equipment or fly rod gear that you'd use for largemouth bass in fresh water. You'll need a maximum of 200 yards of 8-lb. test mono line tipped with a six-inch wire leader testing 20 to 30 lbs. Put a small snap swivel at the end of the leader and take the precaution of painting the swivel black to keep fish from striking at this in lieu of the lure.

You can use both sub-surface swimming and top water popping plugs in

Bluefish can bite fingers badly! Jerry Dominy is careful to use pliers as he removes treble hook from mouth of a three-pounder. He caught fish on a small plastic popping plug fished on top with a light surf spinning stick.

miniature sizes averaging one-half to three-quarters of an ounce in weight. I do well with the Creek Chub "Striper Strike," the Atom "Striper Swiper," and the Arbogast "Jitterbug," the latter a well-known fresh water plug. Among good sub-surface lures, I've scored with Rebel and Nils Master plugs. The popular

Hopkins hammered metal jigs in smaller sizes frequently are real killers.

Don't be afraid to reel quickly on the retrieve! Make a surface popper skitter as fast as you can crank the reel handle. Give sub-surface lures extra action by jigging the rod as you reel. In this shallow water the bluefish will take to the air

You don't need fancy tackle to catch bluefish. Charles R. Meyer took this little fellow on a spoon, flounder rod, and fresh water bait-casting reel. Bluefish like warm water and cannot tolerate temperatures less than 56°.

when it is hooked and treat you to aerial acrobatics worthy of grilse or river-run smallmouth bass.

When bluefish are breaking on the surface in either shallow or deep water, standard trolling methods can be employed. *Never* drive a boat through the center of a school, lest they sound and remain boat-shy. Don't chase the fish back and forth at full throttle. Remain in one spot after fish have sounded. Soon enough they'll be up again and if you are still there you'll reap a small harvest before the fish-chasers come charging back.

Several boats can work a school together if they set up a circular pattern of trolling around the school edges, giving everyone an equal chance at the fish. I like speeds of three to six knots, and this means the speed of the boat through the water, not over the bottom. In relatively shallow water for surface trolling I prefer star drag reels loaded with 20 to 40-lb. test mono line. In deeper waters, Monel wire or leadcore deep trolling line works wonders when the fish won't strike at the surface.

Bucktail and nylon lures may be used bare or with pork rind or squid strips on the hooks. For very big blues, especially at night, rigged eels and eelskins are very effective. Be sure to rig a tail hook in the very tail of the eel or skin to catch the tail-biters. Spoons, plugs, even lures made of rubber surgical tubing all catch blues under right conditions. The best advice in new fishing country is to seek out a local expert and follow his lead.

Tide rips make up over bars and ledges and are prime bluefishing spots. When you find a rip that produces fish, be sure to get ranges on the spot by lining up objects ashore. This way you can return to the bar or ledge area in calm weather when there is no rip. By the same token, be sure to keep your sounding machine going on every rip you fish so you will be able to judge the exact depth of water and character of the bottom.

In trolling a rip, always proceed up-tide, trolling your lures back into the rough water behind the rip face. This is where the fish are most likely to be. Mark your trolling lines with India ink or tiny bits of string tied at convenient distances up from the lure end so you will know exactly how much line is out at any given time. This will enable you to put your lures at the best distance behind the boat for the particular fish in question, or to achieve the proper depth when deep-trolling.

Just as some anglers chum giant blue-

fin tuna, sharks, and mackerel, so others chum bluefish. It's best done at night in areas where there is a resident population of blues living down deep. The famous Seventeen Fathoms grounds off the northern New Jersey coast is a case in point.

Mix ground menhaden with sea water in a GI can to make a thick, gloppy soup. Ladle this overboard in dribs and drabs, continuously, from the anchored or drifting boat. Bait up with chunks of cut menhaden or butterfish. A couple of large split shot on the line will take the bait down properly.

The idea is to work the bluefish up directly astern so they can be seen striking. Some chummers use too much chum, giving the fish free lunch. Some use too little, making "holes" in the chum slick. You must regulate the amount of chum used to meet local current conditions. The chum should be the *hors d'oeuvre* inviting the bluefish to the table, not the main course. *That* is what goes on the hook.

There are several kinds of chum pots on the market that do a good job of dispersing chum down deep or right under the boat, depending on how much line is put overboard when the chum pot is put into action. In a rough sea, the motion of the boat will be enough to make the chum pot slowly spread its contents into the water. In calm weather you'll have to agitate the pot line to obtain chum dispersal.

The fly rod and other very light tackle can be used to good advantage after bluefish have been attracted to the boat by chum. You can frequently hook them by merely lowering the lure or streamer fly into the water. At other times cast out, let the lure or the streamer sink a few feet, then retrieve with a jerky action. Always rig streamers and light spinning lures with a short leader of fine wire. Bluefish can bite through even 80-lb. test mono in one snap.

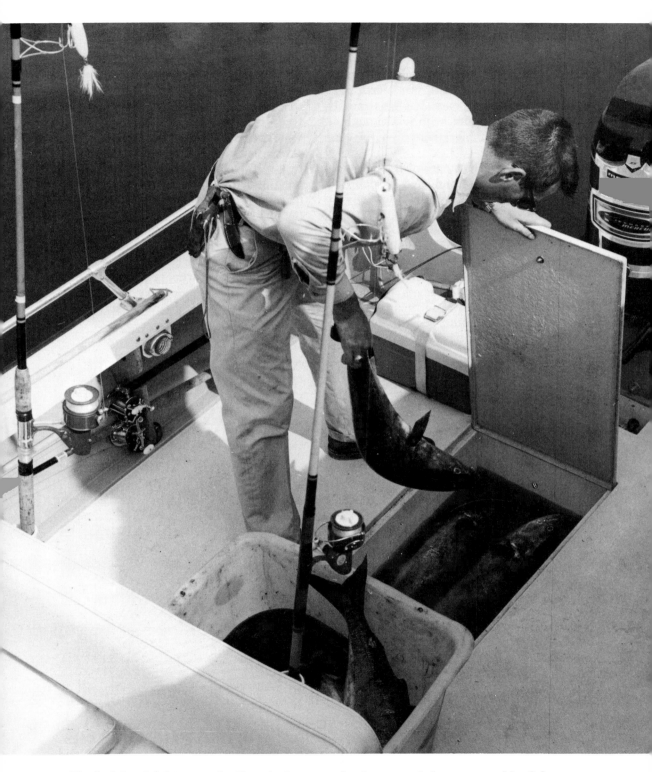

Rhode Island fishing guide Alan Anderson unloads some of the monster bluefish
he has caught off Block Island. Predatory feeders, bluefish are caught by many
methods that include trolling, chumming, and live bait fishing.

PHOTO CREDITS

Jacket photo by S. L. Perinchief

Apelco Company: p. 85

Capt. Stu Apte: p. 115

Bahamas News Bureau: pp. 37, 39, 134

Nelson Benedict: pp. 29, 48, 52, 53, 54, 64, 125, 125, 125

Bertram Yacht Corp.: pp. 22, 22

Victoria Blanchard: pp. 160, 160, 161

Harry Bonner: pp. 32, 141, 141, 143, 144

California Boat Co.: p. 122

Antonio Cesareo: p. 40

City of Miami News Bureau: p. 17

Dr. Oswald B. Deiter: pp. 11, 138

Doty: p. 14

Al Duvernay: p. 118

Dave Edwardes: pp. 18, 129

Ensign: p. 78

Fisher-Pierce Corp.: p. 23

Dennis Good: p. 118

Larry Green: pp. 95, 210, 213, 213

Hatteras Yacht Corp.: p. 21

Huckins Yacht Corp.: p. 45

International Game Fish Association: p. 209

Johnson Motors: p. 122

Lois J. Kennedy: pp. 38, 215, 219

Jerry Kissell: pp. 203, 205

Robert Koliner: p. 96

Lowrance Electronics: p. 82

Charles R. Meyer: pp. 23, 24, 24, 64, 112, 146, 225, 226, 227, 229

Frank T. Moss: pp. 10, 15, 26, 29, 31, 39, 41, 44, 44, 56, 57, 59, 71, 71, 72, 74, 75, 76, 76, 77, 77, 78, 79, 86, 91, 91, 101, 103, 106, 121, 130, 130, 132, 147, 150, 153, 153, 153, 155, 159, 159, 161, 162, 163, 164, 195, 196, 197, 198, 203, 216, 221

Mildred J. Moss: p. 8

Newfoundland Tourist Development Office: p. 15

New York *Daily News:* p. 201

Niel C. Nielsen: p. 12

North Carolina State Development Dept.: pp. 117, 148–149

Nova Scotia Information Bureau: pp. 7, 95

Pacemaker Corp.: p. 89

Perko: p. 47

Norman Phillips: pp. 167, 167, 168

Raytheon Corp.: p. 81

Rock-A-Way Mfg. Corp.: p. 47

Milt Rosko: pp. 109, 111, 147

Sea Bird Yachts: p. 51

Mark J. Sosin: pp. 169–172, 173–176, 177–180, 181–183, 185–187

Sportfishing: pp. 47, 96, 231

Russell Tinsley: pp. 188, 191, 191

University of Miami: p. 218

University of Rhode Island: p. 15

Vexilar Corp.: p. 85

Brian and Ann Vicary: p. 63

Virgin Islands News Service: p. 206

Wheeler Yacht Corp.: p. 18

Hamilton Wright: p. 66

Yachting (Rosenfeld): pp. 21, 31, 32, 42, 60, 69, 69, 103, 157

ADF. Abbreviation for "automatic direction finder."

Air bladder. Gas-filled bladder in fish's body used to maintain depth stability.

Algae. Primitive chlorophyl-bearing water plants.

Anadromous. Types of fish that live most of their lives in salt water, but ascend fresh water rivers to breed.

Anal fin. Single fin on lower body surface between anus and tail.

Anoxia. Condition of being starved of oxygen.

Anterior. Forward part of any object.

Backlash. Tangle of line on reel spool caused by over-run of the spool in casting.

Bait. a) Any natural substance that is used on a hook to entice fish to bite; b) The act of presenting a lure or prepared bait to a fish; c) Any of a large group of small fishes on which larger fish regularly feed.

Bait-casting. The act of casting a prepared bait or lure by means of a specialized revolving-spool reel and light rod, usually known as a "bait-casting rig." Primarily a fresh water technique, but sometimes used on salt water.

Ballyhoo. Balao, a small, thin bait fish widely used as a skipping bait for billfish.

Bearing. The direction by compass of any object as viewed from the observer's position.

Bill. Sword, spike, or spear of a billfish.

Billfish. Any Istiophorid game fish, such as marlin, sailfish, spearfish, and broadbill swordfish, considered as separate from all other fishes by virtue of their bills.

Biological clock. Innate reactive behavior of some fish that appears to be regulated by an inner time-sensitive mechanism.

Bottom fishing. Fishing while anchored or drifting, using heavy sinkers to carry the hooks to the bottom.

Bulldogging. Rapid swinging of the head by a hooked fish that sends repeated heavy shocks up the fishing line.

Butt. Lower extremity of a fishing rod below the reel.

Cast. The act of throwing out a bait or lure by using the rod as a lever to give motion to the bait or lure.

Caudal fin. Tail fin.

Caudal peduncle. Narrow portion of tail just ahead of the caudal fin.

CB. Abbreviation for Citizens Band, certain radio frequencies in the high range reserved for broad public use.

Charter boat. Fishing boat that carries passengers for hire by charging a fixed over-all fee per day.

Chum. Ground or finely chopped bait that is doled overboard for the purpose of attracting fish.

Cockpit. The open, sunken after deck of a sport fishing boat.

Continental shelf. The plain that extends out under the surface of the sea to a depth of about 600 feet and is part of the true continental land mass.

Deboner. A hollow tube about one-half inch in diameter and a number of inches long, with saw teeth cut into the working end, used to core out the backbone of bait fish like mullet.

Demersal. Pertaining to fish that habitually live on or near the bottom of the sea, rather than near the surface.

Dorsal fin. The prominent fore-and-aft fin worn by most fish down the centerline of the back.

Double-line. That portion of the fishing line that is doubled back on itself at the working end, according to specific tackle rules, to gain greater strength.

Drail. A specialized trolling sinker shaped somewhat like a torpedo, but with an offset towing neck.

Drag control. The clutch or brake system of a reel, by means of which the line may be allowed to be drawn out under variable tension.

Drop-back. The act of dropping a trolled bait or lure back to a fish that has missed its strike to give the fish a better chance to try again.

Drop-off. Precipitous underwater cliff or bank, as at the edge of a sunken river channel or edge of the continental shelf.

Ecology. Study of the relationship of living species and their habitats.

Estuary. Bay, sound or large river mouth forming a meeting place for salt and fresh water.

Fathom. Nautical measure equalling six feet.

Fathometer. Registered trade mark name for an electronic sounding machine produced by the Raytheon Corporation.

Feather lure. Lure dressed with or made from feathers.

Ferrule. Male or female metal parts that form a rod joint.

Fighting chair. Large, heavy, swiveling seat or chair equipped with a footrest, used for fighting large fish.

Finning fish. Fish swimming with dorsal and/or tail fin visible above surface of the water.

Fish box. Fixed or portable box kept in boat's cockpit to receive the catch. Usually insulated and equipped with drains.

Fish-finder. Colloquial word for electronic sounder.

Fish well. Fish box built under the boat's deck.

Fishing belt. Adjustable belt supporting a leather or metal cup into which angler may thrust butt end of rod while fishing standing up.

Fishing chair. Lighter version of fighting chair, but without footrest, and sometimes non-swiveling. Has a rod butt gimbal, as does the fighting chair.

Flatfish. Any flounder, fluke, or halibut.

Flat-line. Trolling line fished without benefit of outrigger.

Fly rod. Light casting rod that operates on the principle of casting the line rather than a weighted lure.

Flying bridge. Open, elevated control station, usually atop the deckhouse.

Flying gaff. Very large gaff with detachable head to which is spliced a stout rope or wire cable.

Footrest. Portion of fighting chair on which the feet are placed so as to oppose legs to the pull of rod and line while fighting large fish. Adjustable.

Foul-hook. Act of hooking a fish elsewhere than in the mouth.

Gaff. A strong metal hook mounted on a wooden or metal handle, used to snag fish up from the water so they will not have to be lifted by the leader.

Game fish. Any species of fish that is considered valuable primarily because of its characteristics when caught by hook and line.

Gimbal. Pivoted metal cup equipped with a cross-pin, into which a rod butt may be thrust. Usually mounted on fishing chair or fighting chair at edge of seat, between the angler's knees.

Gin pole. Tall vertical wooden or metal pole equipped with a rope fall for hoisting large fish.

Guide. a) Person who takes anglers out fishing for hire; b) Metal ring or roller on rod shaft through which the line is led.

Halyard. Light rope or line, usually used to hoist flag or outrigger release clip.

Harness. Cloth, leather, or composition vest or belt that is worn around angler's back or shoulders for purpose of taking the weight of the rod via adjustable straps, leaving hands free.

Ichthyologist. One who makes a scientific study of fish.

I/O. Abbreviation for "inboard/outboard," a propulsion system with the motor inside the stern and the drive shaft extending through the stern to a turnable propeller assembly that provides steering and power thrust simultaneously.

Jig. Any small metal lure, heavy for casting or trolling, either plain or dressed with feathers or fibers.

Jigging. a) The act of fishing with jigs; b) Imparting a short, quick, back-and-forth rod action to a lure as it is trolled or retrieved.

kHz. Abbreviation for kilo-Hertz, meaning thousands of cycles per second.

Kite. Special fishing kite used to carry out baits.

Knock-down. The act of an outrigger fishing line being pulled clear of the release clip by fish or angler.

Knot. Nautical unit of speed, one nautical mile per hour, or about 1⅛ statute miles per hour.

Lateral line. Thin, horizontal, wavy line, visible on sides of many fish, that is a sensitive sound and vibration detector.

Leader. Section of wire or synthetic material placed between the hook or lure and the fishing line.

Littoral. A shore or coastal region.

Long-line. Type of commercial fishing gear featuring a very long line equipped with hundreds or thousands of hooks on shorter branch lines.

Loran. A type of electronic navigation system featuring lines of position obtained from comparing the times of receipt of radio signals from paired "master" and "slave" stations.

mHz. Abbreviation for mega-Hertz, meaning millions of cycles per second.

Monofilament. Line made of a single continuous synthetic fiber, usually nylon.

Outrigger. Long pole or shaft fastened to side of boat for purpose of giving lift and separation to trolling lines, usually arranged in matched pairs, port and starboard.

Panfish. Any small, edible, food fish.

Party boat. Boat that carries passengers for hire for fishing, charging so much per person as a fee.

Pectoral fins. Paired fins closest to the gills on underside of fish's body.

Pelagic. Pertaining to fish that spend most of their time in the upper levels of the ocean.

Pelvic fins. Paired fins located on belly behind pectorals.

Pick-up. The act of a fish picking up a bait or lure.

Plankton. Tiny plant or animal life floating freely.

Plug. Lure shaped like a fish, or simulating a fish in action, designed to be cast or trolled, usually made of wood or light plastic.

Radar. Coined word meaning "radio detecting and ranging."

Range. Imaginary line through two visible objects on shore, extended out over the water to the observer's position.

RDF. Abbreviation for "radio direction finder."

Reel. Any mechanical device for storing fishing line on a fixed or revolving spool.

Reelseat. Metal sleeve attached to rod shaft, equipped to receive and lock onto the foot of the reel.

Retrieve ratio. Gear ratio of a reel: a 3–1 retrieve ratio causes the spool of the reel to turn three times for each full turn of the reel handle.

Rocket launcher. Special type of multiple rod holder often used in tournament fishing.

Rod. Any flexible, tapered shaft arranged to carry a reel and fishing line, and used in manipulating the bait or lure to the fish, and in handling the line after hooking the fish.

Rod holder. Metal or plastic tube arranged to receive and hold the butt end of a fishing rod while the rod is being used for trolling, or when it is in the standby condition.

Salinity. Percentage of salt in water.

Scoop. Unit of live bait measure on West Coast, about two-thirds of a bushel.

Seine. Form of vertically hung commercial fishing net.

Shoal. Broad shallow area.

Shooting head. Special weighted headline for flycasting.

Skimmer. The surf or bait clam.

Slick. Thin layer of oil on water surface.

Sound. The act of measuring the depth of water.

Sounder. Any device for measuring water depth.

Species. Scientific term for a group of identical fishes to which the same scientific name is applied. The species is indicated by the second part of the scientific name.

Spinner. Lure containing a revolving or spinning metal leaf.

Spinning. The fishing method that employs a reel with a fixed spool, the line being laid onto the spool by means of a revolving metal arm or bail.

Splice. Method of joining two pieces of rope, rope-laid line, or wire, by means of inter-weaving without using knots.

Spool. The portion of a reel on which line is stored.

Spoon. Thin metal lure shaped like a spoon, equipped with one or more hooks.

Star drag. Reel drag operated by a star wheel.

Stern door. Opening in boat's stern for admitting fish.

Strike. a) The act of a fish attacking or biting at a bait or lure; b) The act of an angler pulling back with the rod and line to hook the fish.

Striking drag. The amount of tension to which a reel's drag is pre-set in anticipation of striking a given species of fish.

Strip bait. Bait made from strip of

fish, pork rind, or similar thin material.

Swivel. Metal device placed between leader and line to form connection and reduce line-twist.

Tag. Small metal or plastic device that is fastened to a fish to identify it for scientific purposes for future recapture.

Tailing fish. A fish such as a marlin or bonefish that frequently exposes its tail in a characteristic manner.

Teaser. An artificial lure-like device designed to entice fish through attractive action.

Terminal tackle. Any part of fishing tackle placed or used at the lower end of the fishing lines, such as sinkers, hooks, leaders, etc.

Thermocline. The transition layer of swift temperature change between warm water near the surface and cold water below.

Tide rip. Visible surf-like condition or clash of water caused by: a) swift current flowing over a reef; b) two opposing currents meeting.

Tip. Upper flexible portion of rod above the reel.

Tournament. Any fishing contest operated according to accepted rules of proper fishing behavior.

Tournament tackle. A grade of tackle considered to be superior by virtue of being built to conform to special tournament requirements.

Tower. Elevated structure for fishing lookout, usually mounted amidships on sport fishing boats.

Toxic. Poisonous.

Transducer. Device that changes electric pulses into sound pulses, and vice versa.

Trawler. Commercial fishing boat that fishes by dragging a net over the bottom of the ocean.

Trolling. The act of fishing by pulling baits or lures through the water behind a moving boat.

Ventral. Pertaining to the underside of a fish.

Weed line. A line of floating sea weeds on the water surface.

Wetland. Coastal intertidal area that is wet at high tide, dry at low tide.

Wire line. Any metallic fishing line.